Canada's 150
Most Famous Great Lakes
SHIPWRECKS

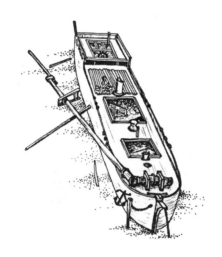

Other Works by Cris Kohl and Joan Forsberg

BOOKS:

Dive Southwestern Ontario! (1985; expanded edition 1988)
Shipwreck Tales: The St. Clair River (to 1900) (1987)
Dive Ontario! The Complete Guide to Shipwrecks and
*   Scuba Diving in Ontario* (1990; expanded edition 1995)
Dive Ontario Two! More Ontario Shipwreck Stories (1994)
Treacherous Waters: Kingston's Shipwrecks (1997)
The 100 Best Great Lakes Shipwrecks, Volume I (1998; updated ed. 2005)
The 100 Best Great Lakes Shipwrecks, Volume II (1998; updated ed. 2005)
TITANIC, *The Great Lakes Connections* (2000)
The Great Lakes Diving Guide (2001; expanded edition 2008)
Diver's Guide to the Kitchen (2003)
Shipwreck Tales of the Great Lakes (2004)
Shipwrecks at Death's Door (2008)
Our World--Underwater, The First 40 Years (Editors; 2010)
The Christmas Tree Ship (2012)
The Wreck of the **GRIFFON** (2014)
Great Lakes Shipwrecks: Recent Discoveries and Updates (2016)

DOCUMENTARIES:

Shipwreck Tales of the Great Lakes (2009)
Great Lakes Shipwrecks of the World Wars (2009)
Tales of Great Lakes Shipwreck Pairs (2009)
The Shipwrecked Whalebacks (2009)
Deep Shipwrecks of the Great Lakes (2009)
Shipwrecks at Death's Door (2010)
Exploring Canada's Great Lakes Shipwrecks (2010)
Thirteen Shipwrecks: The Great Lakes' Worst Maritime Disasters (2011)
Shipwrecks off Whitefish Point (2011)
Shipwreck Tales of Chicago (2012)
TITANIC, *The Great Lakes Connections* (2012)
The War of 1812 on the Great Lakes (2012)
Point Pelee Shipwrecks (2013)
The Great Storm of 1913 (2013)
The Wreck of the **GRIFFON** (2015)
Shipwreck Tales of Georgian Bay (2015)

MAPS:

The 100 Most Famous Great Lakes Shipwrecks (2013)
The War of 1812 on the Great Lakes (2013)
Door County Lighthouses and Shipwrecks (2014)
Lake Superior Lighthouses and Shipwrecks (2014)
Lake Huron Lighthouses and Shipwrecks (2014)

CANADA'S 150
MOST FAMOUS GREAT LAKES
SHIPWRECKS

To Sharon Hill —
Enjoy the shipwreck tales!
Nov. 16, 2018

Cris Kohl
Joan Forsberg

CRIS KOHL
AND
JOAN FORSBERG

Canada's 150 Most Famous Great Lakes Shipwrecks
by Cris Kohl and Joan Forsberg

Published by
Seawolf Communications, Inc.

Photo credits are shown in terms of the author's source for the photograph rather than a specific photographer who might have taken it, except where the photographer is known and specifically named. Photographs are © of any photographers or institutions as indicated, excluding authors Cris Kohl and Joan Forsberg. Artwork is © of the artists as indicated. Text, maps, artwork, and photos by authors Cris Kohl and/or Joan Forsberg are © Seawolf Communications, Inc.

Cover Designs: Cris Kohl and Joan Forsberg

Printed in Canada

FIRST EDITION
5 4 3 2 1

FRONT COVER IMAGE: The wreck of the schooner, *Sweepstakes*, has been lying in these shallow waters of Lake Huron/Georgian Bay at Tobermory, Ontario, since 1885. (Photo by Cris Kohl)

BACK COVER IMAGES (TOP TO BOTTOM, LEFT TO RIGHT): The passenger steamer, *Atlantic*, was sunk after a night-time collision with another ship off Lake Erie's Long Point (Courtesy of the artist, Robert McGreevy); Diver James Taylor examines the ship's wheel on the Lake Ontario schooner, *George A. Marsh* (Photo by Cris Kohl); the freighter, *Edmund Fitzgerald*, at the start of the Lake Superior storm that sank the ship (Courtesy of the artist, Peter Rindlisbacher); the schooner, *Ann Maria*, wrecked in late 1902 at Kincardine, Ontario, on Lake Huron (Kohl-Forsberg Archives); Robert McCracken with the bow of the 1929 Lake Erie wreck, the *N. J. Nessen*, on his farm (photo by Cris Kohl); the luxury yacht, *Gunilda*, stranded on a Lake Superior reef (Kohl-Forsberg Archives); Cris Kohl and Joan Forsberg at Point Pelee on Lake Erie (Photo by Dr. Lara Hernandez Corkrey).

TABLE OF CONTENTS

INTRODUCTION

With the outlook of memorable celebrations in Canada sailing on the horizon for the country's 150th birthday in the year 2017, we decided to bring something a bit different to the party. The idea of writing 150 stories from the more than 2,000 shipwrecks that lie in the Canadian half of the "freshwater seas" known as the Great Lakes metamorphosed gradually from a real-life event, as small a beginning as it was, in July 2016.

For over four decades, scuba divers at Lake Erie's northwest shoreline, near the small community of Morpeth, Ontario, had been diving on and exploring an unidentified, wooden schooner in shallow water, a shipwreck which they had nicknamed, for lack of a better term, the "Morpeth Schooner."

In July 2016, after scuba diving on the wreck with longtime Ontario dive buddies Roy Pickering from Erieau and Allan King from Leamington and videotaping the hull as it lay underwater, Cris Kohl and Joan Forsberg examined the video later, searched through their own extensive files on Lake Erie shipwrecks, and did some additional research on a number of leads, particularly at the far-ranging but unrecognized and/or underrated facilities at the University of Windsor (Ontario). They arrived at a conclusive identification.

The "Morpeth schooner" was the wreck of the Canadian ship named the *Otonabee*.

The twin-masted *Otonabee* (125' x 26'2" x 10'-- that is, having a length of 125 feet, or 37.9 metres; a beam, or width, of 26 feet, two inches, or 7.9 metres; and a draft of 10 feet, or 3 metres), built at Québec City in 1867, was wrecked by strong winds stranding the vessel a very short distance from its destination at the old Morpeth dock on September 7, 1888, while hauling lumber from Collins Inlet on Georgian Bay. No lives were lost, and the cargo was later salvaged, but the 21-year-old schooner was too old and too damaged to recover.

The fact that the *Otonabee* had been constructed in the year 1867 immediately set off an idea to tell this vessel's story in the year of its 150th birthday -- the exact same year as Canada's 150th birthday! This *Otonabee* story led us to create a program that we have presented all over Ontario honouring our nation's birth date. A quick scan of our shipwreck files revealed more and more Canadian ships and shipwrecks that had something to do with the year 1867:

The *Sweepstakes*, launched in 1867 at Burlington (then called Wellington Square), Ontario, and wrecked near Lake Huron's Tobermory in 1885, has, since the 1960s, become the most visited shipwreck in the entire Great Lakes (see pages 136-137 for that story.)

The *Annie Falconer*, launched at Kingston, Ontario, in the spring of 1867 just a few weeks before Canada became a country, and which was located by divers in 1975 in Lake Ontario near Point Traverse west of Kingston, set the scuba diving community on the Canadian side of the Great Lakes abuzz with excitement (read about it on p. 34-35.)

The very first ship that was registered with the government in 1867 under the new maritime rules of the new country called Canada was named the *Mary Ann* -- and this vessel's long life extended well into the 20th century before the ship was scuttled due to old

age in Lake Superior off today's Thunder Bay, Ontario (read its story on page 198.)
There were shipwrecks, too, that occurred in the year 1867, such as the burning of the
Montréal steamer named the ***North*** on the Canadian side of the St. Clair River with
no lives lost. This vessel, however, was raised, repaired, renamed the ***Mary Ward***, and
returned to service, only to be destroyed on Georgian Bay five years later with tragic
loss of lives (turn to pages 150-151 for that story.)
Another significant shipwreck occurred shortly after Canadians celebrated their country's
50th birthday in 1917 -- and this shipwreck was located in the year that the country
again celebrated a significant birthday -- its 100th! However, the story of this wreck
neither began nor ended with either of these events! It is one of the most tragic and
amazing stories ever to emerge from the Great Lakes (read about it on pages 28-29).

The idea of a program celebrating Canada's birthday grew and evolved into a book
that would celebrate MORE than Canada's birthday -- it would celebrate Canada's glorious
and dramatic Great Lakes Maritime History. Working beyond the year 1867, this program
idea gradually developed into selecting, listing, researching and writing the stories of our
choices for the 150 most famous shipwrecks on the Canadian side of the Great Lakes -- a
book for Canada's 150th birthday!

Although spawned for Canada's sesquicentennial year, this book really is, to use a
trite expression, "timeless" -- that is, rather than suddenly cease to be of interest or use to
anyone once the clock strikes the midnight hour that will end Canada's 150th birthday, the
stories in this collection will continue to interest, to amuse and to amaze, to surprise and to
sadden, to haunt and to humble, to enlighten and to entertain, readers for years to come.

In one sense, this book has its roots in the year 1967, when an enthusiastic Canada
celebrated its centennial in so many diverse, thrilling, and happy ways that historian Pierre
Berton called it "the last, good year." As a young man eager and excited to see more of
his country, Cris spent two weeks visiting Ottawa, Montréal, and Québec City during that
summer of 1967, arriving at each destination the old-fashioned way -- by train (but only because the historic business of excursion ships plying the Great Lakes and the St. Lawrence
and Ottawa Rivers had dried up by that time!) Those visits during that famous "Summer
of Love" entailed morning sightseeing at Ottawa's Parliament Buildings and afternoon tea
at the Café le Hibou on Sussex Drive, listening to the house band learn and rehearse songs
from the Beatles' new, groundbreaking Sergeant Pepper album; wide-eyed days spent at
Expo '67 and starry-eyed nights rambling along the bohemian Rue Sainte-Catherine, ut-
terly enthralled by Montréal's European cosmopolitanism; and Québec City's winding
streets, cobbled roads, quaint shops, and restaurants oozing Old World charm.

For Canada's 100th year in 1967, Cris absorbed so much of what those parts of the
country had to offer. For Canada's 150th year in 2017, he was determined to give something back to his beloved country, something that reflected a small part of the nearly four
decades of research, writing, and photography that became his life's work. Joan, also a
Great Lakes Maritime Historian, despite being born in a galaxy far, far away called Brook-
lyn, by traveling extensively and making many friends in Canada, also, long ago, grew to
love the land -- and the water!

Join us for the exciting tales of Canada's 150 Most Famous Great Lakes Shipwrecks!

Cris Kohl and Joan Forsberg
Windsor, Ontario, February 2017

ACKNOWLEDGEMENTS

We are grateful to the following individuals and organizations who provided stunning images, invaluable information, expertise, and insight: Roy Pickering of Save Ontario Shipwrecks; Mike and Georgann Wachter; Ken Merryman and Jerry Eliason of the Great Lakes Shipwreck Preservation Society; Mike Fletcher; Gary Kozak; Allan King; Art Vermette; Ed Fabok; Doug Pettingill; Lloyd Shales; Walter Lewis; Art Amos and Patrick Folkes; Tony Agnello; Richard Tappenden, Jr.; Scott Parent; Darryl Ertel; Jim and Pat Stayer and Tim Juhl of Out of the Blue Productions; artist Adam Henley; artist Peter Rindlisbacher; artist Bob McGreevy; Dan Lindsay of SeaView Diving.com; Wally Peterson; Joe Lark; Ryan LeBlanc; Richard Harvey, a shipwreck diver who also happens to be the mayor of Nipigon, Ontario; Gordon Lightfoot; Phillipe Beaudry; Canada Steamship Lines; Bob McCracken; Bill Humphries; Capt. Robert Campbell; Bill Patterson; Mike Schoger; Rev. Richard Ingalls; the Peter van der Linden Collection; Joan Stickley, the grand-daughter of artist Samuel Ward Stanton, Jamestown, Rhode Island; Jennifer Guerrero; Geoff Kohl; Dr. Lara Hernandez Corkrey; and the late Joyce Hayward, who bequeathed us her Great Lakes photo collection and whom we miss every day.

It is always a pleasure to make use of the following remarkable research facilities and we would like especially to thank their helpful staffs: Library and Archives Canada, Ottawa, Ontario; Ontario Archives, Toronto, Ontario; Toronto Reference Library, Ontario; University of Windsor, Ontario; Windsor (ON) Public Library; Point Pelee National Park; ErieQuest and the town of Leamington, ON; Pelee Island Heritage Centre, ON; Marsh Historical Collection, Amherstburg, ON; Chatham-Kent Historical Museum, Chatham, ON; Moore Museum, Mooretown, ON; Sombra (ON) Museum; City of Hamilton, ON; Rick Nelson, Old Mill Heritage Centre, Kagawong, Manitoulin Island, ON; Nancy Island Historic Site and Wasaga Beach Park, ON; Discovery Harbour, Penetanguishene, ON; Fort Wellington National Historic Site, Prescott, ON; Collingwood (ON) Museum; Craigleith Station Heritage Museum, Craigleith, ON; Fathom Five National Marine Park and Sanctuary, Tobermory, ON; Tory Tronrud, Director, Thunder Bay Museum, Thunder Bay, ON; Belleville (ON) Public Library; Marine Museum of the Great Lakes, Kingston, ON; Kingston (ON) Public Library; Mariner's Park Museum, South Bay, ON; Glen Longacre of the National Archives, Great Lakes Branch, Chicago, Illinois; Robert Graham of the Center for Archival Collections at Bowling Green State University, Bowling Green, Ohio; Runge Collection, Milwaukee Public Library, Milwaukee,Wisconsin; Great Lakes Historical Society, Toledo, Ohio; Northern Illinois University, DeKalb, Illinois; Harrah Historical Society, Harrah, Oklahoma; Oklahoma State Archives, Oklahoma City, Oklahoma.

We thank our family and friends for their encouragement, support, and help on this project, and for tolerating the many hours of travel, patience, seclusion, and absence necessitated by the research, field work, photography, and writing of the text.

Finally, and most importantly, we would like to thank the Sponsors listed on page 221 whose support has enabled this book to be affordable for our valued readers, and for being our partners in the goal of saluting Canada on its 150th birthday.

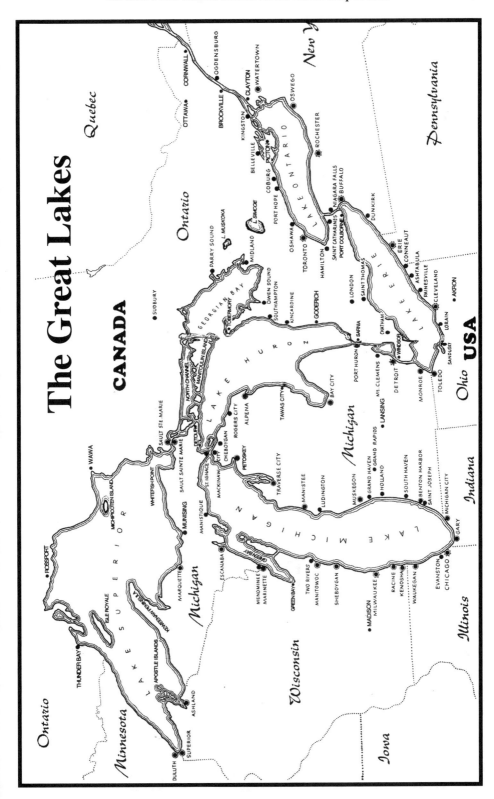

St. Lawrence River

CANADA'S MOST FAMOUS ST. LAWRENCE RIVER SHIPWRECKS

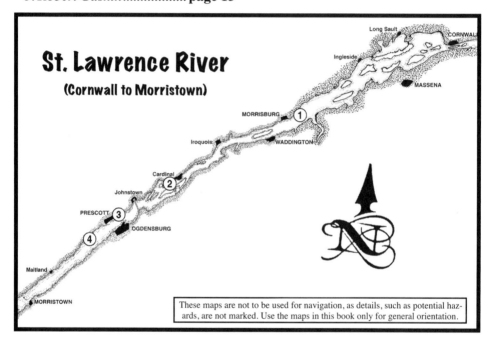

These maps are not to be used for navigation, as details, such as potential hazards, are not marked. Use the maps in this book only for general orientation.

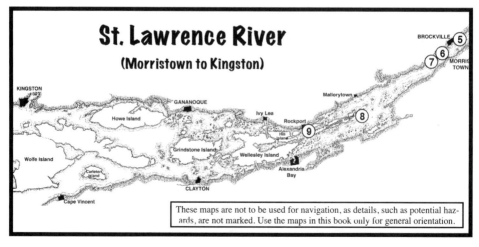

These maps are not to be used for navigation, as details, such as potential hazards, are not marked. Use the maps in this book only for general orientation.

1. *EASTCLIFFE HALL*

JULY 14, 1970   ST. LAWRENCE RIVER

The bulk freight motor vessel, *Eastcliffe Hall,* originally built to a length of 253′4″ (76 metres) in 1954 by Canadian Vickers Shipyards, Ltd., in Montréal, was lengthened to make the ship more commercially competitive when the St. Lawrence Seaway opened in 1959. The *Eastcliffe Hall's* final dimensions, after steel framing and sheeting were welded onto her length by the original builder, were 343′4″ x 43′8″ x 22′8″, with a gross tonnage of 3,335. Twin diesel engines provided 1,280 horse power to move the ship.

The *Eastcliffe Hall* was upbound from Sorel, Québec, for Saginaw, Michigan, with about 4,000 tons (compare this to her gross tonnage!) of pig iron when, at approximately 3 a.m. on July 14, 1970, the ship stranded on some muddy shallows near Crysler Shoal, but kept moving once the crew worked her free. At about 4 a.m., the ship slammed into the 300-ton, concrete buoy abutment at Crysler Shoal, ripping her right side, and sank within three minutes. Nine lives were lost in this tragic mishap: Capt. Richard Groulx, 52, of Montréal, found in the wheelhouse doorway; his 16-year-old son, Alain; Chief Engineer Willie Demers, his wife, Jacqueline, and their 6-year-old daughter, Nathalie; and four crewmen named Lawrence McDougall, 33, from Nova Scotia, Freeman Barter, 29, from Newfoundland, Leonard Harris, 48, from Newfoundland, and Louis Boucher, 59, from Montréal.

The ship sank so quickly that crewmen, lowering lifeboats, were swept off the decks into the river, and sailors in the engine room were blasted through a skylight into the river when inrushing water compressed the air below deck. The 12 survivors clung to debris until they were rescued by Ontario Provincial Police officers who sped to the scene in boats when a local motel owner, who had heard the crash, telephoned them.

The wreck came to rest upright on a slope in 40' to 65' (12.1 to 19.7 metres) of water, with only its six forward masts protruding. The ship's cargo was eventually salvaged, as were its twin propellers. The masts were all removed and the bow superstructure, on the shallowest part of the shipwreck, was dynamited to eliminate the *Eastcliffe Hall* as a navigational hazard. The replacement value of the vessel was set at $2,000,000.

A subsequent inquiry, begun on August 26, 1970, produced a 49-page report revealing that Capt. Groulx's blood alcohol content was very high (0.36 percent), putting him in a "state of plain drunkenness" at the time of the sinking. First Mate Julien Marchand, 45, of Québec, who had been rescued from the crossbar of a mast, had his licence suspended for six months for not observing the captain's condition and taking over command.

The wreck of the *Eastcliffe Hall*, lying just inside the Canadian border in the busy shipping channel, is popular with visiting scuba divers, despite the fast current in the river (3 to 6 knots) and the sometimes poor visibility.

EASTCLIFFE HALL

The wreck today.
(ARTWORK © ADAM HENLEY.
USED WITH PERMISSION.)

The **Eastcliffe Hall** *worked for only 16 years on Great Lakes waters.* (KOHL-FORSBERG ARCHIVES)

2. CONESTOGA

MAY 21, 1922   ST. LAWRENCE RIVER

The wooden, combination passenger and package steam freighter, **Conestoga** (253' x 36' x 16'3"), built for the Anchor Line at an enormous cost, for then, of $90,000 by the firm of Thomas Quayle & Sons at Cleveland, Ohio, was launched on July 6, 1878.

The Anchor Line, experiencing financial difficulties in 1906, sold the **Conestoga** to the Crosby Transportation Company of Milwaukee, which, in turn, sold the ship in 1918 to the Lake Port Shipping Company of Sarnia, Ontario.

On May 21, 1922, the **Conestoga**, loaded with 30,000 bushels of wheat bound for Montréal from Port Colborne, Ontario, caught on fire outside Lock 28 of the Galop Canal about one mile (1.6 kilometre) east of Cardinal, Ontario.

...The blaze broke out when the big freighter was in the lift lock of the canal, but her crew of 22 stood by their posts and succeeded in getting the steamer out of the lock. Several of the crew were badly burned in their efforts. The cause of the fire is unknown.

-- *Daily British Whig,* Kingston, May 22, 1922

The fire apparently began in the engine room, but no lives were lost, and much of the cargo was salvaged. The ship, however, was a total loss, with a reported estimated value of $200,000 for vessel and cargo, either a newspaper misprint, or an incredibly high sum for a 44-year-old, wooden ship, creating suspicion that the vessel was purposely burned to collect a large amount of insurance money.

Scuba divers prepare to leave the shoreline to explore the wreck of the Conestoga, *its exposed steam engine marking its location.*
(PHOTO BY CRIS KOHL)

This shipwreck is easy to locate because part of it sticks out above the surface of the water! The large upper portion of the vessel's 1878 Cuyahoga Iron Works steeple compound steam engine appears intent on exhibitionism as it flashes out from the river and reveals the underwater resting place of the rest of this ship in a maximum of 30 feet (9 metres) of water approximately 80' (24 metres) from shore.

Left: *The 44-year-old* Conestoga *burned to a total loss in 1922.*   (KOHL-FORSBERG ARCHIVES)
Right: *The enormous, four-bladed propeller is a highlight of this site.*   (PHOTO BY CRIS KOHL)

Sponsored by the **ARTHUR CHILD HERITAGE MUSEUM**
125 Water Street, Gananoque, Ontario K7G 3E3
Tel: (613) 382-2535 Email: ivillage@cogeco.net www.1000IslandsHeritageMuseum.com
Come and Explore the Heritage of the Thousand Islands!

3. The Brown's Bay Wreck

Unknown date (circa early 1800s)   St. Lawrence River

Local residents knew for years about an old shipwreck lying in the shallow waters of Brown's Bay on the St. Lawrence River, about 25 miles (40 kilometres) west of Prescott, Ontario. Scuba divers from the Kingston-Brockville area informed federal officials of its location and characteristics in the 1960s. The decision was made by the National Parks Branch, Historic Sites Division (today's Parks Canada), to excavate and conserve this historic vessel.

First, sand that had built up around the hull was removed with underwater "vacuums," after which the wreck was officially documented by archaeologists. Six lifting belts were placed under the hull, again using vacuums to remove the sand, and a specially-built cradle was put in place over the wreck. The fragile wreck was carefully lifted and, on June 2, 1967, was towed upriver to Mallorytown Landing, Ontario. Placed in a tarped gravel pit, the wooden remains were kept wet with a sprinkling system while conservators cleaned it. Then, for about 18 months, the wreck was immersed in a polyethylene glycol/water solution to saturate and preserve the wood, preventing shrinkage and decay. The wreck was then put on display at the St. Lawrence Islands National Park.

This was the first scientific, underwater excavation ever made in Canada, and it led to the development of techniques that were subsequently perfected in their use on numerous projects that followed, giving Canada a leadership role in the research and conservation of waterlogged artifacts.

The boat, 54.5' (16.5 metres) long and 15.5' wide (4.7 metres), was very similar to the **H.M.S.** *Radcliffe* that was built in the Kingston Navy Yard in Upper Canada in 1817. That the Brown's Bay Wreck had been the property of the Royal Navy was indicated by the presence of iron eye-bolts marked with the broad arrow stamp of the British government. There is strong evidence that this vessel was originally used as a British gunboat, and later modified for use as a merchant cargo ship. Its precise identification is still being investigated.

This shipwreck, along with many of the personal and commercial artifacts found on it, is on display at the Fort Wellington National Historic Site in Prescott, Ontario.

Above: *Artist Peter Rindlisbacher's rendition of this vessel's original appearance and use.*

Right: *The actual remains of this historic shipwreck.*

(Photos by Cris Kohl, courtesy of the Fort Wellington National Historic Site)

4. ROTHESAY

SEPTEMBER 12, 1889   ST. LAWRENCE RIVER

Built by J. and S. E. Oliver and launched on February 2, 1868, at St. John, New Brunswick, the wooden-hulled, side wheel passenger steamer, *Rothesay* (193' x 28'8" x 7'9"), operating as a day excursion vessel between the cities of St. John and Fredericton on the St. John River, was removed in 1877 from east coast service and placed on the St. Lawrence River's Montréal-to-Prescott run. The ship was also used as a passenger steamer in the late 1870s, plying the waters between Toronto and the Niagara River.

On the night of September 12, 1889, while returning to Prescott, Ontario, with about 60 excursionists which the steamer had taken to the Gananoque Fair for the day, and when about one mile above Prescott, the *Rothesay* struck the 82-foot-long tug boat named the *Myra*, of the Ogdensburg Coal and Towing Company, at mid-ship, sinking it quickly. The tug was towing the barge, *Mary,* at the time. The tug's Second Engineer Samuel Jardine and Fireman William Sullivan both drowned, while Captain John Martin and First Engineer King Nash survived. Passengers on board the *Rothesay* felt intense consternation, but First Engineer John Miller, heroically working in waist-deep water below deck on the sinking vessel, kept it afloat long enough to allow the ship to steam into relatively shallow water before sinking. No one on the *Rothesay* was injured or killed, a thorough drenching being the worst thing that befell some passengers as they were rowed to shore in small boats.

Left: *The sunken* Rothesay *shortly after the collision.*
Right: *The tug,* Myra, *which the* Rothesay *struck and sank, is seen here towing a barge just like she was doing when disaster struck.*
(BOTH IMAGES: KOHL-FORSBERG ARCHIVES)

The *Myra*, marked with a buoy after it sank in about 40 feet (12 metres) of water, was eventually recovered, repaired, and returned to service, sinking in a collision years later, on August 13, 1930, on the lower St. Lawrence River. That tug was built in 1884 by famous Canadian shipbuilder, Louis Shickluna, at St. Catharines, Ontario.

But the huge, 21-year-old *Rothesay* was too damaged to salvage and was abandoned. The wreck was dynamited in mid-ship in 1901 by the Royal Military College of Kingston to remove it as a hazard to navigation, so little remains intact of that part.

This shipwreck, in just over 30 feet (9 metres) of water, was found on September 25, 1964, by Ottawa scuba divers, and continues to be visited and explored frequently today.

Exploring the massive timbers in the Rothesay's *bow area.* (PHOTO BY CRIS KOHL)

Sponsored by **DIVE BROCKVILLE ADVENTURE CENTRE**
12 Water Street East, Brockville, Ontario K6V 1A1
Tel: (613) 345-2800   Email: charters@divebrockville.com   www.divebrockville.com
Full service dive shop & 1000 Island dive charters with Abucs scubA - April to December

5. *ROBERT GASKIN*

SEPTEMBER 18, 1889   ST. LAWRENCE RIVER

The ***Robert Gaskin*** (132′6″ x 26′3″ x 11′3″), originally a triple-masted, iron-rigged, wooden barkentine, was built by George Thurston for Mr. Robert Gaskin and launched at Kingston, Canada West (later Ontario), on April 21, 1863. Thurston, a shipbuilder since the 1830s, had, in 1862, constructed an earlier vessel for Robert Gaskin named the ***British Lion***, significant as the first ship built on the Great Lakes with wire rigging (but which was wrecked in a storm in 1877 on Lake Erie's Long Point). George Thurston also built the historic ships named the ***Arabia*** (see page 140) and the ***Annie Falconer*** (see pages 34-35).

The ***Robert Gaskin,*** although strongly constructed to Lloyd's of London specifications with the intent of trans-Atlantic travel to Liverpool, with iron knees connecting her deck and hull, and fastened with treenails throughout her construction, spent most of her career transporting grain and stone cargoes, mainly between Milwaukee, Wisconsin, and Prescott, Ontario. By 1886, the ship had been changed to a towed work barge.

In late 1889, this vessel met its ultimate fate by sinking, not once, but a total of three times, off Brockville, Ontario, while being used as a platform for hardhat divers attempting to raise the train ferry propeller, ***William Armstrong***, which had sunk on June 30, 1889, after a portion of her stern dropped out. A 70-foot-long, 8-foot-diameter, steel, salvage pontoon broke loose from the wreck site of the ***Armstrong*** on September 18, 1889, and smashed into the starboard bow of the ***Gaskin***, sinking her virtually on top of the ***Arm-***

strong. The salvage vessel was in need of salvage! On November 11, 1889, the ***Gaskin*** was raised nearly to the surface when a hose coupling on the pontoon detached and dropped the vessel to the bottom again. Twelve days later, the ***Gaskin's*** masts towered high above the water as she was raised and towed about 600' (180 metres) away from the ***Armstrong***. Unfortunately, a rear pontoon which happened to be chained to the keelson tore the ***Robert Gaskin's*** stern away, and she sank for the third and final time at the site she presently occupies.

Incidentally, the ***William Armstrong*** was eventually salvaged the following year (1890), taken to Ogdensburg, New York, for repairs, and returned to ferry service, surviving into the 1930s under the name ***Mons Meg*** before being abandoned due to old age at Trenton, Ontario.

The wreck site of the ***Robert Gaskin***, lying in 60 feet (18 metres) of water, was discovered by divers in 1980, and remains a popular dive site today.

Right: *The wreck of the* **Robert Gaskin**
(ARTWORK © ADAM HENLEY.
USED WITH PERMISSION.)

6. *JOHN B. KING*

JUNE 26, 1930   ST. LAWRENCE RIVER

One of the most severe, loss-of-life, maritime accidents occurred off the northeast side of Cockburn Island in the St. Lawrence River near Brockville, Ontario, on June 26, 1930.

The 140-foot-long (42-metre), 50-foot-wide (15-metre) drill scow, *John B. King*, which, with its 12 steam-driven drills, was reputed to be the largest drilling barge in all of Canada at that time, carried a huge crew of 41 men busily placing underwater charges while at anchor in the main shipping channel of the St. Lawrence River. These men -- drillers, blacksmiths, powdermen, helpers, labourers, and engine room crew -- worked long hours, two shifts every 24 hours, for the J. P. Porter & Sons firm of St. Catharines, Ontario, contracted by the Department of Public Works to deepen and widen the Brockville Narrows. It was customary for many members of the night crew to remain on board during the day, sleeping in bunks that were provided beneath the ship's water line.

A sudden, summer thunderstorm brewed, and, just as the vessel was pulling away from the dynamite-laden site, lightning struck. All of the submerged charges, an estimated 20 tons worth, detonated at once at approximately 4:30 p.m.

The massive explosion rocketed wreckage a couple of hundred feet into the air, and a few minutes later, when the immense cloud of smoke cleared, the ship, reportedly valued at $100,000, was gone, reduced to kindling wood, along with 30 of the men. The U.S. Coast Guard revenue cutter *211*, just over half a mile (about one kilometre) upstream, responded immediately to the frightening sound of the blast and was able to rescue the 11 survivors at the tragic site. Most of the night crew perished as they slept in their bunks.

Among the victims of the dynamite explosion was the ship's mascot, King, a police dog that, a few months earlier, had been awarded a medal for heroism because of his rescue of Jack Wylie, a member of the crew who had broken through the ice while helping load machinery onto the *John B. King.* Wylie, too, died in the blast.

In late November 1930, the J. P. Porter & Sons contracting company erected an imposing, seven-ton monument on Cockburn Island in memory of the 30 men who had died five months earlier. Engraved upon a bronze tablet were the names of these men.

This wreckage, which consists mainly of three large pieces, with heavily twisted metal lying scattered on a slope starting at a depth of 90 feet and dropping to 165 feet (27 to 50 metres), is considered a technical dive due to the depth, the very strong current, and the frequently poor visibility. This site is not for the average or typical scuba diver. This shipwreck site is also considered a grave site, so due respect should be given by any visitors here.

Left: *Port side view of the* John B. King.   (PHOTO COURTESY OF THE EVERRIT SNYDER COLLECTION)
Right: *Starboard side view of the* John B. King.   (KOHL-FORSBERG ARCHIVES)
After the devastating explosion, the intact cook house was towed to Brockville for inspection.

7. *LILLIE PARSONS*

AUGUST 5, 1877   ST. LAWRENCE RIVER

Launched on Monday, September 14, 1868, at Tonawanda, New York, (one Buffalo, NY, newspaper called her "...one of the stongest and best business vessels") [on the Great Lakes], the two-masted, 267-gross-ton, fore-and-after, centreboard schooner, *Lillie Parsons* (132' x 26' x 12'), experienced mishaps during her nine years afloat, such as:

She collided with the schooner, *John Magee*, on May 9, 1870; $600 damage to her.
She was stranded at Devil's Nose, Lake Ontario, on August 24, 1870; pulled free.
She stranded on Point Pelee on October 26, 1871, requiring repairs at Detroit.

The *Lillie Parsons* was loaded with 500 tons of coal when she encountered disaster. Sailing from Black Rock, New York, on Lake Erie, to Brockville, Ontario, on August 5, 1877, the *Lillie Parsons* plowed headlong into a violent squall which heeled her onto her beam ends and shifted her cargo. Just after the crew escaped to safety, the ship struck a rock, filled with water, and sank on a relatively shallow shoal The swift current in the treacherous Brockville Narrows gradually worked the *Lillie Parsons* into deeper water.

The shipwreck lies just off the northwest corner of Sparrow Island, which is about two miles (3.3 kilometres) southwest of Brockville, Ontario. The Brockville Parks Department operates this island's facilities: with prior permission and fee payment, one may camp upon the island, which offers docks, outhouses, picnic tables, and firewood.

The anchor and chain from the *Lillie Parsons* are on land display on Sparrow Island, with the anchor chain trailing down into the water, reaching the wreck itself, thus making it easy for divers to locate and reach this site. The chain ends at the intact, wooden hull, which lies upside-down in 42 to 83 feet (12.6 to 24.9 metres) of water, enabling divers to explore the bottom of the hull and its keel. Other interesting parts of this wreck are the rudderhead, stern deadwood, and the bowsprit still in place. The masts jut out from beneath the overturned hull, and a huge rudder can be viewed at the ship's square stern.

Left: *The* Lillie Parsons *resembled the* Daniel G. Fort, *which was built a year after the* Parsons *by the same builder.*   (KOHL-FORSBERG ARCHIVES)
Right: *A diver examines a boom block on the* Lillie Parsons.   (PHOTO BY CRIS KOHL)

Sponsored by **DIVE BROCKVILLE ADVENTURE CENTRE**
12 Water Street East, Brockville, Ontario K6V 1A1
Tel: (613) 345-2800   Email: charters@divebrockville.com   www.divebrockville.com
Full service dive shop & 1000 Island dive charters with Abucs scubA - April to December

8. *KEYSTORM*

OCTOBER 26, 1912   ST. LAWRENCE RIVER

The steel canaler (meaning it was a near-perfect fit for the old, pre-1932 Welland Canal locks) named the *Keystorm* (250' x 42'5" x 17'5"), built as hull number 836 at Wallsend-on-Tyne, England in 1910, sank on a foggy night two years later on October 26, 1912, when she ran aground at Scow Island Shoal, Chippewa Point, St. Lawrence River. This was nearly due south of Mallorytown Landing, Ontario, and about 12 miles, or nearly 20 kilometres, west of Brockville. The *Keystorm's* crew escaped and, after five hours aground, the ship, heavily loaded with 2,273 tons of coal, slid down a steep slope, coming to rest in 35' to 120' (10.6 to 36.4 metres) of water, with the stern in the deep part.

An investigation determined that both Captain Louis Daigneault and First Mate John Leboeuf were guilty of negligence because their navigational error had caused the accident.

Subsequent efforts to salvage the ship met with failure for a number of reasons, including generally rough weather in 1913, the anchor chains parting when attempts were made to lift the wreck, and the main salvage vessel, the *Reliance*, drifting onto a nearby shoal twice, each time breaking her propeller blades. A hardhat salvage diver, while taking measurements of the wreck's hatches, reportedly brought up her port light to keep as a souvenir in 1913.

In 1917, the wreck was sold to James Robertson & Son of Kingston, Ontario, but the only part of the *Keystorm* to be salvaged was the coal cargo, and not until 1919, seven years after the vessel sank.

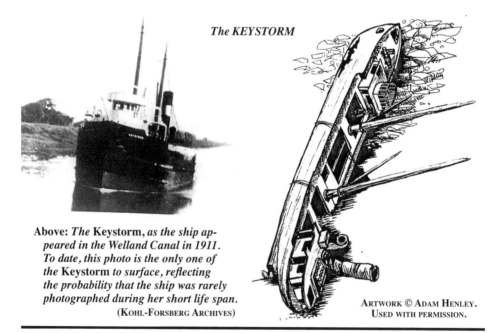

The KEYSTORM

Above: *The* **Keystorm,** *as the ship appeared in the Welland Canal in 1911. To date, this photo is the only one of the* **Keystorm** *to surface, reflecting the probability that the ship was rarely photographed during her short life span.*
(KOHL-FORSBERG ARCHIVES)

ARTWORK © ADAM HENLEY.
USED WITH PERMISSION.

9. *KINGHORN*

MAY 3, 1897   ST. LAWRENCE RIVER

The official name of this shipwreck is *Kinghorn*, not *Kingshorn*, as was reported by the contemporary press. The loss of this 303-gross-ton schooner-barge (131' x 24'8" x 9'1"), about 400' (121.2 metres) off Rockport, Ontario, occurred on May 3, 1897.

The powerful tug boat, *Hiram A. Walker,* towing seven wheat-laden schooner-barges with difficulty down the St. Lawrence River, bound for Montréal, was struck, starting at 11:30 p.m., by a series of the worst squalls to hit that area in years. These bursts of bad weather wrecked three of the seven barges (two at Rock Island Light, and the third stranded on Black Buoy Shoal opposite Alexandria Bay, New York), with the *Kinghorn* leaking so badly that she quickly sank just before Capt. Boyd's tug reached Rockport. It is not often that a tugboat captain loses four of his seven ships in a single tow!

Built in Montréal in 1871, the *Kinghorn* was an early example of composite construction (utilizing both wood and iron in the hull and deck).

Located in 1995 by Ron McDonald, with research assistance from Deb Ring, this wreck sits upright and very (although not perfectly) intact in 80' to 92' (24.2 to 27.9 metres) of water in a very busy, small-boat, shipping channel. The *Kinghorn* does sport a rarity: a ship's wheel lying on the deck! At the stern, the broken-off rudder lies flat, while a windlass adorns the bow. Three bilge pumps, one mounted just forward of each of the three cargo holds, add to the unique nature -- and to the attraction to scuba divers -- of this shipwreck. Much deck planking is missing, providing considerable light and relatively easy access inside the hull. A stove stands upright below deck, anchor chain lies on the forward deck, and authorities are still keeping a lookout for the divers who removed an anchor in 1997.

A tow similar to the one from which the **Kinghorn** *was lost.*   (KOHL-FORSBERG ARCHIVES)

Sponsored by **DIVE BROCKVILLE ADVENTURE CENTRE**
12 Water Street East, Brockville, Ontario K6V 1A1
Tel: (613) 345-2800   Email: charters@divebrockville.com   www.divebrockville.com
Full service dive shop & 1000 Island dive charters with Abucs scubA - April to December

Lake Ontario

The story of ships and shipwrecks on Lake Ontario begins in the 1670s, when the French explorer named La Salle, at Fort Frontenac, or Cataraqui (today's Kingston, Ontario), constructed the first, decked sailing ships ever to ply the waters of the Great Lakes. In fact, the very first shipwreck in all of the Great Lakes occurred in Lake Ontario in early 1679, when one of La Salle's vessels, the *Frontenac*, was stranded and wrecked near present-day Wilson, New York. This took place about eight months prior to the disappearance of La Salle's fabled *Griffon*, the first ship on, and the first ship to be lost in, the upper Great Lakes ("upper" meaning upstream of that enormous, navigational blockage called Niagara Falls).

The most famous shipwrecks in the Canadian waters of Lake Ontario run a wild gamut of types and styles, ranging from War of 1812 fighting ships, one displaying only its dilapidated, skeletal frames today while others lie in amazingly pristine condition in deep water; to many wooden, sailing vessels that mostly succumbed to the fierce and unpredictable nature of lake weather; to wooden steam-powered ships whose mobility depended upon either large, wooden paddlewheels or small, steel propellers; to huge, steel ships that were cut in half to squeeze them through the Welland Canal on their way to serving in a World War on saltwater seas; to sailing ship 'old-timers' which saw their longevities end when they were mercilessly burned as public spectacles; to the huge, excursion ship that became the lake's last, major, floating victim of nautical disaster; and finally to the first ship ever sunk intentionally in the Great Lakes for the express purpose of creating a new, scuba dive site.

CANADA'S MOST FAMOUS LAKE ONTARIO SHIPWRECKS

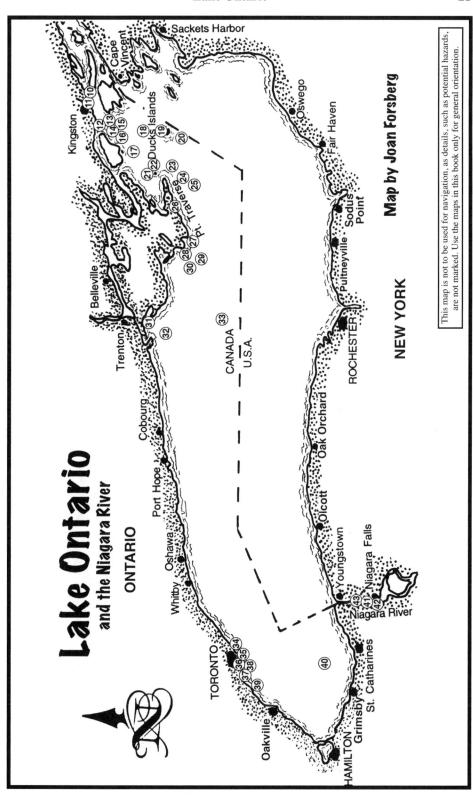

Lake Ontario
and the Niagara River

ONTARIO

Map by Joan Forsberg

This map is not to be used for navigation, as details, such as potential hazards, are not marked. Use the maps in this book only for general orientation.

NEW YORK

CANADA
U.S.A.

Sackets Harbor

Cape Vincent

Oswego

Fair Haven

Kingston

Ducks Islands

Sodus Point

Pultneyville

Belleville

ROCHESTER

Trenton

Oak Orchard

Cobourg

Olcott

Port Hope

Oshawa

Youngstown

Whitby

Niagara Falls

TORONTO

Niagara River

Oakville

HAMILTON

Grimsby

St. Catharines

10. *WOLFE ISLANDER II*

SEPTEMBER 21, 1985   LAKE ONTARIO

The *Wolfe Islander II* ferry, the first commercial vessel purposely sunk in the Great Lakes specifically to create a scuba dive site, is the most visited shipwreck in the lake.

Built at Collingwood, Ontario, in 1946, originally as the *Ottawa Maybrook,* to be presented as a gift from the Canadian government to China, the ship was re-purposed when China declared itself to be a Communist state. Renamed the *Wolfe Islander II* (144'3" x 43'1" x 8'), it replaced the aging, original *Wolfe Islander* as a Kingston ferry.

From 1946 to 1975, the *Wolfe Islander II* carried residents, students, tourists, vehicles, and future shipwreck book writers, while witnessing life (at least two babies were born on this ferry) and death (a deckhand was accidentally killed in 1947). But in late 1975, the ship was replaced by a new one that was, logically, named *Wolfe Islander III*.

The *II* sat idle for nine years. In 1984, the Marine Museum of the Great Lakes at Kingston acquired the ship with the intention of restoring her as a floating exhibit. However, in 1985, the museum unexpectedly acquired the larger, newly-decommissioned Canadian Coast Guard vessel, *Alexander Henry*. They sold the *Wolfe Islander II* for the sum of $1.00 to the Comet Foundation, which planned to turn the ship into a scuba dive attraction. Residents of Wolfe Island, feeling betrayed, fought to stop the subsequent clean-up and scuttling, arguing "heritage betrayal" and "liability problems," but they lost.

On Saturday, Sept. 21, 1985, at 11:48 a.m., the *Wolfe Islander II*, surrounded by a fleet of 100+ horn-sounding boats, sank, after seacocks had been opened, in an "all-weather" area three miles (nearly five kms.) east of Kingston in 85 feet of water. Instead of being scrapped and converted into razor blades, this ship continues to delight visitors today.

The WOLFE ISLANDER II

ARTWORK © ADAM HENLEY.
USED WITH PERMISSION.

Above: *The* Wolfe Islander II *resting upright in Lake Ontario, still resembles a proud ship today.*
Right, top: *The engine room can be examined by divers specifically trained in "penetration shipwreck diving."*
Right, bottom: *The huge, three-bladed propeller attracts dive instructor Marcy McElmon to one of the deepest parts of the* Wolfe Islander II.   (PHOTOS BY CRIS KOHL)

11. *PRINCE REGENT*

ABANDONED CIRCA 1832   LAKE ONTARIO

Left: *The* **Prince Regent.**   (ART BY GEORGE CUTHBERTSON, COURTESY OF THE CANADA STEAMSHIP LINES)
Right: *The* **Prince Regent** *attacked Oswego, NY, in the War of 1812.*   (KOHL-FORSBERG ARCHIVES)

Near the end of the War of 1812, the ***Prince Regent*** was launched at Kingston on April 14, 1814. This impressively huge ship measured 155 feet in length, carried 56 guns (or cannon) on two decks, sported three tall masts, and could transport 500 soldiers and sailors on a single voyage. But after the war, the vessel lay idle. Finally, in January 1832, it was ordered to be sold by the British Navy, but the records of this ship end there. The ***Prince Regent*** was ultimately allowed to sink, abandoned, in an out-of-the-way bay.

Today, the remains of the ***Prince Regent*** lie in about six feet of water at the head of Kingston's Deadman's Bay, with the entire length of the ship's keel and frames remaining at the site. However, nearly 200 years of exposure to winds, waves, and ice have caused the decks and sides of the hull to break off and drift away in slow, natural destruction. What remains of the ship's bones is held together by numerous bolts and nails that are becoming increasingly fragile with age. The steps, or openings, where the three masts were secured to the keel at the bottom of the ship, remain identifiable. The stern post at the western end of the wreck remains identifiable, and, attached to it, are some iron fittings that held the ship's rudder in place. The shallow depth makes the ***Prince Regent*** a popular snorkeling shipwreck lying just off the sandy beach of a public park.

The PRINCE REGENT

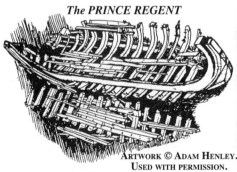 

ARTWORK © ADAM HENLEY.
USED WITH PERMISSION.

Above, right: *The massive frames of the* **Prince Regent,** *mostly covered by aquatic growth by the end of summer, remain a simple reminder of this once-impressive War of 1812 ship.*

(PHOTO BY CRIS KOHL)

12. *Munson*

April 30, 1890   Lake Ontario

Time has left us very few examples of this type of Great Lakes vessel. A dredge was basically a floating steam shovel used to deepen harbours or rivers. It usually scooped its toothy bucket into the soft bottomland, hauled up its dripping, oozing, excavated material, and deposited it onto a barge that worked as a silent partner in harmony with the dredge's activities. The barge was then towed to an out-of-the-way place where its contents could be dumped. The unpowered, unregistered barge and dredge counted on a tug for propulsion.

The dredge, *Munson*, and the tug, *Emma Munson,* both owned by a Mr. E. A. Munson of Cobourg, Ontario, almost always worked as a team. We know, from recently discovered records, that E. A. Munson was able to secure the government contracts for regularly dredging most of the Canadian harbours on Lake Ontario, e.g. in 1881, the Munson dredge and tug were contracted, for the sum of $5,000 (about ten years of average salary back then!) to deepen Belleville harbour. In 1882, they completed the dredging of the channel between Weller's Bay and Lake Ontario near Consecon. In 1883, a $2,000 job was completed at Kingston before the Munson team moved back to Belleville for a $10,000 dredging contract. It was a prolific business that kept all of the Munson elements very busy.

But the dredge, *Munson's*, most important job was deepening the launch area just before the *Minnedosa,* the largest sailing ship ever built on the Canadian side of the Great Lakes, was launched at Kingston in late April 1890. While returning to Belleville after that job, the *Munson* developed a leak, tilted, and quickly sank in 110 feet of water, nearly taking three crew, especially the cook, with it. The *Munson,* upright and very intact, is complete with many workman's tools and considerable china and glassware, items that visiting scuba divers have placed in singular, open areas for future divers to see and appreciate.

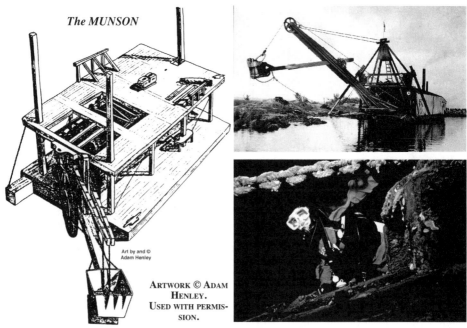

The MUNSON

Art by and ©
Adam Henley

Artwork © Adam
Henley.
Used with permission.

Right, top: *The* Munson *resembled this unidentified dredge.*   (Kohl-Forsberg Archives)
Right, bottom: *Marcy McElmon examines the chains on the bucket arm.*   (Photo by Cris Kohl)

13. *ALOHA*

OCTOBER 28, 1917   LAKE ONTARIO

The schooner-barge, *Aloha* (173' x 32'5" x 12'), built in Mt. Clemens, Michigan, in 1888, began to leak in a fierce, southwest gale early on the morning of Sunday, October 28, 1917, while being towed by the 127-foot-long steam tug, *C. W. Chamberlain*, abreast of Nine Mile Point, nine miles west of Kingston, its destination. The *Aloha* carried a crew of five men, all hailing from Ontario ports, plus 1,100 tons of soft coal loaded at Erie, PA.

Seeing that its tow was awash from the huge waves continually breaking over its bow as it plunged dangerously while racing through the seas, with several feet of water covering the deck because the scuppers and other drains had become clogged by the loose coal which had been piled there, the towing steamer cut the tow line. This was meant to save the *Aloha* from swamping, but it was too late. Ten minutes later, at 6:30 a.m., the *Aloha* sank in 45 feet of water. Only the upper parts of the masts remained visible.

The five crew had donned life jackets earlier, which made it easier for them to remain afloat while the *Chamberlain* turned around to rescue them. Tossed lines saved two crew-members quickly, but 76-year-old Captain Daniel McVicar twice failed to reach or hold onto a rescue line, and he disappeared into the angry waves. His body was found on Simcoe Island the next day. Another crew member drifted atop the ship's dislodged cabin for three hours before being picked up in vicious waves off Simcoe Island by two daring men in a small gasoline launch. The last sailor clung to a protruding mast for six hours before the government steamer, *Grenville,* dared approach the wreck in bad weather to rescue him.

The *Aloha*, launched as a schooner, was converted to a bulk freight towbarge in 1902. Registered at Midland, Ontario, the ship was co-owned by coal interests in Toronto and Captain Stocker of the *Chamberlain*. The *Aloha*, valued at $6,000, was insured.

The *Aloha* was found by well-known, local shipwreck hunters and cousins, Lloyd Shales and Barbara Carson, in August 1964. Most of the *Aloha's* hull is intact, although she was divested of the majority of her small artifacts by scuba divers years ago. Anchor chain sits on the bow, attached to a windlass, and divers can see the original coal cargo by carefully descending into the holds. At the stern, a capstan, steering quadrant, and rudder post lie in the sand. Roman numeral depth markings can be seen on the bow.

Left: *The schooner-barge,* Aloha, *sank in 1917, losing its captain.*   (KOHL-FORSBERG ARCHIVES)
Right: *Schools of fish are attracted to the wreck of the* Aloha.   (PHOTO BY CRIS KOHL)

14. CORNWALL

DECEMBER, 1930   LAKE ONTARIO

This iron-hulled sidewheeler, launched as a floating palace in 1855 at Montréal by builder William Gilbert, experienced several name changes in her career: *Kingston* (1855-1873), *Bavarian* (1873-1895), *Algerian* (1895-1906), and finally, *Cornwall* (1906-1930). She had her share of accidents and rebuilds. As the *Kingston*, she burned at Grenadier Island in the St. Lawrence River on October 26, 1872. As the *Bavarian,* she burned on November 6, 1873, 15 miles (23 kilometres) off Oshawa, Ontario, on Lake Ontario, with the loss of 20 lives. As the *Algerian,* she partially burned in 1905. She was rebuilt in 1872-73, 1873-74, 1895, 1905, and, finally, 1915, when she was outfitted with salvage equipment and converted into a wrecking tug (176'6" x 27'1" x 9'9").

This was quite a transformation from the original vessel, which boasted stained glass windows, pianos and thick carpeting, and which catered to the élite. As a wrecking tug, the *Cornwall* was outfitted with an A-frame derrick, clamshell outfit, steam pumps, air compressor, and other equipment utilized in the salvage profession.

By the late 1920s, the vessel had outlived its usefulness, and in December 1930, she was towed to the ship graveyard off Amherst Island, and dynamited.

The remains of the *Cornwall* were located by Kingston historian and diver, Rick Neilson, who, in 1982, found and interviewed an aging former employee of the Donnelly Wrecking Company which had helped scuttle the *Cornwall* in 1930. Neilson ran zigzag patterns with his boat and depth sounder until he found the wreck in September 1990.

The *Cornwall* sits upright in 73 feet (21.9 metres) of water. Her engine was removed before scuttling, but the two Marine Fire Box type boilers, built in Buffalo, NY, in 1892, remain in place, as do the two, wooden, 10-bladed, 20-foot-diameter paddlewheels. Scattered around the wreck site are a windlass, a ladder, barrels, pipes, tools, and woodwork.

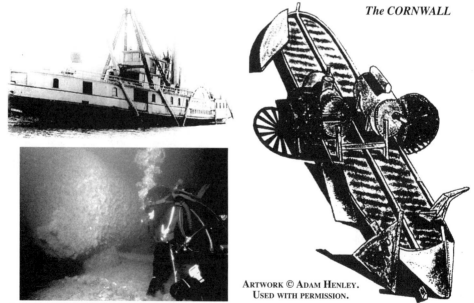

The CORNWALL

ARTWORK © ADAM HENLEY.
USED WITH PERMISSION.

Left, top: *The* **Cornwall's** *final configuration was as a salvage vessel.* (KOHL-FORSBERG ARCHIVES)
Left, bottom: *Doug Pettingill studies the* **Cornwall's** *boiler arrangement.* (PHOTO BY CRIS KOHL)

15. COMET

MAY 14, 1861   LAKE ONTARIO

The elegant, graceful sidewheel steamer, *Comet* (174'8" x 24' -- 45' including the two paddlewheels -- x 10'), was built by George N. Ault of Fisher's Shipyard at Portsmouth (Kingston), Canada West (later renamed Ontario), and launched on June 14, 1848. The *Comet* underwent a name change in 1851, and was known for the next two years as the *Mayflower* before her original name was restored in 1853.

The *Comet* experienced a fair number of casualties during her relatively short life. She sustained damage when she stranded twice during her first season afloat. Her boiler exploded on November 3, 1849, killing three and injuring half a dozen people. On April 20, 1851, the *Comet's* boiler again exploded, this time as she was leaving Oswego, NY, killing eight and sinking the ship. Again, she was recovered, repaired, and returned to service -- but she was no longer considered a lucky ship. This was especially true in 1857, from which time the *Comet* lay idle for three years due to the financial panic.

Bad luck persisted. On May 7, 1861, powerful winds tore the *Comet* from her moorings, slamming her against the Cataraqui Bridge. A week later, with repairs made, she departed for her first trip of the season, and steamed right into her final stroke of bad luck.

On May 14, 1861, Captain Francis Patterson, amidst storm signals and rolling squalls, decided to take his steamer out of the safety of the port. Simultaneously, the American schooner, *Exchange*, was frantically running before the storm in quest of safe haven. In the obscured visibility produced by the foul weather, the bow of the *Exchange* sliced deeply into the hull of the *Comet*. The *Comet* traveled about another eight miles, at which point it became apparent that the sidewheeler was destined to sink, and crew and passengers were ordered to abandon ship. In the haste and confusion of leaving the sinking vessel, two crewmembers were knocked overboard and drowned. All the others quickly jumped into the lifeboat and the yawl, and made for the safety of shore.

The *Comet* lay undisturbed for more than 100 years before two scuba divers, doing a systematic search based upon contemporary newspaper articles, and utilizing two boats and a depth sounder, located this shipwreck in 1967.

The COMET

ARTWORK BY C.H.J. SNIDER.
COURTESY OF THE TORONTO REFERENCE LIBRARY

Right: *The massive paddle wheels of the steamer,* Comet, *rising about 25 feet above the 90-foot-deep floor of Lake Ontario, impress diver Barb Marshall.* (PHOTO BY CRIS KOHL)

16. GEORGE A. MARSH

AUGUST 8, 1917   LAKE ONTARIO

The schooner George A. Marsh *entered Canadian registry in 1914.* (KOHL-FORSBERG ARCHIVES)

Joan Forsberg examines the upright bowsprit on the Marsh.   (VIDEO FREEZE-FRAME BY CRIS KOHL)

Diver James Taylor studies the ship's wheel on the George A. Marsh.   (PHOTO BY CRIS KOHL)

One of the most tragic, unusual, and poignant stories to emerge from the many tales of the Great Lakes involved a schooner lost in a Lake Ontario storm, and a mystery man in a small town in Oklahoma.

The three-masted schooner, *George A. Marsh* (135' x 27' x 9'3"), named after a Great Lakes lumber magnate from Chicago when the ship was launched at Muskegon, Michigan, in 1882, foundered in a furious summer storm with a cargo of coal from Oswego, New York, on August 8, 1917. Reportedly, 12 of the 14 people on board drowned, including Captain John Smith, his new wife, their new baby, five of his children from a former marriage, plus family friends, most of them from the ship's home port of Belleville, Ontario.

The wreck of the *George A. Marsh* was located by Barbara Carson and her team of divers off Amherst Island on October 7, 1967. The wreck sits in 85 feet of water, deep in silt that is easily disturbed. This shipwreck is almost completely intact; besides the many deadeyes, blocks, belaying pins, and tools, there is the ship's wheel and a stove, complete with cooking utensils in place, on the deck. Much of the ship's rigging, a lifeboat, the bowsprit, and pottery artifacts are also in place, with both bow anchors being the only items ever removed.

In 1992, local Picton historian and scuba diver, Doug Pettingill, while exploring some of the shipwrecks in the Kingston area with Cris Kohl, brought to Cris' attention the fact that there was a rumour about the captain of the *George A. Marsh* actually

The GEORGE A. MARSH

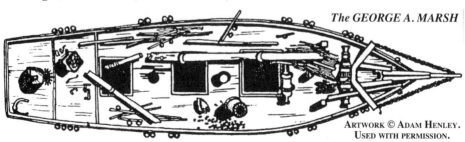

ARTWORK © ADAM HENLEY.
USED WITH PERMISSION.

having survived the sinking.

A few years later, some evidence surfaced, compelling the very curious Cris Kohl and Joan Forsberg to drive to a town called Harrah, Oklahoma, to investigate the rumour that the captain, 49-year-old John Smith, had secretly survived the sinking of the *George A. Marsh* and, in his grief and shame, fled as far away from water as possible to begin life anew.

These railroad tracks at Harrah, Oklahoma, transported Smith into a new life. (PHOTO BY CRIS KOHL)

Exactly how he acomplished this -- and why he went to Harrah -- are part of the *Marsh's* mysteries.

In Harrah in 2002, the authors found information about a mysterious man who had arrived in town in the summer of 1917, opened a bank account at a Harrah bank on August 17, 1917, and started a modest business by selling farm produce that he carried in a horse-drawn wagon to local markets. This man, known locally only as "J. Smith," worked hard and, by the mid-1920s, as the successful proprietor of the Harrah Produce House, owned a warehouse, an ice house, and seven farm produce delivery trucks.

Joan Forsberg points out the location where "J. Smith" operated his business. (PHOTO BY CRIS KOHL)

The authors also tracked down a copy of "J. Smith's" death certificate, indicating that he died on February 23, 1927, from a ruptured appendix. On his deathbed, Smith had confided to his best friend, Walter Wilson, a fellow member of the Masonic Order, who had bankrolled Smith's early days in Harrah, "some of the secrets of his life," including his earlier days as a Great Lakes captain.

He indicated that he wanted his prosperous estate to go to his two children in Canada who were not on board the *Marsh* when it sank. Thus Walter Wilson was entrusted with the task of locating specific people named Smith in a foreign country. With help from newspapers in the Belleville area, Wilson found Smith's children, and mailed them photographs of the deceased man for corroboration. Shockingly, the man in the pictures was, indeed, the father whom they thought had died a decade earlier. Another surprise was that Smith's daughter had married one of the two men who had survived the sinking of the *Marsh*!

Capt. Smith's grave in Harrah; he took many secrets with him in 1927. (PHOTO BY JOAN FORSBERG)

Our further research in Harrah yielded much more information in the census records about "J. Smith," and we also received a description of him from 87-year-old Gwen Wilson, Walter's daughter, who was 12 years old when Smith died, but who clearly remembered her father's friend. A second research trip to Harrah in 2008 produced detailed information about the many items listed in Smith's estate, and the precise location of his business.

Little is known about the time from the sinking to Smith's arrival in Harrah in August, 1917. How did he survive? Did anyone see him? Did anyone talk with him?

Our quest to uncover more of the dead captain's secrets continues.

The Lucky Unfortunate -- Canada's Great Lakes Captain John Smith. (KOHL-FORSBERG ARCHIVES)

17. *City of Sheboygan*

September 15, 1915   Lake Ontario

The three-masted schooner, *City of Sheboygan* (135′2″ x 27′4″ x 10′), was launched at Sheboygan, Wisconsin, on July 5, 1871. Until the spring of 1915, the *City of Sheboygan* was engaged in the lumber-carrying business on Lake Michigan; at that time, however, business slowed down, and Captain Edward McDonald of Toronto purchased the vessel for use on Lake Ontario in the mineral feldspar trade.

In late September 1915, the old *City of Sheboygan* was loaded with 500 tons of feldspar mined just north of Kingston, Ontario. One local sailor later told the press that he thought the ship was "heavily overloaded" when a tug towed her out into the open waters of the lake.

Captain McDonald attempted to run into the lee, or protected, side of Amherst Island to get out of the storm. He lost the race. The four men and the captain's wife (who worked as cook) were all lost to the powerful wind and waves when their ship slipped out from under them and sank 105 feet to the bottom of the lake.

After the storm, only the tops of the masts remained above the water as silent sentinels marking the site of the tragedy. The first body to be found was that of the captain's wife, Mrs. McDonald, the ship's cook, on Wednesday, October 6, 1915, ten days after the sinking. Only one other body, that of a sailor, was found.

The wreck of the *City of Sheboygan* was located by a team of divers led by Lloyd Shales and Barbara Carson in the early summer of 1963. The wreck is deep and, hence, well-preserved and mostly intact. The ship's wheel and anchor are the only items that have been removed, and they are on exhibit at a local museum. The ship's masts, rigging, and most other items, including deadeyes, are present on the wreck.

Left, top to bottom:
The schooner City of Sheboygan. *Lloyd Shales and Barbara Carson, with the* Sheboygan's *wheel in 1963, soon after they found the wreck.*
(Both Kohl-Forsberg Archives)

Doug Pettingill examines the wreck.
(Photo by Cris Kohl)

Lloyd Shales in 1995 with a photo of a lookalike ship to the City of Sheboygan, *the* Ford River. (Photo by Cris Kohl)

18. *John E. Hall*

DECEMBER 13, 1902   LAKE ONTARIO

On December 13, 1902, the steamer, *John E. Hall*, commanded by Capt. Timothy Donovan of Oswego, NY, cleared the port of Charlotte (Rochester), New York, towing the schooner, *John R. Noyes,* commanded by Capt. Donovan's son. Both ships were bound for Canada, both vessels carried cargoes of coal, and it was the final voyage for both.

A mid-December crossing of Lake Ontario has always been a risky prospect. When the gales blew relentlessly, the snow flew blindingly, and making headway became impossible, the steamer cast off its tow, signaling a case of "every ship for itself." Unfortunately, the engineless *John R. Noyes* also carried no sails, bobbing aimlessly at the mercy of the wind and the waves. The Charlotte Lifesaving crew, enduring enormous hardship, reached the northward-blown schooner and rescued the crew at about noon on December 15th. The *Noyes* continued drifting northward, with the abandoned hull eventually sweeping onto the Canadian shoreline near Salmon Point, where it broke up.

The steamer, *John E. Hall*, also succumbed to the storm, disappearing with her entire crew. About a week after the *Hall* went missing, wreckage washed ashore at Stony Point, New York, diminishing all hopes for the safety of the ship's crew.

On December 24, 1902, one local newspaper, reflecting the despairing mood, under the heading, **ALL HOPE IS GONE**, noted that "...Captain Charles Ferris and the tug *Ferris* arrived here Saturday night with a cupboard from the galley of the steamer, which Capt. George Donovan identified as belonging to his father's steamer, and other wreckage. The wreckage was found on the south side of the Main Ducks...."

The *John E. Hall* (139' x 28'6" x 10'9"), valued at $15,000, was built at Manitowoc, Wisconsin, in 1889 by Hanson & Scove.

The empty steamer, John E. Hall, *washed ashore in Canada; her crew was never seen again.*
(ARCHIVES OF ONTARIO)

19. *John Randall*

November 16, 1920   Lake Ontario

The 194-gross-ton, wooden propeller, *John Randall* (104'4" x 22'5" x 7'7"), built in 1905 by the Shelby and Youlden Company of Kingston, Ontario, carried a cargo of coal from Oswego, New York, towards Belleville, Ontario, when she encountered a severe storm on November 16, 1920, off Main Duck Island. Captain Harry Randall (the son of the man, also a Great Lakes captain, after whom this ship was named) steamed the vessel towards shelter in School House Bay. There, the ship leaked and sank, leaving only the wheelhouse above water. Another report indicated that the ship's stern struck a rock that angled the ship partially out of the water, causing it to break in two; the four men on board were stranded at the forward end of the sunken vessel for ten hours. With the lifeboats washed away, the life-jacketed crew (the captain and three sailors) abandoned ship on a large hatch cover and reached the safety of the island, about half a mile away, with assistance from Cecil Bongard, who had sighted the spars of the *Randall* and rushed to the scene; he was a relative of Fred Bongard, the Main Duck Island lighthouse keeper.

"The biggest job," Mr. Bongard reportedly said later, "was to get the survivors to the lighthouse residence, a mile away."

The crew, suffering heavily from exposure, reached the warm shelter of the lighthouse, where they remained the guests of the Fred Bongard family for nine days before the heavy gales subsided and Mr. Bongard could transport them to Point Traverse on the mainland.

Modern communication capabilities being in their infancy in the early 1900s, meaning there was no telephone line or wireless (radio) set on Main Duck Island, there was no way of informing the outside world that the *John Randall's* crew was safe. Captain Randall's father, meanwhile, on the mainland, had enlisted the aid of spiritualist Eva Fay, who was appearing at Kingston's Grand Opera House, who informed the worried captain that his son and crew were safe and happy, but that their ship had sunk near an island. How right she was, and how joyful the father must have been when his son returned alive!

Lying in shallow water, the *Randall's* coal cargo (valued at $2,400), and its machinery and fittings, were easily salvaged, leaving only the bare, broken hull in the bay to be ravaged by nature and time.

Unfortunately, exactly a year after his experience on Main Duck Island, Captain Harry Randall did not have the same fortune when he commanded the wooden propeller named the *City of New York*.

Left: *The* John Randall, *built in 1905, was wrecked in 1920.*   (Kohl-Forsberg Archives)
Right: *Underwater videographer, Jim Stayer, shoots the* Randall's *flattened remains.*
(Photo by Cris Kohl)

20. *CITY OF NEW YORK*

NOVEMBER 25, 1921   LAKE ONTARIO

To replace the loss of the *John Randall* in 1920 (read that story on the preceding page), Captain Harry Randall purchased one of the oldest, wooden vessels afloat on the Great Lakes. The *City of New York* (136' x 27'6" x 11'6"), launched at Cleveland in August 1863, in the midst of the U.S. Civil War, carried passengers and freight between Chicago and Ogdensburg, NY, before being converted (with her cabins removed) to a bulk freight carrier in 1881 hauling primarily coal and lumber. Harry Randall bought this ship from the Lake Shore Sand and Gravel Company of Toronto for $15,000. Due to high rates for such an old vessel, Randall carried no insurance on the *City of New York*.

In the very early hours of Thursday, November 24, 1921, the *City of New York* steamed out of the harbour at Oswego, NY, heading for Trenton, Ontario, across the lake. Accompanying her were two other steamers, and, with heavy snow blowing, all three ships headed to Main Duck Island to take advantage of its protective lee side. Two steamers reached the island, but, by then, the lights from the *City of New York* had disappeared. Initial hopes that the old steamer had found safe anchorage elsewhere soon faded.

On Saturday, November 26, 1921, Captain Fred Baldwin of the steamer, *Isabella,* arrived at Oswego with a lifeboat that he had picked up in the lake. In that oarless lifeboat were five lightly-dressed bodies, all from the *City of New York*: Mrs. Harry Randall (31 years old, and the only one wearing a lifebelt) and four sailors, ages between 17 and 31. The men's bodies were found huddled under the seats, while Mrs. Randall's body was "hanging over the side of the boat, with her hands in the water." The bodies of Captain Harry Randall, his ten-month-old daughter, and 14-year-old Stanley Pappa were never found.

Interestingly, when the ship was first reported missing, Captain John Randall reportedly returned to spiritualist Eva Fay for information about his son and his vessel. The fortune-teller told him that the *City of New York* had sunk, and that his son's body would not be recovered. The wreck of the *City of New York* has, nearly a century after its loss, not yet been located.

EIGHT PERSONS PERISH IN LAKE

Steamer City of New York Lost off Stoney Point With Entire Crew.

FIVE BODIES IN YAWL

Capt. Harry Randall, His Little Son, and Boy of 12 Still Missing.

KINGSTON, Nov. 27.—Latest developments in the loss of the steamer City of New York, which foundered ten miles off Stoney Point while on her way from Oswego to Trenton with a cargo of phosphate, show that eight lives were lost. Five bodies were found in the yawl, picked up late Friday afternoon by the steamer Isabella H., and Captain Harry Randall, his ten-months-old child, and Stanley

Left: *The* City of New York, *58 years old when it sank -- was very old for a wooden ship!*
Right: *The tragic finding of five bodies in a lifeboat made headlines across the Great Lakes.*
(BOTH: KOHL-FORSBERG ARCHIVES)

21. ANNIE FALCONER

NOVEMBER 12, 1904   LAKE ONTARIO

The two-masted schooner, *Annie Falconer* (108' x 24' x 9'), was built at Kingston by George Thurston and launched on May 22, 1867 (just a few weeks before Canada became a country!). Mr. Daniel Falconer named his new vessel in memory of his late wife, Mary Ann ("Annie") Falconer, nee Baker (1832-1860), seven years after her death. What a strong and memorable love theirs must have been! Their young daughter, also named Annie, christened the ship and, according to reports, swung the christening bottle, but missed the ship! The vessel glided down the launch ramp anyway. Pessimists viewed this as an ill omen, but the *Annie Falconer* enjoyed a long life with comparatively few problems.

One accident was almost the *Falconer's* undoing. The ship ran aground at Weller's Bay, Ontario, on October 14, 1893, during a violent storm that sank numerous other ships, and spent the winter there high and dry. Fortunately, it was a mild winter with no devastating storms; she was pulled off that shore with little damage the following April 21st.

The *Annie Falconer* foundered in a violent storm off South Bay Point about 1.5 miles north of False Duck Island, near Timber Island, 25 miles southwest of Kingston, on Saturday, November 12, 1904. At that time, she was underway with a cargo of soft coal bound from Sodus Point, New York, to Picton, Ontario.

The *Falconer* had begun to leak about ten miles off False Duck Island, and the crew pumped frantically while the captain steered the ship towards Timber Island in an effort to purposely run her aground rather than lose her in deep water. They didn't make it. The ship sank about halfway between False Duck Island and Timber Island.

The crew of seven escaped the sinking schooner in the ship's yawl boat at about 2 p.m. that Saturday, and landed on inhabited Amherst Island to the north at 7:30 p.m. after a frighteningly desperate run. They had nothing but their hats and cupped hands with which to bail out the freezing water from their frail, old yawl boat. The first mate, James Sullivan, died of exposure shortly after landing on Amherst Island when he wandered away from the rest of the crew in the darkness. The survivors found shelter in a nearby farmhouse and, the next day, Captain Murray Ackerman, the *Annie Falconer's* owner and master, telephoned the results of the disaster to his wife and the mate's family and friends. The captain and crewmembers were local boys, all hailing from nearby Picton.

THE ANNIE FALCONER FOUNDERS

Between False Duck and Timber Islands Saturday Noon.

Every fall brings with it November gales that inflict more or less damage to navigation—vessels go to the bottom never to rise again; and the life of many a dear one lost forever. The mighty gale that swept old Lake Ontario on Satur-

Left: *The schooner,* Annie Falconer, *from a painting by Gibbons.*
Right: *The sad news in the* Picton Gazette *on Nov. 15, 1904.*   (BOTH: KOHL-FORSBERG ARCHIVES)

According to insurance records, in 1875, the *Annie Falconer* was valued at $8,000; in 1882, $6,000; by 1890, only $4,500. At the time of her loss in 1904, the aging *Annie* had an estimated value of only $1,000; 37 years is considered old for a wooden ship, even on the Great Lakes. At the time of her loss, her coal cargo, appraised at $1,500, was worth considerably more than the ship!

Barbara Carson, Audrey Rushbrook, and Doug Pettingill located the wreck of the *Annie Falconer* in 1975. This shipwreck is one of the best and most popular explorations that wreck divers can experience anywhere in the Great Lakes! The wreck sits upright on a mud bottom in about 78 feet (23.6 metres) of water about 1.5 miles north of the False Duck Island Light, and is very well preserved, with deadeyes, anchors, blocks, chain, and the ship's wheel in place. Her stern broke off, but it lies within visible range at an angle to the main hull. Limited shipwreck penetration is possible in the forward portion. There is much to see at this incredible site!

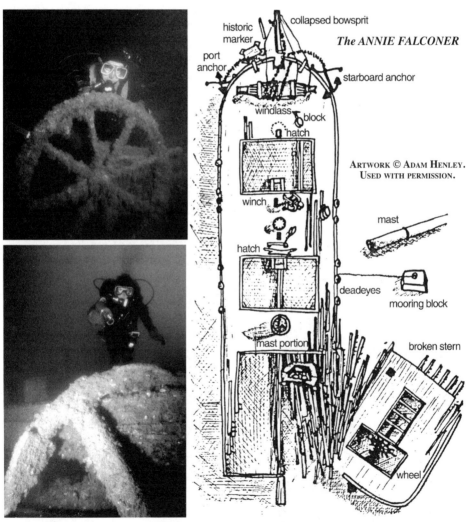

The ANNIE FALCONER

Artwork © Adam Henley. Used with permission.

Left, top: *Doug Pettingill, co-finder of the wreck of the* Annie Falconer, *takes a turn at "steering the* Annie," *something many hundreds, if not thousands, of scuba divers have done.*
Left, bottom: *Pat Stayer studies the port bow anchor on the* Annie Falconer. *About two weeks later, the heavy anchor lost its grip on the rail and fell to the lake bottom.* (Photos by Cris Kohl)

22. OLIVE BRANCH

SEPTEMBER 30, 1880   LAKE ONTARIO

A mystery ship succumbed to wild Lake Ontario waves in an early autumn storm on September 30, 1880, sinking between Main Duck Island and False Duck Island. Several schooners, initially unaccounted for after the storm, turned up safely over the next five days, leaving only one missing. To verify its identity, one schooner captain sailed his ship close to the wreck, lowered a boat, and recovered the lost vessel's fly (a small flag used for indicating wind direction) from the topmast of the sunken ship sticking out of the water, and the ship's identity was established as the *Olive Branch*.

Operating primarily as a barley carrier, the *Olive Branch* had been loaded with coal before she left Oswego, NY, bound for Kingston. She encountered bitterly severe weather, and sank off False Duck Island. All on board were lost: Captain Aull of Kingston, the female cook from Belleville, plus two French sailors, and one from Oswego, NY.

The uninsured -- her insurance policy had expired on September 15th, two weeks before her loss! -- two-masted schooner, *Olive Branch* (92'4" x 22' x 8'), was built in Picton, Ontario, in 1871. At the time of loss, although only nine years old, she was rated in the low category of B1 by the underwriters, being valued at only $3,000.

In 1961, local maritime historian, Willis Metcalfe, met a Kingston scuba diver named Guenter Wernthaler and, with charts in hand, discussed the probable resting place of the *Olive Branch*. A dot was penciled onto the chart, and Mr. Wernthaler, with his depth sounder and his boat set for discovery, excitedly proceeded to the spot and located the shipwreck within a half hour of searching. The *Olive Branch* is intact, sitting upright at the base of a shoal down which the ship appears to have slid. The original accounts placed the wreck in about 70 feet of water, but she now rests in 98 feet. A sidescan sonar image of the steep slope off the wreck's stern suggests a skid mark left by the vessel when it slipped down that slope into deeper water. These impressive physical remains remind us of this tragedy.

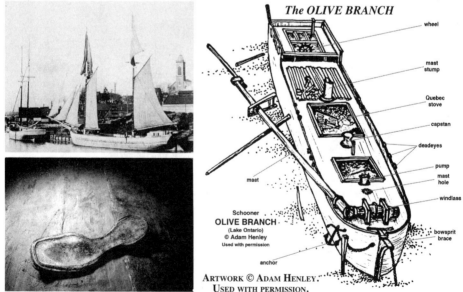

Left, top: *The schooner,* Olive Branch, *resembled this vessel, the schooner,* **J. H. Stevens,** *which was built in Milan, Ohio, in 1859 and was abandoned in 1908.*   (KOHL-FORSBERG ARCHIVES)
Left, bottom: *A grim reminder that the crew perished on the* **Olive Branch.** (PHOTO BY CRIS KOHL)

23. *MANOLA* (BOW)
DECEMBER 3, 1918   LAKE ONTARIO

Left: *The* Manola, *as captured on film by noted photographer Louis Pesha.*

Right: *All hands were lost when this half a ship sank.*

(BOTH: KOHL-FORSBERG ARCHIVES)

ELEVEN ARE DROWNED WHEN VESSEL SINKS

The Bow Section of the Minola Went Down at Duck Island.

Watertown, N.Y., Dec. 4.—Eleven men, comprising the crew of the bow section of the freighter Minola, are believed to have been drowned when that section of the boat went down in Lake Ontario, near Duck Island, Monday night, in a terrific gale and blizzard.

News of the disaster was brought into Cape Vincent yesterday, by the Government tug Michigan, which was towing the Minola. The captain of the Michigan reports that within five minutes after the lines parted, the Minola foundered. The sea was

The story of the *Manola* is a tale of how one ship became two shipwrecks in different lakes!

Built in 1890 by the Globe Iron Works Company of Cleveland, Ohio, the steel steamship, *Manola* (282'4" x 40'3" x 21'2"), received very favourable reviews when launched, with one newspaper calling the ship a "magnificent specimen of marine architecture" specially designed for the iron ore trade and capable of cruising at 12 knots fully loaded.

After 28 years of service on the Great Lakes, the Manola was sold to the Emergency Fleet Corporation of the United States Government in early 1918 to be used for the war effort (World War One) on the Atlantic Ocean. The ship, too long to pass through the locks of the old Welland Canal, with its 250-foot (75.8 metres) maximum length, had to be cut in two, to be re-assembled at Montréal once it emerged from the canal and crossed Lake Ontario. But Lake Ontario proved to be the most challenging portion of the voyage.

Snowstorm conditions developed while the two halves of the *Manola* were being towed across Lake Ontario on December 3, 1918. The towline unexpectedly parted and the bow half of the *Manola* suddenly toppled over and plummeted to the lake depths, taking with it the eleven men who were on board. All died, and only one body was ever found. Ironically, World War One, for which the *Manola* was cut in half and towed through the canal and across the open lake, had ended just a few days earlier!

The stern half of the *Manola* was used in a rebuild, the resulting ship being named the *Mapledawn*, which was wrecked in Georgian Bay in 1924 (see page 154).

In 1976, local maritime historians and underwater explorers Barbara Carson and Doug Pettingill located the *Manola's* bow half in 82 feet (25 metres) of water off Point Traverse, Ontario. Despite this shipwreck lying upside-down, many items of interest, including anchors, brass portholes, and pulleys, interest visiting divers.

Left: *Doug Pettingill, one of the discoverers of the* Manola, *poses under an anchor on this upside-down shipwreck.*

Right: *Doug Pettingill with the* Manola *bell which he recovered and donated to a local museum.* (BOTH PHOTOS BY CRIS KOHL)

24. R. H. RAE
AUGUST 4, 1858   LAKE ONTARIO

The three-masted, merchant bark of 344 tons, the ***R. H. Rae*** (136'5" x 23'2" x 11'2"), was launched on October 5, 1857, at the famous shipyard of Louis Shickluna at St. Catharines, Canada West (which later became Ontario). This vessel, however, was not built by him, but rather by Donaldson & Andrews, who had purchased the shipyard in late 1856 for $60,000 when Shickluna planned to retire; he changed his mind and re-acquired his yard

The huge windlass is only one item of interest on or near the bow of the **R. H. Rae**. *Other attractions include the ornately-carved bow stem and copper-capped samson posts.*

Marcy McElmon positions herself between the two, wooden tubes that served as part of the ship's bilge pump system.

The **R. H. Rae's** *huge rudder rests on a twisted angle. Other items of interest on this wreck include winches, blocks, and an 1857 toilet* (ALL PHOTOS ARE BY CRIS KOHL)

for the same sum a year later, but not before the *R. H. Rae* was built and launched, making her historically unique based solely upon this background.

The *R. H. Rae* was the first Canadian ship to utilize a self-reefing topsail design, which avoided having to send sailors aloft to do this dangerous work.

The *Rae,* however, sank during her first full season of operation about two miles (three kilometres) south of Point Traverse, in a situation also considered unique. White squalls appear suddenly and forcefully on the Great Lakes, usually during summer months. It was just such a violent, unexpected, three-minute-long blast of wind which capsized and sank the *R. H. Rae* "in about 20 fathoms of water," at 11:30 a.m. on August 4, 1858. The crew, with great difficulty, saved themselves in their lifeboat.

In 1976, maritime historians and shipwreck hunters, Barbara Carson and Audrey Rushbrook, located the *R. H. Rae,* keeping the location a secret, but, in 1980, in collaboration with the Marine Museum of the Great Lakes at Kingston, offered this shipwreck to Jacques Cousteau during his only expedition to the Great Lakes. Many artifacts, including the ship's wheel, were raised for display in the museum. Unfortunately, Cousteau lost a diver on this shipwreck.

This shipwreck location returned to secrecy, known but to a few divers, until being relocated 16 years later on July 25, 1996, according to a sign placed with *Rae* artifacts in the Marine Museum, "using sidescan sonar by a team lead by Chris *[sic]* Kohl..." who gave the location to a local charter boat operator so that "...sport divers were finally able to visit the wreck."

25. *Ocean Wave*

April 30, 1853   Lake Ontario

Built at Montréal in 1852 by E. D. Merritt for the brewery baron, John Molson, and launched on May 22 of that year, the 241-ton *Ocean Wave* (174'2" x 26' x 11'7") joined six other steamers that ran between Montréal in Canada East and Hamilton in Canada West.

This fine, upper-cabin sidewheeler, traveling between Hamilton and Ogdensburg, NY, on the evening of April 29, 1853, transported 26 passengers, a crew of 31, and a cargo of 1,500 barrels of flour, 200 kegs of butter, 80 barrels of ham and pork, and miscellaneous freight. A fire, apparently started from smokestack sparks which alighted on the roof of a freshly repainted cabin, started at 2 a.m., when most people had retired to bed.

One crewmember used an axe to chop an opening in the blazing cabin to free the passengers, but strong breezes whipped the flames into a frenzy, and the entire ship was soon enveloped. People desperately jumped overboard clinging to anything that would float, such as furniture or planks. The captain, upon awakening, evaluated the fire to be beyond control, so he promptly seized two flour barrels, jumped overboard, and kicked towards shore; this behaviour was exonerated by the subsequent inquest. The *Ocean Wave* sank at about 6 a.m., taking 28 lives (13 passengers and 15 crew) with her. One passenger, Mrs. Stevenson, tragically lost her three children, all under the age of six. Despite being hampered by the intense heat from the flaming steamer, the schooners, *Emblem* and *Georgianna*, assisted with rescues, as did a Point Traverse farmer who rowed out in his little boat. The first person he picked up was the *Ocean Wave's* captain.

The fire broke out when the *Ocean Wave* was two miles (3.2 kms.) from land near the Ducks, but the wind blew the vessel about six miles (9.6 kms.) offshore. A team of divers, including Barbara Carson and Doug Pettingill, located this shipwreck in 1991, south of Point Traverse, upside-down in 153 feet of dark water.

DESTRUCTION OF THE STEAMER OCEAN WAVE ON LAKE ONTARIO.—DESCRIPTION ON PAGE 330.

The Illustrated News, *from New York City, on May 21, 1853, provided its readers with this dramatic depiction of the steamer,* Ocean Wave, *ablaze on Lake Ontario.* (Kohl-Forsberg Archives)

26. *ATLASCO*

AUGUST 7, 1921   LAKE ONTARIO

The barge, *Atlasco,* slid down the launch ramp originally as the steamer *Russell Sage* (218' x 32'8" x 13'4") in Buffalo, New York, on May 21, 1881. The *Sage* was one of the old-style package freight steamers without arches, hauling mostly package freight between Buffalo and Toledo on Lake Erie. The *Russell Sage* caught on fire at her dock at Oswego, NY, on November 2, 1912, and she burned to the waterline.

The hulk of the burned-out *Russell Sage* remained at Oswego until 1917, when the Barge Ireland Company of Montréal purchased the remains for rebuilding as a barge, and renamed it the *Atlasco*, under which name she lasted four years. On August 7, 1921, the *Atlasco* foundered in a storm off Ostrander Point with a cargo of coiled wire, along with the barge, *Condor*, with no lives lost. Both barges were being towed by the steamer, *Macassen*, which rescued all the people on them before cutting them loose. The *Condor* washed ashore and today lies embedded in the shoreline, some of it visible, while the *Atlasco* sank in 43 feet (13 metres) of water. The steamers, *Cornwall* and *City of New York*, as well as other ships, salvaged half of the wire cargo; the rest remains on the shipwreck today. Commercial fisherman Doug Harrison gave local maritime historian Doug Pettingill the coordinates to this "obstruction" in 1990, and Doug became the first diver to see this wreck.

Left to right: *The barge,* Atlasco, *was launched as the steamer,* Russell Sage. (KOHL-FORSBERG ARCHIVES). *Doug Pettingill descends to the* Atlasco *shipwreck. Diver James Taylor examines the many, large coils of wire that remain on the shipwreck.*   (PHOTOS BY CRIS KOHL)

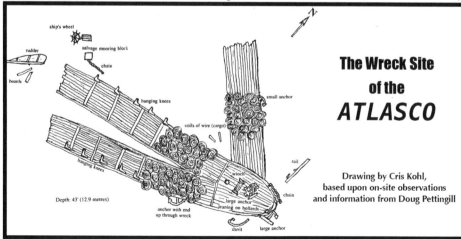

The Wreck Site
of the
ATLASCO

Drawing by Cris Kohl,
based upon on-site observations
and information from Doug Pettingill

27. *FRANK C. BARNES*

NOVEMBER 2, 1915   LAKE ONTARIO

Only a few weeks after the tragic sinking of the *City of Sheboygan* (see page 30), a wooden tugboat of the Canada Steamship Lines, the *Frank C. Barnes* (66'7" x 16'3" x 7'2"), foundered with the loss of all five hands while enroute from Port Dalhousie to Montréal. Young (he was merely 30 years old) Captain Bert LaRush planned this as his last run of the 1915 season, but instead, it "proved to be his last venture in this world."

An eyewitness had reported seeing the tug on Tuesday, three miles below Point Petre, southeast of Gull Pond, "and when he first saw her, she was going very slow with but little steam and a gale of wind. This was about ten or half past ten in the morning. Then he turned round and looked at her again and she had disappeared altogether."

Captain Donnelly, from nearby Kingston, took his wrecking vessel, the *Cornwall* (see page 26 for its story) out on the lake in search of the missing tugboat on Sunday, November 7, 1915, but found no trace of the *Barnes*.

A week later, the unidentified body of a man wearing a *"Frank C. Barnes"* lifebelt washed ashore at Consecon, Ontario; this body, which remained unidentified, was sent to Toronto and buried at the Metropolis. On November 15, 1915, a portion of the pilothouse of the *Frank C. Barnes* was found ashore near Oswego, on the other side of the lake.

Another body from the *Barnes* was found off Salmon Point on Sunday, November 21, 1915. A local resident was looking after his boats early that morning when he noticed a body floating in the water. With assistance from some neighbours, he retrieved the corpse and sent it to Picton, where it was identified as a sailor from the *Barnes*.

The body of the Japanese cook, Harry Yips, aged about 35 years, was found on the lakeshore at Cressy, Ontario, on November 28, 1915, according to one newspaper, "in a good state of preservation" with "a small amount of money and a gold chain, with a $10 gold piece as a charm." No one claimed the body, so it was buried in Glenwood Cemetery (which likely kept his valuables as payment for interment). The man who had found Yips' body had seen another floating in the high seas near the shore, but could not recover it.

The 46-ton *Frank C. Barnes*, built in 1892 at Manistee, Michigan, was sold to Canadian interests in 1906. This little shipwreck has not yet been found.

The Foundered Tug, Frank G. Barnes

Body Found at Consecon and Portion of Pilot House Washed Ashore

(Canadian Press Special)

OSWEGO, Nov. 15.—A portion of the Pilot house of the tug, Frank G. Barnes, which foundered two weeks ago while on the way from Port Dalhousie to Montreal, was found on the shore near here today.

The body of a man was washed ashore at Consecon on Sunday. He had

The tug, **Frank C. Barnes,** *sank with all hands in 1915. The* **Belleville Daily Intelligencer,** *on Nov. 15, 1915, provided one of numerous accounts of the lost boat.*

(BOTH KOHL-FORSBERG ARCHIVES)

28. *JESSIE*

OCTOBER 31, 1871   LAKE ONTARIO

The loss of the two-masted, Port Stanley schooner, *Jessie* (121'6" x 23' x 10') with all hands on October 31, 1871, prompted the Canadian government to construct the lighthouse at Salmon Point (earlier named "Wicked Point" due to its notorious danger to navigation) and establish the first lifeboat, or lifesaving station, on the Canadian side of Lake Ontario, and probably in the entire Great Lakes system.

Heavily loaded with 13,000 bushels of wheat, the *Jessie* sought shelter from the storm on Lake Ontario and somehow successfully sailed across the shallow bar into Sandy Bay near Salmon Point. She dropped her anchors and headsails (or jibs), and left her lower sails in place. The wind, however, shifted from the southeast to the west, and the *Jessie* was unable to exit the bay, a place which then became her captor rather than her protector.

Newspapers said the ship "dragged her anchors and struck bottom" about 500 feet (150 metres) from shore. The relentless fury of the wind and the waves gradually tore apart the *Jessie,* with her crewmembers clinging to the ship's rigging in hopes of imminent rescue by the terror-stricken spectators gathering helplessly along the shore.

The twin-masted schooner, **Jessie,** *resembled this schooner, the* **Thomas Dobbie,** *launched as the* **Comanche** *in 1867, and abandoned at Deseronto, Ontario, in 1905.*
(KOHL-FORSBERG ARCHIVES)

At approximately ten o'clock in the morning, all hopes were suddenly dashed when the ship appeared to break in two, her spars falling in different directions, nine human beings (not eight, as had been initially reported) being enveloped by the angry seas. Two or three of the sailors kept themselves above the waves for a few minutes, but all lost their struggles for life. One powerful man, apparently an expert swimmer, was carried parallel to the beach by the current in his attempt to reach shore, but disappeared just before he attained the halfway point to land. His body washed ashore a short time later, while another male body, presumably from this crew, was found a month later. The other seven crewmembers were never located, the assumption being that their bodies had been taken by the undercurrent into deep water off Salmon Point.

Fragments of the ill-fated vessel littered the beach for about half a mile, with one witness reporting to the press that "nearly every timber seemed to be completely rotten -- in fact, we scarcely saw a fragment amongst the tens of thousands that we could not pound to pieces and pulverize with a small mallet."

The *Jessie* was built in 1854-55 by famous St. Catharines shipwright, Louis Shickluna, at Port Robinson, Ontario.

29. *NORTH WEST* (BOW)

NOVEMBER 28, 1918   LAKE ONTARIO

Left: *The enormous, impressive* North West *was needed for service in World War One.*
Right: *Due to her length, the ship had to be cut in two to get her through the old Welland Canal.*
(BOTH: KOHL-FORSBERG ARCHIVES)

Happening under similar circumstances as the *Manola* (see story on page 37), but exactly four days prior to the *Manola's* loss, the sinking of the bow half of the huge, steel ship named the *North West* resulted in lives lost.

The 4,244-gross-ton, steel *North West* (358' x 44' x 24'), built in 1894 at Cleveland, Ohio, received considerable media coverage praising its gargantuan merits, from its quadruple expansion steam engine to its enormous hull. In 1902, its original boilers were replaced by ten scotch boilers, giving some idea of the ship's size and power.

The ship, however, burned in the harbour at Buffalo, NY, on June 3, 1911, and it sat idle for years, until the USA's entry into World War One in April, 1917. This action led to plans to use the *North West* for the war effort on the Atlantic Ocean. The oversized ship was cut in two at Buffalo in late October 1917, in order to float the huge pieces through the Welland Canal, with plans to reconnect the two parts once they reached Montréal. After a prolonged delay, during which the ship's ownership changed four times, the two parts were towed across Lake Ontario. However, the bow half sank on November 28, 1918.

In transit, when the weather worsened, the man in charge cut his bow loose from the towing tug off Rochester, NY, and dropped anchors to ride out the storm. But this bow broke away and drifted across the lake. As the weather worsened, the bulkheads broke in. The men took to a makeshift raft, which overturned when close to shore, but all made it to land. They wandered for miles along the Canadian shore before finding shelter, but not before two of the men died on the beach. This bow half, according to contemporary newspapers, sank in 100 feet (30 metres) of water, "a short distance off the Prince Edward County shore," but it was reportedly located there recently in over 200 feet (60 metres).

TWO SAILORS DIE OWING TO EXPOSURE

The Terrible Experience of Crew of the Lost Steamer Northwest.

Trenton, Dec. 2.—Charles Jardine and George Fryon, sailors, of Buffalo, are dead, and Capt. McMinn and the remainder of his crew of nine are lying in farmhouses some distance from Trenton recovering from the effects of exposure following the sinking off the Scotch Bonnets, a point in Lake Ontario some distance from Trenton, of the bow section of the steamer North West. The bow end of the steamer cut loose from her tow some distance from Rochester during a storm on

Left: *The loss of two lives was reported by the Belleville newspaper on Dec. 2, 1918.*
Right: *The* North West's *stern was rebuilt as the* Maplecourt, *later a U-boat victim in the Atlantic on Feb. 6, 1941.* (BOTH: KOHL-FORSBERG ARCHIVES)

30. ZEALAND

NOVEMBER 7, 1880   LAKE ONTARIO

On November 10, 1880, a grim report emerged from Lake Ontario:

> **...The schooner, *Guiding Star,* Capt. M. Griffith, arrived** [at Port Dalhousie] **from Oswego and reports having passed pieces of cabin, bedclothes, water tank and barrels of flour. The flour was made by and marked Z.W. Tyson & Co., Clarksburgh, Ont.**
>
> **One of the crew says they passed the schooner *Ariel* picking up the flour. The lake was filled with portions of the wreck and is suppposed to be that of some propeller bound from Toronto to Kingston. Pieces of white railing were also picked up....**

A day later, it was ascertained that this wreckage off Long Point in Prince Edward County, Ontario, came from a ship named the *Zealand*, which had left Toronto bound for Montréal on November 6, 1880, with a cargo of grain and flour. The *Zealand's* master was Captain Zealand, who had purchased the ship in 1874, after it had suffered a serious fire at Hamilton in 1873, giving the rebuilt vessel his family name.

The 361-gross-ton, wooden propeller, *Zealand* (136' x 26' x 12'), was built by Hyslop & Ronald and launched at Chatham, Ontario, on Nov. 3, 1871, as the *City of Chatham*. It was the right length to fit the locks of the Welland Canal; hence it was called a "canaler."

Critics denounced the type of vessel represented by the *Zealand*, e.g. "The canal style of craft continues to furnish the horrors. Other craft go ashore, are dismasted, waterlog, sink, etc., etc., but the only craft that go down with all hands are the canalers...." (*Chicago Inter Ocean,* November 11, 1880.) When another "canaler," built by the same builder in Chatham, Ontario, went down in Lake Huron with nearly all hands within three weeks of the *Zealand's* loss, the criticism of canalers, specifically those built in Chatham, multiplied. Read the story of the sinking of the *Simcoe* on page 165.

Captain Zealand's son, living in Hamilton, publicized the offer of a $200 reward for his father's body. The reward was never collected. The wreck has also not been found, despite rumours that wreckers, searching for another ship, found the hull in the 1890s

MARINE INTELLIGENCE.

Further Positive Proof of the Danger of the Canal Style of Craft.

The Propeller Zealand Still Unheard From and Doubtless Lost with All Hands.

Various Disasters and News from the Recent Wrecks on This and the Other Lakes.

Left: *The* Zealand, *as drawn by maritime historian C.H.J. Snider.* (TORONTO REFERENCE LIBRARY)
Right: *The* Zealand *drew the dramatic, multi-headlined, journalistic attention that the press usually afforded to vessels lost with all hands.*   (KOHL-FORSBERG ARCHIVES)

31. *BELLE SHERIDAN*

NOVEMBER 7, 1880   LAKE ONTARIO

WHERE THE "BELLE SHERIDAN" POUNDED TO PIECES

On November 7, 1920, the Toronto Telegram *newspaper printed a commemorative, 40th anniversary story on the loss of the* Belle Sheridan. *The above drawing of the vessel and the map, which indicates where the ship first dropped anchor to ride out the storm, and where she ultimately grounded and broke up, are from that source.*   (KOHL-FORSBERG ARCHIVES)

The two-masted, 256-ton schooner, *Belle Sheridan* (123' x 22'8" x 10'2"), built at Oswego, NY, by Andrew Miller in 1852, was overhauled, repaired, and rebuilt several times during her 28-year career, including slight damages from the inevitable collisions with other ships. Then this vessel faced the same storm that sank the *Zealand* (see page 44).

In 1877, now 25 years old, the *Belle Sheridan* sank in a waterlogged condition at a Toronto dock at the foot of Church Street. In July 1878, the *Belle Sheridan* was offered for sale by order of the Maritime Court, and the vessel was reportedly purchased by John Lamb for $900. He, in turn, sold the ship to Capt. James McSherry in February 1880, who, along with his four sons, rebuilt the *Belle Sheridan* and returned her to service.

Unfortunately, it was a short service.

The press reported later that year, on November 9, 1880, with some inaccuracies:

> **A private dispatch states that the schooner *Belle Sheridan* is a total wreck at Weller's Bay, and that six of the crew -- probably all hands -- are lost. The victims are Captain McSherry, Mate McSherry, two seamen named McSherry, and two seamen whose names are not known. The male members of the McSherry family, who hail from Toronto, are all lost by this disaster. Captain McSherry was the father of the three other men of that name. The *Sheridan*...was owned by Captain McSherry, rated B1 [in insurance ratings], and was valued at $6,000. Whether insured is not known....**

Four of Captain McSherry's sons were working on board: John, 21 years old; James, 18; Thomas, 17; and Edward, 13. Jack Hamilton and Samuel Boyd rounded out the crew. To ride out a severe storm, the *Belle Sheridan* dropped her anchors at the mouth of Presquile Bay, but they failed to hold, and the ship was dragged by strong winds to Beecroft Point near Weller Bay. Although the ship ran aground only about a hundred yards, or metres, from shore, and hundreds of people gathered in an effort to assist the stricken crew, 18-year-old James was the sole survivor. Holding tightly onto a huge timber, he jumped overboard and swam madly for shore, arriving more dead than alive before being transported to a nearby farmhouse for warmth and food.

In 1933, portions of the *Belle Sheridan's* deck and ribbing were raised and returned to their home port of Toronto.

32. SPEEDY

OCTOBER 8, 1804   LAKE ONTARIO

The sailing ship, *Speedy,* was built in 1796 at Cataraqui (Kingston), and sank in a storm on the night of October 8, 1804, while transporting numerous prestigious politicians and influential others a distance of 93 miles (150 kms.) from Toronto (then called York) to the newly-surveyed district capital named Newmarket (which, at this point in history, consisted only of a courthouse; the planned town later failed to materialize) at Presquile.

The foundation of this sailing trip was to deliver a prisoner to justice at the new courthouse. An Ojibway Indian named Ogetonicut had been arrested for the clubbing murder of a trader named John Sharp at Lake Scugog. On board the *Speedy,* the chained prisoner was confined deep in the hold, while the notables, including the Honourable Thomas Cochrane, Judge of the Court of King's Bench in Upper Canada; Robert Gray, the Solicitor-General of Upper Canada and his slave, Simon Black; Angus MacDonald, treasurer of the Upper Canada Law Society; John Fiske, High Bailiff of York; and others, enjoyed more comfortable quarters above.

The Speedy *under sail.*
(ARTWORK BY GEORGE CUTHBERTSON)

Somewhere close to Presquile, during a storm, the *Speedy* sank with the loss of all on board. Some of her spars and her compass box were the only items that washed ashore. Why she sank may never be known. Some argue that the *Speedy* may have struck a "needle" rock which rose close to the surface from the lake bottom. One imaginative, colourful legend is that Ogetonicut, nicknamed "Mad Dog," in his zealous determination never to hang for the murder of a white man, clawed a hole into the bottom of this wooden vessel with his nails and teeth, sending himself and those on board into infinity when the ship sank. A local marine/archaeological firm has long claimed to have found the *Speedy's* broken and scattered remains, with some compelling evidence -- but not yet with the "smoking gun" evidence that would absolutely identify it.

The Speedy *struggling in the storm that sank her.*   (COURTESY OF ARTIST PETER RINDLISBACHER)

Sponsored by **LIGHTHOUSE BOOKS**
65 Main Street, P.O. Box 190, Brighton, ON K0K 1H0
Tel: (613) 475-1269   ligboo@bellnet.ca   www.facebook.com/LighthouseBooksBrighton
We sell new releases, award winners, bestsellers, local authors, and children's favourites.

33. *ICEBERG*

AUGUST 17 (?), 1857   LAKE ONTARIO

There is a shipwreck somewhere at the bottom of Lake Ontario that has a strong connection to the famous Franklin Expedition, lost in Canada's Arctic in the late 1840s. With the recent discoveries of Franklin's Arctic ships, the ***Erebus*** and the ***Terror,*** it seems appropriate to bring the story of the ***Iceberg*** to the surface now.

However, this tale begins with a man of noted physical stamina named John Rae (September 30, 1813 - July 22, 1893), who worked for the Hudson's Bay Company as a Scottish explorer of northern Canada beginning in 1846, and is perhaps best remembered as the man who brought disturbing news to England regarding the fate of the Franklin Expedition members in 1854. Through Inuit (native) connections, he found the remains of about 30 members of the Franklin Expedition who had starved to death over the winter of 1850-51. With them, he found a small, silver plate engraved with Franklin's name. Evidence, such as human bones cut by knives or axes, indicated that cannibalism had taken place. Back in

Left: *Famous Arctic explorer, John Rae, was determined to return to the Arctic for more discoveries.* **Right:** *The "Arctic exploration" brigantine,* Iceberg, *built at Kingston for Rae in the spring of 1857, disappeared on Lake Ontario that summer!* (BOTH: KOHL-FORSBERG ARCHIVES)

England, the thought of British explorers turning to cannibalism was abhorant and impossible to believe, particularly by Lady Franklin (John's widow). Only after she learned that her husband had died long before the cannibalism took place did she warm to Rae, who was finally given the huge monetary prize that was offered for finding the expedition's fate.

With this money, Rae returned to his two brothers in Hamilton, Canada West, with plans to keep exploring the Arctic for more Franklin evidence and to find the elusive Northwest Passage. Rae decided to build a special ship for Arctic exploration.

Constructed at Kingston, Canada West (later Ontario), and launched on Sunday, June 21, 1857, Rae's brigantine, ***Iceberg***, measured a relatively small 117 tons, carpenter's measurement. While local newspapers gave provided information about the new ship, perhaps the best description came from the *New York Daily Times* on June 25, 1857: "...She is heavily built -- strength being more necessary than beauty, considering the severe work she is destined to perform. Yet her appearance in the water is particularly graceful...." But because it was too late that year to sail this impressive ship to England, outfit her, and proceed to the Arctic, Rae decided to put his new vessel, which had cost him $6,450 to build, to work in the Great Lakes' freighting trade for the remainder of 1857.

However, Rae's vessel did not complete the shipping season on the the inland seas. The ***Iceberg***, hauling a coal cargo from Cleveland to Kingston, traversed the Welland Canal into Lake Ontario on August 12, 1857, and headed across the open lake towards Kingston at the other end. A storm arose, and the ship and its seven crew members were never seen again -- another example of Great Lakes violence having been underestimated. Some wreckage washed ashore in eastern Lake Ontario. Rae did no more Arctic exploration.

34. ALEXANDRIA

AUGUST 3, 1915   LAKE ONTARIO

The sidewheel steamtug named the *Alexandra* (161'7" x 25'2" x 8'1") was built by Auguste Cantin in Montréal in 1866 for the purpose of towing barges on the Ottawa River between Montréal and Ottawa, and the ship's name was changed ever-so-slightly to *Alexandria* in 1883. In the course of her 49-year-long career, she did move to different work areas, and she did encounter some problems, including being wrecked off the Scarborough cliffs early in her career, on November 6, 1880, from which the vessel was quickly released, repaired, and returned to service. A subsequent rebuild at Picton, Ontario, increased her dimensions and tonnage somewhat.

The paddlewheel steamer, Alexandria, *was built at Montréal in 1866.*   (KOHL-FORSBERG ARCHIVES)

On Tuesday afternoon, August 3, 1915, bound from Port Hope to Toronto with a partial cargo of general merchandise, mostly pickles, vinegar, potatoes, canned tomatoes, and sugar, the *Alexandria* encountered severe weather, became stranded at the base of the Scarborough Bluffs approximately 600 feet (180 metres) off shore, and broke up from the severe pounding just off the narrow beach area; specifically, a large bow section and a similarly sized stern section broke away from the hull. All 22 men (this was a huge crew!) on board survived, some by swimming ashore, and others using the lifeline that the crowd of people on shore had managed to get to the stricken vessel.

After the storm, the collapsed vessel remained an interesting local site, lying on her port side, helplessly embedded in the bottom, proclaiming her anguish with the loud presence of her huge boiler, iron girders, and oak timbers. Before long, every valve, nut, and bolt was removed by local swimmers as proof of their daring, or simply collected as souvenirs. Rumour has it that many cellars were well-stocked with vinegar containers and canned goods from the *Alexandria,* while many of her huge timbers, useless as part of a shipwreck back in those unappreciative days, were retrieved for shed construction. With the wreck lying so openly in such shallow water (maximum 10 feet, or 3 metres), the hull soon broke up, and the *Alexandria* stopped looking like a ship when most of it disappeared beneath the waves.

Left: *It was at the base of the Scarborough Bluffs that the* Alexandria *met her demise.*
Right: *The shallow wreck of the* Alexandria *was a total loss.*   (BOTH: KOHL-FORSBERG ARCHIVES)

35. *REUBEN DOUD*

AUGUST 24, 1906   LAKE ONTARIO

Constructed of strong white oak by builder Cecil Gibson at Winneconne, Wisconsin, in 1873 for a company called Doud & Vance, and named after Mr. Reuben Doud (1830-1877), the major owner of Wisconsin's Wolf River Transportation Company and co-owner of the lumber firm of Doud & Vance in Racine, the three-masted schooner, *Reuben Doud* (137' x 26' x 11'5"), within two months of her launch, ran aground at Lake Erie's notorious Point Pelee, but was recovered, repaired, and returned to service. The *Doud* was also temporarily wrecked near Pelee Island in 1900. In between her Pelee misadventures, the ship lost her centreboard on Lake Michigan, stranded at Goderich, and collided with at least one other vessel, all requiring repairs of varying degrees.

The *Reuben Doud* gained a reputation as being a ship that was difficult to steer and handle, earning the nickname "bull of the woods." Another source gives the (unlikely) reason for the nickname being the fact that the ship could easily pull in and out of small, wilderness harbours.

In 1901, the aging schooner was purchased by the Conger Coal Company for use in the Toronto coal trade, and was refitted at Windsor, Ontario, while on her way down to her new home on Lake Ontario. Strangely enough, this refitting left her mainmast shorter than her foremast, and a peculiar, triangular "square" sail flew atop her foremast, both oddities for a schooner. Along with her relocation to Lake Ontario came her proclivity for difficult handling, and the *Doud* had trouble keeping captains.

The *Reuben Doud*, loaded with a coal cargo and sailing under the command of Captain John Joyce, approached Toronto's Eastern Gap on the evening of August 23, 1906, attempting to enter the harbour. However, an anchored dredge obstructed the gap's entranceway. The *Doud* waited until early morning the next day to try to sail past the dredge. But at the most critical point, there was a lull in the wind, and the *Doud* lost headway. An attempt to return the ship to the open waters of Lake Ontario resulted in the vessel grounding, and soon she unshipped her rudder. The wind then swung the schooner around and drove her in towards the beach about half a mile west of the piers. Toronto Island resident, Captain William Ward, commanded the government lifeboat that rescued all seven people on board the *Doud* before the 33-year-old sailing vessel broke apart.

While the upper sections of the schooner quickly broke to pieces and scattered, the bottom portion of the *Reuben Doud's* hull still lies submerged in the sands off the Ward's Island beach. The "bull of the woods" had finally been tamed.

Left: *The* Reuben Doud *looked smooth and impressive under sail.*   (KOHL-FORSBERG ARCHIVES)
Right: *C. H. J. Snider's dynamic drawing of the* Doud's *loss.*   (TORONTO REFERENCE LIBRARY)

36. NORONIC

SEPTEMBER 17, 1949   LAKE ONTARIO

To keep up with the huge popularity of Great Lakes steamship excursions in the early 1900s, the Northern Navigation Company of Canada spared no expense in 1913 to build a ship in the yard of the Western Dry Dock and Shipbuilding Company at Port Arthur (today part of the city of Thunder Bay, Ontario, the largest city on Lake Superior). This was the birth of the passenger steamer, *Noronic* (362' x 52' x 24'8"), destined to become the company's flagship and called the "Queen of the Fleet"-- but doomed to be remembered as one of Lake Ontario's worst Death Ships.

This nearly 7,000-gross-ton ship, which could accommodate 562 passengers in comfortable staterooms located on six decks, entered regular service placed on the run between Detroit, Windsor, and Sarnia, heading to the more distant Sault Ste. Marie, Port Arthur, Fort William, and Duluth on Lake Superior, with occasional evening excursions offering dinner, dancing, and moonlight. The *Noronic* joined the company's two other crown jewel vessels, the *Hamonic* (see page 120 for that ship's story) and the *Huronic*, all of which became part of the Canada Steamship Lines fleet.

Ten thousand people watched the historic launch of the passenger steamer, Noronic, *at Port Arthur, Ontario, on June 2, 1913.*

The luxurious *Noronic* provided music rooms, a writing room, a childrens' playroom, a chapel, and observation rooms for the comfort and convenience of her passengers. The fancy dining room on board the palatial *Noronic* was so large that it could serve 272 people at one time, about half the passenger capacity. This luxury ship's staterooms had beds, as opposed to bunks, and most rooms were equipped with baths and running water, luxuries not usually found on board Great Lakes ships build in 1913. A variety of onboard activities included games, dances, and masquerade parties.

The Noronic, *with its huge size, more closely resembled an ocean liner rather than a Great Lakes vessel.*

The *Noronic's* peak years were during the "roaring" 1920s, and, after surviving the bleak years of the Great Depression in the 1930s and World War Two in the early 1940s, the ship competed with a few other remaining vessels, plus millions of automobiles that had attracted people's time and money, for diminishing traveler dollars.

But it all ended suddenly one night in 1949.

Inside the Noronic, *delighted passengers found luxury furnishings.*
(ABOVE PHOTOS: KOHL-FORSBERG ARCHIVES)

Close to the end of the season in 1949, three charters were planned from Detroit and Cleveland to Toronto and the Thousand Islands, and back. A total of 524 passengers and a crew of 171 were on board the *Noronic* when it docked at Pier 9 in Toronto on September 16, 1949. Captain William Taylor, at 66, a 43-year employee of Canada Steamship Lines and master of the *Noronic* for the preceding eight years, and about half of the passengers, went out on the town in Toronto that evening. Just after 1:30 a.m., a man enjoying a drink in the lounge with his daughter strolled through C deck's starboard side when he saw blue-gray smoke issuing from a small linen closet. Finding the door locked, he located a bellboy who had a key to unlock it, and they tried to smother the fire with an extinguisher and a faulty fire hose before seeking a ship's officer.

This is probably the most famous and the most widely published of the dramatic photographs of the Noronic's demise.

Suddenly, with terrifying speed, the fire leaped out, roaring and crackling in both directions along the heavily varnished and painted floors and the tinder-dry woodwork of the 36-year-old ship. The fire alarm sounded, but precious time had been lost. Several passengers, including women and children, slid down ropes to the safety of the dock, suffering rope burns in the process. Many passengers who had no time to dress escaped in their night clothes down several ladders placed by the Toronto Fire Department, which had arrived within minutes of the call. Before long, thousands of gallons of water were pumped into the burning ship in a futile attempt to extinguish the spreading flames, and soon the *Noronic* listed and sank at her stern. Captain Taylor, who had returned to the ship just before the fire broke out, suffered injuries when he helped many people escape the flames.

The Noronic was blackened, with debris and ashes lying a foot deep on a deck with melted lifeboats still on their davits.

The next day, with the flames extinguished and the burned-out hull cooled enough, firemen finally dared to board the *Noronic*. Theirs was the grim task of removing cinderized bodies lying in foot-deep ashes and melted glass, or from scorched mattresses where passengers had died. Some bodies crumbled into ashes when firemen tried to move them. The magnitude of the disaster became evident; aside from the many bodies that were found, the ship itself proved to be a visual disaster from bow to stern. Below deck, dining room tables looked like so many burned stumps in a forest fire. Steel supports twisted like drinking straws gave mute evidence to the inferno's intensity. Despite numerous tales of fortune and heroism, the reality that 119 people had lost their lives in a cruise ship fire could not be equated or explained.

Many bodies could be identified only by such things as wedding rings, necklaces, clothing, and melted eyeglass frames.

Nearly all of the victims were US citizens; only one Canadian died in this tragedy. Truly shocking was that all of the dead were passengers; not a single crew member had perished. The censured Captain Taylor chose to retire.

This tragic fire essentially spelled the end of excursion ship travel on the Great Lakes.

The Noronic's hull was raised and towed to Hamilton, Ontario, for scrapping.
(ABOVE PHOTOS: KOHL-FORSBERG ARCHIVES)

37. Toronto Spectacle Ships

1928 - 1934   Lake Ontario

In the Great Lakes, especially in the early 1900s, many old, wooden, unseaworthy ships were removed from sight by being allowed to sink quietly along out-of-the-way river banks or along the edge of harbours, or towed out into deep water and scuttled (purposely sunk). But occasionally, someone with a passion for fire decided to make a flaming spectacle out of an old veteran.

Although ships were purposely burned in several areas of the Great Lakes, the high number of such spectacles reached a pinnacle in Toronto in the late 1920s-early 1930s.

The popularity of such spectacles began in the late summer of 1928 with the little-advertised torching of the 160-ton, 22-year-old steamer, *Missisiquoi* (87'3" x 20'9" x 5'4"), built in 1903 at Noyan, Québec.

Above, left: *The* Missisiquoi *was intentionally burned in August 1928.*
Above, right: *The* John Hanlan *was set ablaze at Sunnyside on July 20, 1929.*
Below, left: *The* Jasmine *was publically torched on August 3, 1929.*
Below, right: *The* Clark Brothers *was set on fire on July 1, 1930.*
(All Images: Kohl-Forsberg Archives)

Having proved popular, more burning spectacles were planned by the organizers, who searched for old wooden ships to put to the torch. They found two of them in the form of a pair of Toronto's longtime, ferry boats, the *John Hanlan* (71' x 16' x 6') built in 1884 at Dalhousie, Ontario, and the *Jasmine* (112'4" x 219" x 7'4") built as the *William M. Alderson* in 1884 at Port Burwell, Ontario, renamed *A. J. Tymon* from 1892 to 1902, the *Ojibway* from 1902 to 1906, and the *Jasmine* since 1906. Reportedly Toronto's Works Commissioner endorsed the city's recommendation to destroy the pair of veteran boats with the curt words, "Let Sunnyside have them and put a match to them."

And that is exactly what happened at Toronto's very popular Sunnyside Amusement Park, with the *John Hanlan* being destroyed in front of thousands of paying customers just after midnight on July 20, 1929, following the "tossing of torches from motor boats and dropping of bombs from an aeroplane," and the old steamer, *Jasmine*, providing a similar performance at the same place while anchored 100 yards outside the seawall, starting at midnight at the beginning of August 3, 1929, a local newspaper reported, "loaded up with dry wood and empty barrels, saturated with gasoline, and set alight with large torpedoes,... fired from the shore on wires which will stretch across the water from the old bandstand to her decks." The following year, despite rain, a crowd of 25,000 people packed Sunnyside's shoreline once again to see the small steamer, *Clark Brothers* (40' x 8'9" x 3'4", built in Toronto in 1890), go up in smoke during the first hour of Dominion Day, July 1, 1930.

By this time, public opinion was slowly changing, and the destruction of the next vessel met with opposition. A classic Great Lakes schooner, the *Julia B. Merrill* (128' x 26'5" x 8'4"), built at Wenona, Michigan, in 1872, hauled grain and lumber. The ship was sold to Canadian interests in 1910, and was an incredible 59 years old when the vessel was burned at Sunnyside Park as a public spectacle on July 2, 1931. Letters of outrage over the burning appeared in Toronto newspapers, mostly over the destruction of history, but one practical person, aware that the Great Depression was in progress, argued that the lumber from the *Merrill* would have kept many families warm that winter.

The public burning of the schooner, Julia B. Merrill, (left) *met with opposition.* (KOHL-FORSBERG ARCHIVES)

Below, left: *The Lyman M. Davis--the last commercial schooner.*
Below, middle: *Thousands of attendees bought commemorative pins to remember the burning of the* Davis.
Below, right: *The Lyman M. Davis had her timbers soaked in oil, dry wood piled on her deck, and rockets and fireworks attached to her rigging to thrill the crowd.* (ALL: KOHL-FORSBERG ARCHIVES)

Spectacle organizers laid low for three years. Finally in 1934, another candidate was found -- it turned out to be the last, commercial Great Lakes schooner in existemce.

The 225-gross-ton *Lyman M. Davis* (123' x 27'2" x 9'4"), built at Muskegon, Michigan, in 1873 as a lumber schooner, was sold to Canadian interests in 1913. The City of Toronto denounced the planned burning of the *Davis* when organizers tried to pass it off as a city centennial celebration. Toronto ferry boats had been one thing in 1929 and 1930, but this ship was truly historic! Thousands of people signed petitions to save the *Davis* in a drive led by maritime historian C. H. J. Snider. But nothing worked, and the ship was burned on June 29, 1934. This "grand light" served only to show Sunnyside's dark side.

38. KNAPP'S ROLLER BOAT

ABANDONED 1907?   LAKE ONTARIO

Frederick Augustus Knapp
(1854-1942)
(KOHL-FORSBERG ARCHIVES)

If you thought that whalebacks were bizarre-looking craft -- take a look at Knapp's Roller Boat!

Over the course of several years in the late 1800s, a few "roller steamer" type ships were conceived, but only two were actually constructed: one in France in 1896, and one in Toronto in 1897. Both were unsuccessful.

Knapp's design featured a large, steel cylinder inside another one, with the outer cylinder, which was powered by steam engines inside the inner cylinder to make it revolve, being equipped with a series of narrow paddles. The balanced, bevelled, inner cylinder which remained level, besides containing the steam engines, also held the passengers. Theoretically, this design could travel nearly twice as fast as a conventional steamship, using much less fuel.

Frederick Augustus Knapp was a lawyer, born in Prescott, Canada West, in 1854, and educated at Montréal's McGill University, but his passion was inventions. Knapp had his strange vessel, measuring 110 feet (33.3 metres) in length and 22 feet (6.7 metres) in diameter, built at the Polson Iron Works in Toronto, and launched on September 8, 1897. Thousands watched from the Toronto shoreline as the "boat" reached the speed of three miles an hour on its first test run. It performed better the following spring (1898) with wider paddles. Always the dreamer, Knapp hoped to impress his idol, Queen Victoria, with this ship that he felt certain would prevent the seasickness to which she was so prone whenever she went on a boat, and that this would earn him a knighthood. He also planned to build an 800-foot-long version, 200 feet high, that could carry 30,000 U.S. troops to Cuba for the Spanish-American War.

But nothing further came of his plans, other than more testing between Toronto and Prescott, with less than acceptable results. Back in Toronto, breaking free from its mooring in 1907, the roller boat struck and damaged the passenger ship, *Turbinia*. To pay for repairs, the boat was sold. But the hull was never claimed, and it lay abandoned in the shallows of Toronto Bay for decades. In the late 1920s, it was buried by the shoreline extension. Today, the hull reportedly lies under Lakeshore Blvd. between Richardson and Lower Sherbourne Streets. In the end, people called Knapp's Roller Boat something else: "Knapp's Folly."

Left: Knapp's Roller Boat *was a steel cylinder built in Toronto.*   (KOHL-FORSBERG ARCHIVES)
Right: *Canadian maritime historian C. H. J. Snider drew this version of* **Knapp's Roller Boat**
in motion, possibly while being tested off Toronto.   (TORONTO REFERENCE LIBRARY)

39. *SLIGO*

SEPTEMBER 5, 1918 LAKE ONTARIO

The long life of this three-masted vessel (138′ x 23′ x 11′8″) started in 1860 at St. Catharines, Canada West (later Ontario), when the bark, named the ***Prince of Wales***, slid down the launch ramp of the famous shipbuilder, Louis Shickluna.

This ship reportedly made several trans-Atlantic crossings before being converted into a "three & after" schooner at her original shipyard in 1863. Eleven years later, after being rebuilt at St. Catharines, the vessel was renamed the ***Sligo*** and was registered as a new ship on April 11, 1874. In 1893, the ***Sligo*** saw her final transformation, this time into a bulk-freight schooner-barge, at the James Simpson Shipyard at Port McNicoll, Ontario.

The Sligo *at Kincardine, Ontario, harbour, early in her career.* (KOHL-FORSBERG ARCHIVES)

A fierce gale parted the towline between the ***Sligo*** and the towing tug, ***New York***, on September 5, 1918. Loaded with 90 tons of limestone, the 58-year-old ***Sligo*** foundered. No lives were lost.

When Toronto diver, Don MacIntyre, located the resting place of the ***Sligo*** in 1985, he tried hard to keep it a secret for fear of wreckstrippers tearing it apart. Despite his efforts, some irresponsible divers managed to find it, and by 1986, the wreck was half-stripped, with most of the cutlery, dishes, deadeyes, tools, and personal belongings of the crew having disappeared. Instead of limiting access to save the rest of the shipwreck, it was opened up to everyone in the diving community. Before long, every diver knew what was left on the wreck, and anybody removing anything would face the the diving community's resentment and run a greater risk of getting caught (after all, it IS illegal).

The SLIGO

ARTWORK © ADAM HENLEY.
USED WITH PERMISSION.

40. *HAMILTON* AND *SCOURGE*

AUGUST 8, 1813   LAKE ONTARIO

The historic War of 1812 vessels named the *Hamilton* and the *Scourge* lie close to one another in 289 feet (86.7 metres) of Lake Ontario water off St. Catharines, Ontario.

The *Hamilton* was originally launched as the 112-ton merchant schooner named the *Diana* in 1809 at Oswego, New York. At the outbreak of the War of 1812 between the United States and Great Britain, the *Diana*, with its carved figurehead (a rarity on Great

The Hamilton *and the* Scourge, *part of the U. S. fleet, underway on Lake Ontario.*
(COURTESY OF THE ARTIST, PETER RINDLISBACHER)

Lakes vessels) of Diana, the classical Greek goddess of seemingly contradictory elements: the hunt and motherhood, was purchased by the U.S. Navy, renamed *Hamilton* after the Secretary of the Navy, Paul Hamilton, and equipped with 10 cannons. The majority of these artillery pieces were six-pounders (meaning they shot cannonballs weighing six pounds), but one was a 24-pounder, and another a 32-pounder. The *Hamilton* usually carried a crew of 50 men.

The 110-ton vessel known as the *Scourge* was originally built in 1811 at Newark, or Fort George, later Niagara-on-the-Lake, by the British as the merchant schooner, *Lord Nelson*. The bow figurehead is an ornately carved figure in a striding pose, supposedly of Lord Nelson, the most celebrated British naval hero of his day, who lost his life in the Battle of Trafalgar in 1805. This figurehead depicts him as the "complete" hero with two arms, although he had, in well-known reality, lost his right arm in 1797, before he became a hero! Two weeks before a state of war was officially declared, the U. S. brig, *Oneida*, captured and confiscated the *Lord Nelson* as she carried a load of flour from Prescott to Niagara. Taken to Sackets Harbor, New York, and equipped with nine cannons (one 32-pounder and eight 12-pounders), the Americans renamed

The Hamilton *and the* Scourge *closely resembled the ships in this C. H. J. Snider drawing.*
(TORONTO REFERENCE LIBRARY)

the *Lord Nelson* the *Scourge*.

Unfortunately, these vessels were not used to carrying extreme weight like navy personnel and their armament, such as cannons, and in a squall on August 8, 1813, the *Hamilton* and the *Scourge* capsized with the loss of most of their crews. Only 19 men were saved from the combined crews of 72 sailors on board these vessels. The accidental sinking of the *Hamilton* and the *Scourge* was the greatest single loss of life on the Great Lakes during the War of 1812, outnumbering the lives lost in the Battle of Lake Erie a month later.

The *Hamilton* and the *Scourge* were found through the determination of Dr. Daniel Nelson, of St. Catharines, Ontario, a diver and an avocational archaeologist who, inspired by the work in Europe on the Swedish warship, *Wasa*, and the *Mary Rose* project in England, became the driving force behind the discovery of these two historic, War of 1812 vessels in Lake Ontario. His quest began in 1971 and ended in 1975 when, with the use of side scan sonar, the two wrecks were located and identified. Several expeditions (such as the Cousteau Great Lakes expedition in 1980, a National Geographic expedition in 1982, and a Robert Ballard -- he's the man who found the *Titanic* in 1985 -- experimental satellite television broadcast live on site in 1990 to schools) have been impressed by the condition of these vessels and the historic artifacts in place on each of them.

 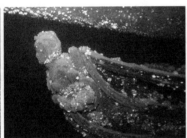 

Above, l. to r.: *This sidescan sonar image shows one of the the bowspritted War of 1812 ships with a lifeboat lying along its stern; the carved figure of Diana at the* **Hamilton's** *bow; the carved figure of Lord Nelson on the* **Scourge.**
Below, l. to r.: *A cat's head was, literally, carved onto the end of this anchor cathead; a hatch; transom windows.*   (ALL IMAGES ARE COURTESY OF THE CITY OF HAMILTON, ONTARIO)

The *Hamilton* and the *Scourge* are historic vessels beautifully preserved at the bottom of Lake Ontario with cannons, cannonballs, swords, grapeshot, axes, deadeyes, masts, a carvel-built lifeboat, and exquisitely-carved figureheads. The stories of these two ships generate an appreciation of the maritime heritage of Canada and the United States when both were young, struggling nations. The City of Hamilton, Ontario, received ownership of these military vessels from Washington, D. C. (on condition that any human remains that may be recovered be returned to the USA for interment at Arlington National Cemetery), but plans to raise these ships for public exhibition have been put on hold. The shipwrecks themselves are likely too fragile to be moved without enormous archaeological losses. Unfortunately, the threat of pillage from technical divers who are disrespectful is a problem, despite Ontario declaring these shipwrecks to be strictly off-limits to any visitation.

The question remains -- now that we've got them, what do we do with them?

Niagara River

While the word "Niagara" is universally recognized as one of the most famous waterfalls in the world (not to mention THE traditional place to go for a honeymoon), the river that runs just before and continues just after the Falls, despite being lesser known, is also quite historic. Here are the most famous shipwrecks associated with "Niagara," both the Falls and the river.

CANADA'S MOST FAMOUS NIAGARA RIVER SHIPWRECKS

Left: *The original, 91-foot-long* Maid of the Mist, *built in 1846 on the U.S. side of the Niagara River, served initially as a ferry across that river, becoming a tourist boat running close to the Falls only after the first bridge across the river, in 1848, ended the ferry business.*   (KOHL-FORSBERG ARCHIVES)

This next Maid of the Mist, *only 100 tons and built in 1854, felt the pinch of difficult economic times by 1860, and the owner decided to sell the ship. But the vessel was locked between two violent, vessel-unfriendly waters, namely Niagara Falls and the chaotic part of the Niagara River, with its two sets of rapids and a frightening whirlpool. A Montréal company purchased the boat, but only on condition that it be delivered to Lake Ontario, 12 miles (19.5 kms.) down-river, out of its natural enclosure. On June 6, 1861, Captain Joel Robinson and two crew members succeeded in taking the ship down the rough river, with only minor damage, such as a missing smoke stack, broken off in the wildest part of the journey. It came close to becoming a shipwreck. But this vessel survived, and was scrapped in 1875.*   (KOHL-FORSBERG ARCHIVES)

41. *CAROLINE*

DECEMBER 29, 1837   NIAGARA RIVER

It has long been bragged by both countries that Canada and the United States, sharing the longest, "undefended" border in the world, have been free of hostilities against one another since the War of 1812 ended in December 1814. That, however, is simply not true.

In 1837, a quarter of a century after the start of the War of 1812, certain elements in the USA supported Canadian rebels who, tired of the British "old boys' club" attitude and the corrupt and impenetrable control in the governments of Upper and Lower Canada (today's provinces of Ontario and Québec respectively), decided that they wanted reform to make the Canada colonies more democratic, perhaps even independent of Great Britain, and they were determined to foment rebellion towards that end.

The 71-foot, sidewheel steamer, *Caroline,* formerly the *Carolina,* built in New York City in 1822, became a dramatic victim of politics and Niagara Falls. Canadian rebels, led by William Lyon Mackenzie from Toronto, a fed-up politician who now headed the Reform Movement in Upper Canada and enjoyed widespread U.S. support, used this U.S. vessel as his supply ship and, with 200 followers, declared Navy Island, on the Canadian side of the Niagara River, to be the "Republic of Canada." British loyalists in Canada, fearing an American invasion in support of the Canadian rebels, torched the *Caroline* at Fort Schlosser, NY, just across the river from Navy Island, and cast it adrift towards the Falls, on December 29, 1837. One person, a black American, was killed in the fray. His body was displayed at Buffalo, NY, to rally support for the Canadian rebels against the British.

In revenge for the *Caroline*, Americans burned the British steamer, *Sir Robert Peel,* in the Thousand Islands in the spring of 1838 (see page 203 for that story).

The rebellions in Upper and Lower Canada were nipped, the Canada colonies becoming neither independent nor part of the USA. The British sent Lord Durham to the New World to study the problems. His 1840 report did little more than insult the French-Canadians so seriously that they wrote their histories and literature, strengthened their French culture, and increased their population dramatically by having enormous families for many generations. Their slogan, "Je me souviens," remains on their licence plates to this day.

Left: *The steamer,* Caroline, *as depicted by Canadian Maritime Historian C. H. J. Snider, early in the 20th century.*   (TORONTO REFERENCE LIBRARY)
Right: *Although attempting to depict a dramatic part of Canadian-American history, this late-1800s painting is over-dramatized and unreal; the ship was unmanned, so no victims could have fallen off the bow of the plunging vessel, as indicated by the two "stick men," and most sources state that the ship stranded above the falls, burned itself out, and broke up before going over the Canadian side of Niagara Falls in pieces.*   (KOHL-FORSBERG ARCHIVES)

42. THE BARGE

AUGUST 6, 1918   NIAGARA RIVER

The most visible and the most viewed shipwreck at Niagara is the steel scow that has been wedged in the rushing waters and the rocks just above the edge of Niagara Falls for about 100 years.

On August 6, 1918, this nameless scow, which was carrying gravel, broke loose from its towing tug, the *Hassayampa* (1910-1934), after the tug stranded about a mile and a half upstream. Horrified watchers on shore saw the powerless scow with two men on it being swept swiftly down the centre of the shallow, rock-strewn Niagara River towards the ominous precipice of Horseshoe Falls. The scow moved downstream so quickly that there had been no time to find and throw a rope to the men on board. At first, it appeared that the two acted frenzied, shouting and jumping into the air, but they seemed to calm down, as if resigning themselves to their fate, as their vessel neared the edge of the Falls.

Then, just opposite the Power House building, the scow appeared to slow down, and, finally, it quivered and stopped, appearing to have struck a rock. With the scow stationary, at least temporarily, the two men walked up and down the deck aimlessly while the hundreds of shoreline onlookers grew to the thousands.

The two Buffalo, New York, men on board the scow, Gustav Luffberg and James Harris, stopped the scow's drift to the falls by dropping an anchor and opening the dumping doors. Efforts to get a thick rope to the marooned mariners from shore met with failure due to the overwhelming current. There was talk of having aviators try to rescue the men, but the only thing a biplane could do (helicopters had not yet been invented) was to drop a line to the scow. With darkness came the realization that the rescue would have to wait until morning, but a searchlight was played on the wreck all night to offer the two men some encouragement. Thousands on shore kept an all-night vigil.

That night, the two men worked hard rigging up some barrels with ropes. In case the scow broke loose from its perch, the men hoped that the barrels, into which they would quickly climb, would stay stationary in the rapids until they could be rescued.

In the morning, a breeches buoy line was finally connected between the Power House building roof and the scow. Gus Luffberg, the 48-year-old Swede, told Harris, "You go ahead. I'll stay behind and man the ropes. I know how to handle them better than you." Both men soon returned to shore safely. During their rescue, breeches buoy lines became snarled, but William "Red" Hill untangled them, allowing the rescue to happen.

Left: *The scow in 1918 when it first stranded above Niagara Falls.*   (KOHL-FORSBERG ARCHIVES)
Right: *The steel scow in modern times, a bit worse for age and wear.*   (PHOTO BY CRIS KOHL)

43. *MAID OF THE MIST, I* AND *II*

APRIL 22, 1955 NIAGARA RIVER

Millions of visitors to Niagara Falls have taken one of the daring boats from a down-river dock right up to the churning, mist-clouded foot of mighty Niagara Falls. Historically, the vessels that carried tourists so close to the Falls in the first 150+ years of that enterprising activity have all been given the mild-mannered name, *Maid of the Mist,* a reference to a First Nation woman who, according to legend, took a canoe over the Falls, and who can still be seen as a misty figure at the cataract's base, reaching ever upwards to her lover.

The very first *Maid of the Mist* operated from 1846 until 1854, while the second one ran from 1854 to 1860 (see page 58). After a 25-year hiatus, a new, 71-foot-long, wooden, propeller-driven *Maid of the Mist* was built in 1885, followed in 1892 by a 76-foot-long running mate, *Maid of the Mist II*. Trapped for their entire careers as tourist boats in that narrow strip of the Niagara River between the falls and the whirlpool rapids, these two ships, the longest-running of a long line of *"Maids of the Mist,"* burned to total losses on April 22, 1955, while being fitted out in dry dock at the marine railway (or incline railway, which takes tourists up and down the steep cliff to the water's edge) for the new season.

A large team of 26 workers was giving the two, aging ships a $75,000 upgrade when a fire started in the starboard corner of one of the vessels, probably from the sparks of a welder's torch. The fire spread so quickly that the 26 men could not quell it with fire extinguishers. The Niagara Falls fire department quickly wheeled to the scene with full equipment, several trucks descending the narrow roadway from Queen Victoria Park to the riverside dock. Sadly, while directing operations, 55-year-old Fire Chief John Shapton, a 33-year veteran, suddenly turned command over to his assistant captain, and asked his son, also a fireman, to drive him to hospital, where he died of a heart attack 90 minutes later.

The actual damage to the two boats was estimated to be about $100,000, and the replacement cost was stated to be $300,000. Despite the fact that only the superstructures on the boats were burned away, leaving the main decks and the heavy, oak hulls undamaged, both vessels were scrapped due to their advanced ages (70 and 63 years old respectively) and the strict requirements that would update them. They were partially insured.

Each vessel had made 13 trips a day, carrying about 50 passengers each time, to the foam and spray at the base of the Falls. No new ship was ready by the usual opening date of early May, so a temporary, single-decked ship that could carry 40 passengers was used until a new, replacement *Maid,* with its 100-passenger capacity, was launched on July 28th. Several more have followed since then.

Left: *The* Maid of the Mist *in its earlier years on the Niagara River in the 1920s.*
Right: *Both the* Maid of the Mist *and the* Maid of the Mist 2, *with their superstructures burned away, on the day after the fire in April 1955.*   (BOTH IMAGES: KOHL-FORSBERG ARCHIVES)

Lake Erie

Despite the fact that Lake Erie was the last of the five Great Lakes to be seen or "discovered" by European explorers, it has the highest number of shipwrecks (or close to the highest -- Lake Michigan's rising number is hot on the heels of Lake Erie's); Lake Erie has about 1,800 shipwrecks in it.

The variety of famous Lake Erie shipwrecks on the Canadian side begins, chronologically, with the tale of the Wilkins Expedition of 1763, which lost at least 15 of its cannon-mounted, undecked lake boats off Rondeau while heading to Fort Detroit, and runs a full gamut of several luxury, excursion steamers from the 1850s, and continues with a wide variety of schooners, steamers, and propellers, (many lost off those two, major natural obstructions to navigation called Long Point and Point Pelee), all the way to steel freighters lost in the Black Friday Storm of October 1916, including a large portion of a Point Pelee-area shipwreck that spent years in a farmer's field, plus an unusually-designed whaleback steamship, and the long-lost and much-sought, steel, railroad car ferry, one of the largest shipwrecks in Lake Erie, which sank with the loss of all 30+ hands in December 1909; this huge, relatively modern ship, lying in the shallowest of the Great Lakes for well over a century, has not yet been found.

Canada's Most Famous Lake Erie Shipwrecks

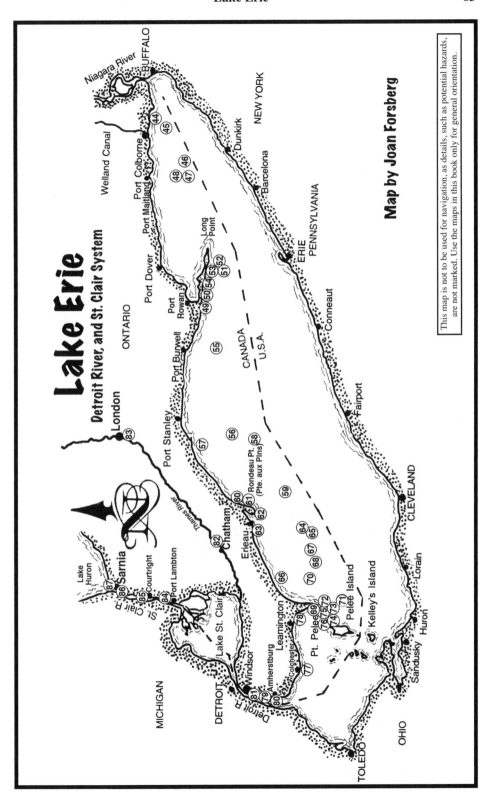

Lake Erie

Detroit River, and St. Clair System

Map by Joan Forsberg

This map is not to be used for navigation, as details, such as potential hazards, are not marked. Use the maps in this book only for general orientation.

44. *RALEIGH*

NOVEMBER 30, 1911   LAKE ERIE

This shipwreck is located about three-quarters of a mile (1.2 kms.) off shore, near Sherkston, Ontario, approximately four miles (6.5 kms.) east of Port Colborne, just west of the Point Abino Lighthouse, in nearly 30 feet, or 9 metres, of water.

The wooden freighter, *Raleigh* (227'3" x 34' x 15'), was constructed at the Quayle & Martin Shipyard in Cleveland, Ohio, in 1871, for use in the bulk freight trade.

On November 30, 1911, the *Raleigh,* having just cleared the Welland Canal and hauling a load of pulpwood to Erie, Pennsylvania, broke her rudder in severe winds several miles east of Port Colborne, at which point Captain Harry Beauvais of Cleveland ordered both anchors dropped in an effort to save the old ship. Violent waves caused the cargo to shift, and the hatch covers were blown off. The persistent winds soon forced the anchor lines to part, and the *Raleigh* ran aground. The ship was then wrecked in the heavy seas, and it gradually broke apart. The crew launched both yawl boats and abandoned ship, seven people in the larger boat and five in the other, but the breakers capsized the larger boat, drowning the cook and his wife. The 35-year-old chief engineer from Detroit, also in this larger boat, despite being a poor swimmer, made it back to the wrecked *Raleigh*. Several attempts to rescue him in the heavy seas failed, and he soon disappeared from the wreck, placing the total number of lives lost at three. The bodies of the cook and his wife reportedly washed ashore still clutching each other. The chief engineer's body was also found.

The ship's boiler, engine room machinery, propeller, bow winch, rudder, and anchor chains remain at the wreck site. The ship's anchor, recovered by divers in 1975, has been put on public display at the Port Colborne museum. The ship's wheel, capstan, and other artifacts are also in the museum.

The wooden steamship, **Raleigh,** *launched in 1871, had a long, 40-year career on the Great Lakes.*   (KOHL-FORSBERG ARCHIVES)

45. *C. B.* BENSON

OCTOBER 14, 1893   LAKE ERIE

The sturdily-built, three-masted barquentine, ***C. B. Benson*** (136′5″ x 26′ x 13′), constructed in 1873 at Port Clinton, Ohio, suffered from wanderlust.

A year after her launch on Lake Erie, she crossed the Atlantic Ocean with a heavy cargo of corn -- she had only 18 inches of freeboard and, because her centreboard construction was deemed unsuitable for ocean voyaging, she could obtain no insurance. But it was a gamble she took, crossing the ocean from Québec City to Cork, Ireland, in 32 days. The ship then spent seven years plying the trade routes between the British Isles and South America, taking coal south, and returning north with phosphate.

The ***Benson*** returned to the Great Lakes in 1881, working there for a dozen years before being overpowered by a shallow, freshwater sea named Lake Erie in a violent storm that sank the steamer, ***Dean Richmond***, plus several other ships, around the Great Lakes. The ***Benson*** sank on October 14, 1893, taking all seven people on board with her, including Captain John Duff, who reportedly had helped build the ship 20 years earlier.

This shipwreck, found by divers in the late 1990s, sits upright in 87 feet (26.4 metres) of water, approximately six miles (ten kms.) south of Port Colborne, Ontario. The vessel displays many traditional nautical items, such as deadeyes, blocks, rails, a bilge pump, lifeboat davits, an anchor, and the ship's wheel.

IN EIGHTY FEET OF WATER

SCHOONER C. B. BENSON AT THE
BOTTOM OF LAKE ERIE.

HER CREW OF SEVEN UNDOUBTED-
LY WENT DOWN WITH HER.

NO WORD FROM THE SCHOONER
RIVERSIDE SINCE FRIDAY.

The Leighton is Accounted For—Other Missing Vessels Turn Up—Notes.

Buffalo, October 18.—The schooner lost
off Port Colborne in Gravelly Bay is the
C. B. Benson. It was her topmasts, painted black, that have been reported by ves-

Left, top: *The* C. B. Benson *was constructed on Lake Erie, but built for ocean crossings.*
Right: *After her multi-year, ocean adventures, the* Benson *returned to the Great Lakes.*
Left, bottom: *Reports of the loss of the* C. B. Benson *were mingled with stories about many other ships lost in the same, wide-ranging storm.*   (ALL: KOHL-FORSBERG ARCHIVES)

46. CARLINGFORD

NOVEMBER 12, 1880   LAKE ERIE

The three-masted, 12-year-old, wooden schooner, *Carlingford* (154'7" x 31'1" x 12'3"), loaded with 26,500 bushels of wheat from Duluth for Buffalo, collided with the new, 237-foot-long, iron propeller, **Brunswick**, hauling 1,500 tons of coal from Buffalo to Duluth. The accident occurred in eastern Lake Erie in the early morning hours of Saturday, November 12, 1881, when the **Brunswick** struck the *Carlingford* near her port bow, abeam the foremast, and the sailing vessel sank in 95 feet of water head foremost in 20 minutes. Surprisingly, the iron **Brunswick** sank, too, but not before it steamed six miles (10 kms.), reaching U.S. waters. It lies in 120 feet. Three lives were lost from the **Brunswick**, and one, a sailor from Newfoundland who recklessly ran back into the ship to retrieve his clothing, on the *Carlingford*.

The 470-ton *Carlingford*, launched at Port Huron in August 1869, had a difficult first season: she lost a sailor on Lake Erie in early November, and later that month, she broke in two at North Manitou Island in Lake Michigan, but was salvaged, repaired, and returned to service the following year.

The *Carlingford* was one of the many found shipwrecks located by wreck hunter/side-scan sonar expert, Gary Kozak, originally from Windsor, Ontario, during his eight-year quest to find the steamer, **Dean Richmond**, in the early 1980s.

Above: *The three-masted* Carlingford, *in the only photo of this ship known to exist.*   (KOHL-FORSBERG ARCHIVES)

Left: *Ohio diver Joyce Hayward moves along the* Carlingford's *zebra mussel-encrusted rail on this wreck close to the middle of Lake Erie.*   (PHOTO BY CRIS KOHL)

47. *GEORGE C. FINNEY*

NOVEMBER 15, 1891   LAKE ERIE

The two-masted schooner, *George C. Finney* (136'7" x 26' x 10'8"), launched on August 22, 1866, at Oswego, New York, departed Toledo on the evening of November 14, 1891, for Buffalo with a cargo of 21,000 bushels of wheat. The ship never reached her destination. Sunk by a storm, presumably on November 15, 1891, all seven people on board (the captain, five sailors, and a female cook) were lost. The sinking occurred approximately 15 miles off the Grand River at Port Maitland, Ontario. The vessel was owned and captained by Thomas Riordan of Buffalo, who, with his passing, left behind a widow and four grown-up children. It was reported on November 28, 1891, that two of Captain Riordan's sons "...went to Port Colborne, and taking a tug, visited the scene of the wreck. They identified the masts positively, as they had helped fit her out." The 25-year-old *Finney* herself was valued at $6,000, and was insured for $5,323 between two underwriters, while the wheat cargo was also covered by insurance. None of the seven bodies was ever found.

Eight months after the *Finney's* loss, a note in a bottle was found near Ashtabula, Ohio. On both sides of a large sheet of note paper, in pencil, were printed these words:

I, Pat McCarty, on this awful night in November write this letter to inform the one who finds it that the boat I am on is about to founder. Her name is the FINNEY, and I am going to Dave Jones' locker. Tell my wife that I leave all my possessions to her. She lives in Michigan. The waves are so high now that I can hardly write. The Captain was washed overboard just now. Goodbye.

Pat McCarty was First Mate on the *George C. Finney*. This note was sent to Captain Riordan's widow, who planned to forward it to Mrs. McCarty if she could be located.

The *George C. Finney* had a long history of accidents, including stranding off Lake Michigan's South Fox Island in 1874, colliding with the schooners, *Jennie White,* in 1883, and *Niagara* in 1884, and being damaged by a waterspout off Port Colborne in 1889.

In late 1889, the ship was converted to a three-masted schooner. The *Finney's* three, relatively new masts still stuck out of the water a week after she sank in 1891. Today, the masts are down and most of the ship's decking has disappeared, washed away with the passage of time, but the wreck still sports a windlass, anchors, a winch, and a bilge pump.

Above: *The* George C. Finney *resembled the schooner,* Horace H. Badger, *which was built a year after the* Finney, *and which sank in Lake Erie in 1903.* Right: *The media reported the severe loss of life from the storm that sank two scows and the* Finney.
(BOTH: KOHL-FORSBERG ARCHIVES)

LOST ON THE LAKE.

Twenty-Four Men Probably Victims of the Gale.

FATE OF THE SCHOONER G. C. FINNEY

Her Captain and Crew Almost Certain-ly Drowned—Two Scows with Eighteen Others Missing—Four Laborers Killed by a Caving Trench—A Heroic Italian Loses His Life Trying to Save His Fellow Workmen—Four of the Gang Badly Hurt—Fatal Railway Accidents.

BUFFALO, Nov. 23.—There is little doub that the schooner George C. Finney has gone down with all hands. She left To-ledo on the evening of Nov. 14 with about 21,000 bushels of wheat for Buffalo, and was last seen a few

48. *NIAGARA*

DECEMBER 5, 1899   LAKE ERIE

The comparatively small, 348-gross-ton, wooden propeller named the *Niagara* (135'6" x 26'3" x 12'2"), built by Melancthon Simpson and launched on July 31, 1875, at St. Catharines, Ontario, foundered with all 16 hands in a snowstorm off Port Maitland, near Long Point in eastern Lake Erie, on December 5, 1899, while upbound from Parry Sound, Ontario, to Buffalo, New York, with a cargo of lumber and shingles at the time of loss.

But it took a while to piece together the identity of this lost vessel. It was evident that a ship had met with disaster, as several vessels reported steaming through debris fields floating off Long Point. Wreckage included lumber, shingles, and pieces of a wooden steamer. The *Niagara*, last seen by another steamer on December 5, 1899, struggling off Long Point, was the only vessel unaccounted for by December 8th. Records indicated that there were 16 people on board the *Niagara*, but initially, only Capt. Henry McClory's name was known. By the next day, seven of the 16 names had been pieced together. More wreckage was found, including a lifeboat washed ashore near Port Colborne.

Then a message in a bottle was picked up about half a mile east of the Port Colborne piers. Pranksters with a macabre sense of humour had, for decades, been planting fake messages in lakes after disasters for the cheap thrill of "making the news," but this note was deemed to be real. It read, on one side,

Expect to go down any minute. Capt. McClory. Good-bye.

and on the other side,

Steamer *Niagara* foundered about three miles from Port Maitland.

During the remainder of December 1899, only two bodies from the *Niagara* were found, both men in their early 20s, one identified by his initials tattooed on his arm.

Besides the infamy gained from the tragic sinking in 1899, the *Niagara* had one accomplishment like no other. When the ship was 15 years old, she tried something quite different and daring -- she left the freshwater seas, ventured into salt water, steamed all the way down to Havana, Cuba, and returned to the Great Lakes on May 6, 1890, with such an enormous number of Cuban cigars for a company in Milwaukee that the customs duty on the cargo amounted to $5,480! Perhaps we should remember this fact as a positive achievement of this small steamship to counter-balance the enormous tragedy of her loss.

The wooden propeller, **Niagara,** *sank with all hands in December 1899.* (KOHL-FORSBERG ARCHIVES)

49. *CONDUCTOR*

JANUARY 24, 1854   LAKE ERIE

This is a story more about a courageous woman than about a shipwreck.

In 1848, at the age of 17, Abigail Jackson married widower Jeremiah Becker, a fisherman and trapper at Lake Erie's Long Point. Life was not easy for the pioneers in the rough cabin that Jeremiah had built, reportedly from lumber that washed up on shore, with Abigail caring for the six children from his previous marriage, while producing eight more children of their own. But the powers-that-be must have felt that Abigail did not have enough work to do -- so they sent her a shipwreck.

The 250-ton schooner, *Conductor,* constructed in 1849 in the wilderness along Pigeon Bay, near the future site of Leamington, Ontario, and rebuilt in 1853 at nearby Amherstburg, where the ship was owned, was heading to Toronto with 10,000 bushels of wheat. Captain Robert Hackett rightfully distrusted the weather; that evening, November 24, 1854, winds stranded his ship just half a mile off the south shore of Long Point near Port Rowen, tearing away their yawl boat. With breakers lifting and pounding his ship, Hackett knew the vessel was doomed -- and perhaps he and his crew, as well.

Abigail Becker, seeing their distress, had her children carry blankets, a kettle, and tea to the beach, where they built a fire. One by one, the crew members jumped into the freezing, rampaging waters, swimming towards shore. Abigail waded halfway out in shoulder-deep water to meet each exhausted one and to assist them to shore, until all were safe.

Abigail's story spread quickly. She received many rewards: a banquet in Buffalo, NY, provided her with $500 in sailor donations, among additional cash gifts she received later; humanitarian groups gave her gold medals; and Queen Victoria wrote her a letter with a gift of 50 British pounds. Abigail was able to buy a 50-acre farm near Long Point.

This was all well-deserved -- especially considering that Abigail Becker did not know how to swim. The heroic actions of this 23-year-old, that happened because the powers-that-be sent her a shipwreck, made the remaining 51 years of her life easier.

Left: *Abigail Becker (1831-1905) remained a determined woman, even in her old age.*
Right: *While no known photograph of the schooner,* Conductor, *appears to exist, that vessel closely resembled the* Aurora, *pictured here. For the first four years of its life, the* Conductor *sported twin masts, as pictured; in her fifth and final year, she was converted to a three-masted topsail schooner.*   (BOTH: KOHL-FORSBERG ARCHIVES)

50. MARY JANE

NOVEMBER 19, 1881   LAKE ERIE

In Great Lakes lore and music, there is the story of the "Black Dog of Lake Erie." While some people take paranormal tales, or "ghost stories," seriously, most individuals are aware that "grains of salt" must be taken with any meal consisting of accounts that sprang from creative, over-active, and/or gullible (some would even say "warped") imaginations that would also have us believing in things like a "Witch of November." It has been our experience that a listener's caution must be doubled when such yarns originate from sailors.

First, some background on the "Black Dog of Lake Erie" legend. Supposedly a black Labrador or Newfoundland dog (or a St. John water dog) fell overboard from a ship in the Welland Canal in the mid-1800s. The crew, assuming that their mascot had exceptional swimming capabilities, left him to swim alongside the vessel the entire length of the lock while they cheered him on. Once they reached the end of the lock, the exhausted dog was crushed in the gate. This jam caused a long delay for the ship as the crew struggled to extricate the dog's body to free the gate. According to the story, the crew was thereafter haunted nightly by the howling of the dog they had failed to rescue. The story soon started that the ghost of this dog would often appear on ships just before they ran into trouble.

This fantasy element was actually applied to the real loss of an actual ship on Lake Erie. In November 1881, the three-masted, 345-ton schooner named the *Mary Jane* (135' x 23'3" x 12'), with her cargo of telegraph poles from Port Hope, east of Toronto (where the *Mary Jane* was owned), passed through the Welland Canal bound for Erie, PA. While the vessel was being towed out of the canal at Port Colborne, Ontario, at 8 a.m. on Saturday, November 19, 1881, dockside workers claimed they saw a black dog run across the *Mary Jane's* deck, and vanish. As the ship continued, the morning rain turned into evening snow squalls, and the favourable northeast breeze became deadly southwest gales. That evening, the ship stranded and wrecked near Port Rowan, close to the Long Point Cut. All nine people on board the *Mary Jane* perished. Cargo and wreckage, with the wind shifting yet again, was blown ashore as far away as the U.S. side of the lake.

The *Mary Jane*, built in 1862 by prolific shipbuilder, Louis Shickluna, at St. Catharines, Ontario, was valued at $5,500 at the time of loss.

Added to the superstition was the fact that the *Mary Jane* began its voyage from Port Hope on a Friday (the "bad luck" day to start any voyage, according to sailors). Even without the fatal hound visiting their vessel, the crew would have been in trouble!

The 135-foot-long, 345-ton **Mary Jane** *resembled this vessel, the 139-foot-long, 344-ton* **Emerald**, *which was built in 1872 at Port Colborne, Ontario, and which foundered off Port Hope, Ontario, on November 29, 1911.*

(KOHL-FORSBERG ARCHIVES)

51. *St. James*

October 25 (?), 1870   Lake Erie

When the mini-sub, *Clelia,* was lowered in June 1994, from the deck of the research ship, *Edwin Link,* to view a shipwreck, nicknamed "Mystery Schooner X," resting upright in deep water off Long Point, few could imagine the variety of "facts" that would be reported in many Ontario newspapers about this schooner's discovery.

Most media sources reported something along the lines of, "Fishermen were the first to notice the schooner's presence, having occasionally caught their nets on its masts." But this shipwreck in 164 feet of water was one of the many found in 1984 by wreck hunter, Gary Kozak, originally from Windsor, Ontario, and a Klein sidescan sonar expert, employed by that company, since the mid-1970s, during his quest for the *Dean Richmond,* a steamer lost in Lake Erie in a storm in 1893, reputedly with a valuable cargo.

In 1994, Brantford's Dan Lindsay and dive team members, John Veber and Ray Stewart, were instrumental in the investigation and identification of this shipwreck. Thanks to them, Toronto maritime historian, Art Amos, with assistance from Patrick Folkes, Bill McNeal, and Bob Graham, was able to ascertain, from the tonnage numbers stamped into the main beam ("226 76/100"), that this vessel was the two-masted schooner, *St. James* (118' x 25'), built in Milan. Ohio, in 1856, and mysteriously lost in foul weather with all hands and its cargo of 14,000 bushels of wheat. The *St. James* had left Toledo, Ohio, bound for Oswego, New York, on October 23, 1870, and was never seen or heard from again. Surprisingly, this tragedy never received the usual, big headlines that newspapers used when a ship disappeared with all hands.

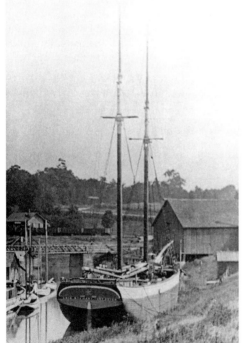

While the wreck of the *St. James* sits upright in 164 feet of water, both masts, which remain upright, rise to a depth of 81 feet from the surface. This magnificent shipwreck is complete, with both ship's anchors in place at the bow, plus bow chains, deadeyes, rigging, the ship's wheel, two bilge pumps, one wooden, one iron, and an ornately-carved, scroll figurehead. The ship's cabin and its roof are still in place, a rare feature on an older, wooden shipwreck, considering that escaping air pressure, created by the rapid displacement of interior air by rushing water when a ship was sinking, usually "blew off" such deck items from their mounts. This strongly suggests that the *St. James* sank slowly, giving that displaced air below deck time to escape without causing damage to the vessel.

The two-masted St. James *resembled the* Erie Stewart (117' x 23' x 10'), *which was built at Port Dover, Ontario, in 1874, but sank on October 7, 1907, at Southampton, Ontario, after missing "the gap" and ramming the breakwall. This wreckage still lies there in a maximum of 18 feet of water.*   (Kohl-Forsberg Archives)

Art Amos and Dan Lindsay co-authored a prize-winning report, titled "The Discovery of the *St. James*," outlining their work on, and investigations into, this shipwreck.

52. *ATLANTIC*

AUGUST 20, 1852   LAKE ERIE

Left: *The mid-19th-century paddlewheel steamer, the* **Atlantic,** *as drawn in the 1890s by famous East Coast artist, Samuel Ward Stanton, who died on the* **Titanic.**

(PERMISSION FOR USE GIVEN BY JOAN STICKLEY, SAMUEL WARD STANTON'S GRANDDAUGHTER)

Right: *A contemporary lithograph of the steamer,* **Atlantic.**   (KOHL-FORSBERG ARCHIVES)

This was one of the worst disasters in Great Lakes maritime history.

The luxurious sidewheel steamer, *Atlantic* (265'7" x 33' x 14'6"), built at Newport (now Marine City), Michigan, in 1849, sank with enormous loss of life (about 150 people perished from the approximately 420 who were on board) after a night-time collision with the steamer, *Ogdensburg*, on August 20, 1852. Both vessels continued on their separate ways, but the *Ogdensburg* turned around when her captain heard the screams of the *Atlantic's* panicked passengers when they became aware that their ship was sinking.

The *Atlantic* catered to both the travelling rich, offering them 85 First Class staterooms, and, with an abundance of open and affordable deck space, to newly-arrived immi-

COLLISION BETWEEN THE STEAMER ATLANTIC AND PROPELLER OGDENSBURG ON LAKE ERIE, N.Y.

The collision between the **Atlantic** (on left) *and the* **Ogdensburg** *was depicted by an artist for the September 11, 1852, issue of* **Gleason's Pictorial Drawing Room Companion,** *a popular weekly newspaper.*   (KOHL-FORSBERG ARCHIVES)

Above: *Many newspapers reported the controversial story about Lale Erie's* Atlantic. (Kohl-Forsberg Archives) Right: *Mike Fletcher with the U.S. flag and buoy that he had removed from the wreck of the* Atlantic *in Canadian waters.* (Photo by Cris Kohl)

Above: *Mike Fletcher and dive-buddy David Barrington stand with maritime artist Bob McGreevy, impressed by the detailed artwork in his painting of the steamer,* Atlantic. (Photo by Cris Kohl)

grants of modest means. The fact that many of the passengers were Norwegian immigrants who did not speak or understand English helped create the ensuing chaos during the sinking. Commands meant to save their lives were not comprehended by the immigrants.

All of the people who drowned actually did so before the *Atlantic* sank. In the 1850s, very few people went to the beach (a tan signalled that you were a common labourer forced to work outdoors; "pale white" was the skin colour that reflected wealth), nor did people venture into shoreline water (because few knew how to swim, and any leisure time that could be found was spent domestically with family).

No one remained below deck when the ship sank, so no one went down with the *Atlantic.* The *Atlantic* carried no insurance; its owner offered the shipwreck for sale "as is," but no buyer came forward.

Subsequent salvage descriptions made for fascinating stories, such as the competition between hardhat divers Johnny Green and Elliot Harrington in the 1850s to recover the ship's strongbox. Much later in modern times, the *Atlantic's* 1984 discoverer, Mike Fletcher, then living in Port Dover, Ontario, fought California pirates in the early 1990s who claimed that they had just discovered this "treasure wreck" (as their business brochures seeking funding proclaimed it to be), despite it being in Canadian waters and their claim to the rights to salvage everything on it. Eventually the courts ruled against them.

The famous/infamous *Atlantic* has a major feature: the ship's giant paddlewheels rise dramatically from the lake bottom, where the wreck sits upright, but its hull and decking have collapsed to the point where penetration inside the shipwreck is no longer possible. A double ship's wheel lies flat in the silty bottom. The twin smokestacks have tumbled, and thick mud and silt have accumulated on the wreck.

As with all Great Lakes shipwrecks, the "treasures" lie in the stories.

PHILIPS' SUBMARINE, 1851.
By favour of the *Illustrated London News.*

The experimental submarine tested -- and lost! -- in Lake Erie during efforts to salvage the wreck of the Atlantic. (Kohl-Forsberg Archives)

Lodner Phillips, an early submarine inventor from Michigan City, Indiana, built the first sub ever seen in the Great Lakes. In 1853, he tried to use it to reach the Lake Erie wreck of the Atlantic *in about 160 feet of water, but his 20-foot-long submarine leaked at a depth of 100 feet. He lowered the unmanned sub to the lake bottom by means of ropes as a test to check for leaks, but, in attempting to lift it, the lines broke. Somewhere at the bottom of Lake Erie, and likely embedded in the bottom, rests this very historic, early submarine.*

53. *IDAHO*

NOVEMBER 6, 1897   LAKE ERIE

The story of the wooden, steam propeller named the *Idaho* (220'6" x 31'4" x 13'7") is one of tragedy, with 19 lives lost -- and determination, with two survivors.

In the early afternoon of Friday (yes, a Friday departure, inviting bad luck!), November 5, 1897, the 34-year-old *Idaho* left Buffalo, New York, headed for Milwaukee on Lake Michigan, loaded with general merchandise, such as coffee, sugar, hardware, and Christmas toys. Fresh winds followed the ship into the open waters of Lake Erie, but by the time the vessel reached Long Point, a powerful storm had started. Feeling confident, Captain Alexander Gillies remained underway, rather than ducking into the protected waters of Long Point Bay and anchoring until the storm passed.

Shortly after passing the Point, the pounding that the *Idaho* took opened her seams, and she began to leak badly, quickly reaching the point where pumps and bucket brigades could no longer stem the intake. The water soon extinguished the boiler fires, and the ship, drifting towards Long Point in hurricane conditions in the middle of the night, sank faster than expected. Of the 21 crew members, only two reached safety by climbing the mast that remained above water level. For eight hours they clung to that mast, their hair and clothing encrusted with ice, before the five-year-old, 330-foot-long, steel freighter, *Mariposa*, downbound with grain from Chicago, attempted a rescue. Finding it impossible to launch a small boat, Captain Frank Root skilfully steamed his enormous freighter, facing right into the cyclonic winds and mountainous waves, up against the *Idaho's* wooden mast, plucking the two men to safety in one of the Great Lakes' most daring manoeuvres.

Before the 1897 navigation season closed, a tug determined the resting place of the wreck of the *Idaho* in 60 feet (18 metres) of water by dragging, and placed a buoy to mark it. In June 1898, the underwriters recovered a large amount of the *Idaho's* cargo. The cargo, totaling $45,000 in value, included $17,000 in barreled sugar (of which only the outer two inches of each barrel were damaged) and $20,000 worth of coffee, which was green and thus recoverable. The old ship, itself valued at only $15,000, had had some repairs made to her twice in her long career, but had never been rebuilt, raising eyebrows as to the wisdom of facing such a storm in such a vessel.

Left: *The 915-ton* **Idaho,** *built at Cleveland, Ohio, in 1863 (during the middle of the U.S. Civil War) never received a rebuild.* **Right:** *Captain Frank D. Root, of the steel freighter,* **Mariposa,** *took heroic action to rescue the* **Idaho's** *two survivors.*   (BOTH: KOHL-FORSBERG ARCHIVES)

54. *CITY OF DRESDEN*
NOVEMBER 18, 1922   LAKE ERIE

Launched (with some difficulty) into the Detroit River at Walkerville, Ontario, near Windsor, on April 20, 1872, the 132-gross-ton, wooden propeller, *City of Dresden* (93' x 23'2" x 8'8"), was built to replace the similarly-sized *Alexander Watson*, which had burned at the head of Walpole Island in the nearby St. Clair River on June 29, 1871. The new ship, like the previous one, serviced the communities of Wallaceburg, Dresden, and Windsor. It switched, starting in 1886, to servicing Amherstburg, Leamington, and Pelee Island.

Fifty years after its launch, the *City of Dresden,* now an old ship with its best years far behind it, went out with a bang, not a whimper, an exit befitting its launch location.

On November 18, 1922, a strong, southwest gale pounded the upbound *City of Dresden* until her seams opened, sinking her in 30 feet of water five miles west of Port Rowen, Ontario, near Long Point. Captain J. E. McQueen, the ship's owner, and his crew, five men total, all from Amherstburg, took to their lifeboat, but not before one of the sailors was swept away by a large wave, and was never seen again. Early reports indicated the *City of Dresden* was carrying a cargo of coal.

While women from nearby farms helped rescue the sailors in their lifeboat from the strong undertow, the true nature of the *City of Dresden's* cargo became apparent as the ship broke up. Waves carried case after case of whiskey to shore, keeping men along the waterfront busy "rescuing" the cargo. Farmers fetched their horsedrawn wagons and trucks, while others arrived with sacks to gather up the liquor bottles. Prohibition was then in full force in both the USA and in Ontario, and local residents eagerly saw to it that their "medicinal needs" for a long time to come would be satisfied. Nearly every bottle in the 500 cases of Canadian alcohol on board the *City of Dresden* found a good home, or was cached in the surrounding swamps. When law enforcement officers arrived on the scene, little remained for them to seize. Clearance papers indicated that the $50,000 cargo of the *City of Dresden* had been shipped from Belleville, Ontario, on the order of a Montréal firm, and was consigned to Mexico. But at the time of her sinking, the *City of Dresden* was heading deeper into the Great Lakes towards the Detroit River, in the opposite direction from Mexico.

The City of Dresden *had an unusually long life -- and ended it loudly!* (KOHL-FORSBERG ARCHIVES)

55. *Sylvanus J. Macy*
November 23, 1902   Lake Erie

The 752-gross-ton, wooden, bulk freighter, *Sylvanus J. Macy* (164'6" x 31'8" x 11'4"), named after Sylvanus Jedediah Macy (1833-1903), a railroad and coal industry executive, was launched in July 1881 at Marine City, Michigan. Two months later, on September 20, 1881, the *Macy* collided with the Canadian schooner, *Victor,* on the Detroit River opposite Walkerville, Ontario, sinking the sailing ship (which was recovered, repaired, and returned to service). This was not a good first season on the lakes for the *Macy*. But after her first year, the *Sylvanus J. Macy* enjoyed 20 years of relatively worry-free work, enduring only the usual minor strandings and repairs. That changed, however, in 1902.

The *Sylvanus J. Macy* left Buffalo, NY, on Saturday, November 22, 1902, with the huge barge, the 243-foot-long, four-masted *Mabel Wilson*, in tow. Both ships were fully loaded with coal cargoes bound for Kenosha, Wisconsin. Both ships were due to pass Detroit on Monday, November 24, 1902. Both ships encountered severe storm conditions that Saturday night off Long Point. Neither ship appeared at Detroit. Concerns mounted.

On Thursday, November 27, 1902, two events occurred: steamers coming up the lake reported passing through five miles of wreckage off the west side of Long Point, and the *Mabel Wilson* was found safely anchored off Bar Point, near the mouth of the Detroit River. Just as the storm had threatened to sink both ships, the tow line between the *Wilson* and the *Macy* went slack. It was never ascertained if the line broke due to the violent weather, or if the *Macy* released or cut the line to the *Wilson* because the *Macy* was sinking. She never saw the *Macy*, which had been her tow steamer for the previous five years, again.

The yawl boat of the *Macy,* found floating upside-down 20 miles to the west of Long Point, was recovered and taken to Detroit on December 6, 1902. Evidence indicated that the 14 crew members on the *Macy* "must certainly have lost their lives in the open small boat as, when it was found, although bottomside up, it showed signs of having been occupied," according to one Detroit newspaper.

In July 1903, eight months after the sinking, one body, that of the *Macy's* Engineer, Walter F. Gregory, of Detroit, was found, recovered, and taken to Detroit.

The *Mabel Wilson*, which sailed safely to Detroit after being cut loose from the *Macy*, became waterlogged and sank, with no lives lost, less than four years later, on May 26, 1906, at the Cleveland breakwall.

The Sylvanus J. Macy *experienced a major difficulty in her first year, but went on to enjoy two decades of virtually untroubled work -- until the year 1902.*
(Kohl-Forsberg Archives)

56. *THEODORE PERRY*

JULY 22, 1887   LAKE ERIE

High seas in a strong, summer storm struck a wooden propeller towing four former schooners on Lake Erie on July 22, 1887. The steam vessel, the **D. W. Powers** (built in 1871, abandoned in 1910) towed, in order, the **B. B. Buckhout** (built in 1873, wrecked in Lake Huron's North Channel in 1912), the **Senator Blood** (built in 1863, abandoned in 1909), the **Theodore Perry**, which was the oldest of all these ships, and the **Wyandotte** (built in 1856, abandoned in 1909). All carried coal cargoes from Buffalo to Saginaw. Suddenly, the tow line attached to the **Theodore Perry's** bow broke.

While the **Wyandotte**, behind the **Perry**, fared well on its own, the starboard seams of the **Perry** had opened from the violent wave action and the strain of the tow line, and the ship and its heavy, 300-ton, coal cargo sank in five minutes, taking with it five of the seven people on board (one of them was a passenger). An enormous wave tore the pilot house from the deck, taking the ship's female cook with it. Captain McCormick quickly jumped onto the floating pilot house, but his efforts to save the cook failed. The mate, Hugh Deering, clung to a section of the foredeck. These two survivors were picked up eleven hours later by the passing propeller, *Alaska*.

The press denounced the **Theodore Perry,** valued at $5,000, as a "floating coffin."

Today, the wreck of the **Theodore Perry**, lying in 80 feet (24 metres) of water about 25 miles east of Rondeau, features intact railings, two pumps, the remnants of a mast, the coal cargo, a windlass with chain, the impressive starboard anchor, and the ship's wheel. As with most wooden ships that were advanced in age at the time of loss, the **Perry** appears to have "shivered its timbers," with much of it lying in broken disarray.

The three-masted schooner, **Theodore Perry** (137′4″ x 25′8″ x 10′7″), was built by the famous firm of Bidwell & Banta at Buffalo, New York, in 1855, during the time when sailing ships were at their peak of popularity on the inland seas. However, 32 years later, wooden, propeller-driven steamers, or what schooner sailors referred to as "stink pots," ruled lake commerce, and sailing ships, even those that had been demoted to bulk cargo tow-barges (and that covered most of them), were gradually fading from the scene.

The **Theodore Perry's** enrollment documents were surrendered at Port Huron, Michigan, on March 31, 1888, with the farewell words, "Foundered, total loss."

Left: *The* **Theodore Perry** *closely resembled the schooner,* **Southampton (1860-1901).** *No archival photograph identified as the* **Theodore Perry** *has surfaced.*   (KOHL-FORSBERG ARCHIVES)
Right: *Roy Pickering uses his underwater light to brighten the* **Theodore Perry's** *steering wheel.*   (VIDEO FREEZE-FRAME BY CRIS KOHL)

57. MARQUETTE & BESSEMER NO. 2

DECEMBER 7-8, 1909   LAKE ERIE

When Cris Kohl arrived at the Marysville, Michigan, home of longtime wreck hunter and diver, Bill Patterson, in January 1987, tape recorder in hand, to interview him about his shipwreck experiences, Bill immediately "broke the ice" by bluntly asking, "Has anybody found that *Marquette & Bessemer No. 2* yet?" The finding of this lost ship has been on the minds of many people, even those who live beyond close proximity to Lake Erie!

During the treacherous, howling blizzard of December 7-8, 1909, the enormous railroad car ferry, *Marquette & Bessemer No. 2* (338' x 54' x 19'5"), went missing with all 32 people on board.

Depending upon one's source of information, there were anywhere from 31 to 38 people on board this ship, which regularly carried railroad cars between the Ohio town of Conneaut and the Ontario town of Port Stanley. On this trip, she had on board 26 hopper cars loaded with coal, one with iron castings, and three containing steel.

The *Marquette & Bessemer No. 2* required <u>two</u> triple expansion steam engines, producing 2,280 horsepower, <u>four</u> large Scotch boilers, and <u>twin</u> propellers, all built by the American Ship Building Company to propel the combined weights of her steel hull and her heavy cargoes. Built in Cleveland in 1905, this 2,514-gross-ton vessel was only four years old at the time of her loss.

The **Marquette & Bessemer No. 2** *pulling out of the harbour at Conneaut, Ohio. The wide open stern would have severely disadvantaged the ship in rough weather. Captain Robert McLeod, who perished with his crew when the ship sank, is inset.*   (KOHL-FORSBERG ARCHIVES)

On this last crossing, there reportedly was one passenger among the large number of crew, a man who supposedly carried a satchel with $50,000 in cash in it to conclude a business deal in Ontario. He, and his satchel, of course, were lost when the ship sank.

Great Lakes newspapers carried much information about the disappearance of this ship, in part because there were more vessels sunk with loss of life during this particular storm (for example, the *Clarion*; see pages 92-93). The *Duluth Evening Herald*, on December 11, 1909, after describing the destruction caused by this cruel storm elsewhere on the Great Lakes, reported:

> **General Manager Leslie of the company** [which owned the *Marquette & Bessemer No. 2*] **said:**
>
> **'It is my opinion that the heavy sea broke the key which held the** [railroad] **cars in place, and weighed heavily with coal, they rolled in the stern of the boat, overcoming her keel. She probably turned turtle and sank without a minute's warning. This theory is borne out by the fact that the men were splendidly drilled, and only a short time would have sufficed for them to launch the boats which with proper handling would ride almost any storm.'**

The theory that the ship sank so suddenly that there was no time to launch the lifeboats was disproved with the discovery of one of her lifeboats about 15 miles (23 kms.) off the Ohio shore. In it were nine bodies, all *Marquette & Bessemer No. 2* sailors, frozen stiff in death. Three other lifeboats were eventually located, two off Port Burwell, Ontario, and another smashed against the breakwall at Buffalo, New York. All were empty. The body of Captain Robert McLeod was found at Long Point about a year after the sinking.

There is the possibility that the heavy ship has, over time, sunk into the soft Lake Erie bottom, as other ships have done, such as the barge, *Raphael*, sunk in 1966 with a half-a-million dollars' worth of steel (by the 1980s, only about six feet of this wreck protruded above the lake floor), and the 2,139-gross-ton, wooden freighter, *C. B. Lockwood*, which foundered in a storm in 1902 and is now 15 feet under the lake bottom. (See the sidebar called "There's Something About Erie -- Disappearing Acts" in the book, *Great Lakes Shipwrecks, Recent Discoveries and Updates,* by Cris Kohl and Joan Forsberg). However, information recently found by the authors of this book suggests that the *Marquette & Bessemer No. 2's* profile rose fairly high off the lake bottom in 1940, and that coal from this ship's railroad cars regularly washed up at one location following storms in the 1950s.

The wreck of the *Marquette & Bessemer No. 2* has become one of the greatest mysteries of Lake Erie, if not THE greatest. The question remains: How do you lose a 338-foot-long, steel ship in the shallowest of the five Great Lakes, and not be able to find it after decades of searching by various people? The answer appears to be complicated.

Left: *One of the lifeboats from the* Marquette & Bessemer No. 2 *that came ashore in Canada.*
Right: *The nine bodies found in the drifting lifeboat.*   (Both Images: Kohl-Forsberg Archives)

58. MERIDA

OCTOBER 20, 1916   LAKE ERIE

$25.00
Reward

The Lake Carriers' Association will pay a Reward of
$25.00 for each body recovered after this
date from the wrecks of the

Steamers

Merida and Colgate

which foundered on Lake Erie Friday, October 20th,
1916. Telegraph or Telephone information at our
expense to the undersigned or to

GEO. A. MARR
Secretary Lake Carriers' Association
Cleveland, Ohio

Dated Detroit, Mich., November 1st, 1916.

WILLIAM LIVINGSTONE
President Lake Carriers' Association
2217 Dime Savings Bank Building
DETROIT, MICH.

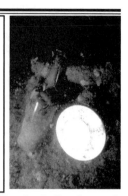

The **Merida** *was an enormous vessel. The Lake Carriers Association of Cleveland offered rewards for the recoveries of any bodies from the* **Merida** *and the* **James B. Colgate**. (BOTH: KOHL-FORSBERG ARCHIVES). Right: From the captain's cabin on the wreck of the* **Merida** *came a half-filled bottle of whiskey and a dinner plate; that corked bottle still contained 1916 air!* (PHOTO BY CRIS KOHL)

Lost with all 23 hands and its iron ore cargo in the notorious Black Friday Storm of October 20, 1916, the *Merida* (380' x 45' x 26'), was the largest ship of her kind on the Great Lakes when she was built by F. W. Wheeler & Company and launched at Bay City, Michigan, on May 1, 1893. A steel freighter with wooden deck houses, she could make 14 miles an hour, but her double steel hull, her good speed, and her five watertight bulkheads could not save her from the 1916 storm that claimed four ships and 51 lives on Lake Erie.

At the Soo on October 19, 1916, the *Merida's* captain had been remonstrated for overloading his vessel, but was allowed to proceed. The steam propeller, *Briton*, was the last ship to see the *Merida* at about 12:30 p.m. on October 20th, approximately 25 miles east of Point Pelee. The *Merida,* already struggling, steamed another 30 miles before sinking. The first *Merida* bodies were recovered three days after the storm, while fish tugs from Port Stanley towed in the *Merida's* floating pilot house with the brass bell still attached. This was enough evidence to prove the tragic fate of the *Merida* and her entire crew.

Many years after the sinking, on April 15, 1975, a commercial fisherman named Larry Jackson from Port Stanley, Ontario, pulled up an old, steel railing in his torn and rust-stained nets. He had accidentally (and at a price!) discovered the final resting place of the *Merida*, although it would be several years before scuba divers would finally explore and positively identify the shipwreck. A recovered brass capstan cover clearly revealed the ship's name in large letters, while huge, brass letters on both sides of the shipwreck's bow spelled out her name. A gold watch was found on the deck close to where the wheelhouse once stood, and a lightbulb from below deck still worked perfectly on land after being under water for 75 years!

The *Merida* rests upright and intact in about 80 feet (24 metres) of water near the middle of the lake halfway between the Canadian harbour towns of Erieau and Port Stanley. A hinged-fluke anchor remains mounted flat in place on the bow, where a large capstan and numerous brass portholes can be seen. Stanchions and railings, for the most part, remain intact. The *Merida's* "spine" (her keel) appears to have snapped, probably from the weight of her heavy, iron ore cargo, and most of the hull at midship is buried in the bottom of Lake Erie, with the bow and the stern sticking out and up at tortured angles. With the entire middle of the ship buried and out of sight, it is surprisingly easy to lose this huge shipwreck completely while attempting to swim from one end of it to the other.

59. *James B. Colgate*

October 20, 1916   Lake Erie

The **James B. Colgate** *was a whaleback steamer, a type of vessel built in the late 1800s unique to the Great Lakes, that turned heads in many harbours.* (Kohl-Forsberg Archives)

The *James B. Colgate* (308' x 38' x 24') was a whaleback, meaning that it was of a rounded design offering minimal resistance to wind and waves; the seas just washed over her steel deck. These "pig boats," as they were disrespectfully nicknamed (because their "nose" resembled that of a pig), were the brainchild of Captain Alexander McDougall of Duluth in the late 1800s. A total of 42 whalebacks were built on the Great Lakes.

Launched on September 21, 1892, the *James B. Colgate* foundered in the Black Friday Storm of October 20, 1916, which also sank the *Merida* (see preceding page). Every one of the 20 sailors on board the *Colgate*, excluding Captain Grashaw, perished in the sinking. Grashaw miraculously clung to a makeshift raft for over 30 hours before he was finally rescued by a passing railroad car ferry.

The wreck of the *Colgate* was located by Wheatley commercial fisherman, Len Cabral, while he was moving his boat to Erieau in the summer of 1991. The wreck, 12 miles (18 kms.) southeast of Erieau, lies nose-embedded and upside-down in 80 feet of water.

The survival of the **Colgate's** *Captain Grashaw became legendary.* (Kohl-Forsberg Archives)
Gary Smith shines his light on the **Colgate's** *overturned hull.* (Video Freeze-frame by Cris Kohl)

60. THE 1763 WILKINS EXPEDITION BOATS

NOVEMBER 7, 1763   LAKE ERIE

The historic marker in Rondeau Provincial Park reads:

The WILKINS EXPEDITION 1763

On November 7, 1763, a fleet of small boats carrying nearly 700 officers and men of the 60th and 80th Regiments under Major John Wilkins, was forced ashore by a violent storm about three miles east of this point. The expedition had set out from Niagara on October 19 to relieve the British post at Detroit, commanded by Major Henry Gladwin, which was then under siege by a powerful force of Indians led by Pontiac. Some seventy men and twenty boats with most of the supplies were lost in the storm. Wilkins and the survivors reached the shore where they buried the dead and encamped for five days before returning to Niagara.

Erected by the Ontario Archaeological and Historic Sites Board.

A year after the failed Wilkins Expedition to relieve the troops at Fort Detroit, the Bradstreet Expedition, following the south shore of Lake Erie this time rather than the north shore, succeded in reaching Detroit. That expedition, too, encountered losses off present-day Cleveland. One of this expedition's lake boat's cannons was located by a diver in the 1970s and was on display in a scuba shop for years. Only one of the metal rings, located at the base of this four-foot-long, 168-pound cannon, was visible above the sandy lake bottom, and the diver spent much time fanning away the sand that covered this artifact. Even the Smithsonian Museum in Washington, D.C., expressed interest in this historic cannon.

The largest of the Wilkins lake boats was about 60 feet (18 metres) in length, and these vessels were primarily sailed rather than rowed. Each lake boat was equipped with at least one cannon, either at midship or at the bow, and sometimes at both locations. None of the Wilkins' Expedition lake boats has been found, and they could very well be buried, after 250+ years on the bottom, by the shifting sands off Rondeau. But they are still out there, somewhere in Lake Erie, awaiting discovery.

If even one of the 20 lost Wilkins Expedition boats-with-cannon(s) is located, it will be one of the oldest, European-built vessels found to date in the Great Lakes (La Salle's ships from the 1670s, the *Frontenac,* definitely in Lake Ontario, and the *Griffon,* possibly in Lake Huron -- see pages 170-171 -- and a few others would pre-date it.)

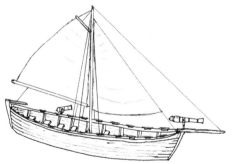 

Left: *The Wilkins Expedition of 1763, and the Bradstreet Expedition of 1764, travelled down Lake Erie from Niagara towards Fort Detroit in open sailing boats like this, which could also be rowed if necessary.*   (KOHL-FORSBERG ARCHIVES)
Right: *This cannon came from the 1764 Bradstreet Expedition.*   (PHOTO BY CRIS KOHL)

61. *PICTON*

SEPTEMBER 22, 1882   LAKE ERIE

The 248-gross-ton, paddlewheel steamer, *Picton* (158' x 26' x 8'), was built in 1870 at Mill Point, Hastings County, Ontario, at a cost of $45,000. In its early career, this vessel operated mainly between Belleville, Ontario, and Montréal. In 1872, the ship was purchased by the Bay of Quinte and St. Lawrence Navigation Company at Picton, Ontario; for that reason, the *Lake Underwriters List of Canadian Hulls* for the year 1873 listed the *Picton's* home port as Picton, Ontario, and its value at $29,000. In 1877, the vessel was rebuilt with the addition of upper deck cabins, and operated at the western end of Lake Ontario, running mainly between Toronto and Port Dalhousie.

In September 1882, a re-location was planned for the *Picton* -- the ship was selected to replace the *Asia* (see pages 162-163) on the Owen Sound to Sault Ste. Marie run.

On its way to Georgian Bay, the *Picton* was wrecked. On September 25, 1882, one newspaper reported:

> The owners of the propeller, *Asia*, recently lost, seem to be particularly unfortunate. They chartered the sidewheel steamer, *Picton*, of Picton, Ontario, to take her place, and while on her way there, the *Picton* went ashore at Rondeau Point, Lake Erie.

Captain Dunn blamed this accident on "the compass going wrong two points that ran her [the *Picton*] into the rocks." She was a total loss, but carried $15,000 in insurance. Most of the small cargo of 25 tons of general merchandise was recovered before the ship broke up.

The 158-foot-long Picton *was similar in appearance to this vessel, the 163-foot-long* City of Sandusky *(formerly the* Jay Cooke*), which was built in 1868 in Detroit and abandoned there in 1895.*   (KOHL-FORSBERG ARCHIVES)

62. LYCOMING

OCTOBER 21, 1910   LAKE ERIE

Left: *The unidentified "Erieau Wreck" proved to be the steamer,* Lycoming.
Right: *The closest newspaper to the shipwreck reported its loss.* (BOTH: KOHL-FORSBERG ARCHIVES)

Long popular with local scuba divers, the "Erieau Wreck" was discovered in 1977 by gas divers from Toronto working commercially in the area. An intense survey, undertaken by Kent Divers Association of Chatham, Ontario, in 1990, under the leadership of then-President Roy Pickering, concluded that the wreck was that of the propeller, *Lycoming*.

The wooden, bulk freight steam ship, *Lycoming* (251' x 36' x 15'3"), built by Frederick N. Jones at the F. W. Wheeler & Company yard in West Bay City, Michigan, in 1880, caught on fire while at the dock at Erieau on October 21, 1910. The flaming ship was towed out into the lake to save the dock from burning.

Because the ship sank in only 28 feet of water, more than a century of winds, waves, and ice have broken up the wooden hull completely. However, large hardware items form the most interesting parts of this shipwreck: the steeple compound steam engine, the enormous boiler, a capstan (see photos below), anchor chain, and a four-bladed propeller.

The *Lycoming* was the sister ship of the *Conemaugh*, which, coincidentally, lies off Point Pelee, a relatively short distance up the Lake Erie coast from the *Lycoming* (see page 91.) A Save Ontario Shipwrecks historic marker was placed with the *Lycoming's* capstan.

The Lycoming's *capstan (a mechanical, ratcheted, rotating device used to "winch," or pull in, a line), in a project organized by Roy Pickering, was raised, cleaned and restored over the course of one winter, and returned to the wreck site the following spring.* (PHOTOS BY CRIS KOHL)

63. *COLONIAL*
NOVEMBER 12, 1914   LAKE ERIE

The 1,713-gross-ton, wooden propeller, *Colonial* (244'5" x 36'3" x 22'9"), launched on March 18, 1882, at Cleveland, Ohio, sprang a leak off the Rondeau Peninsula in central Lake Erie on November 12, 1914. Captain Cooper beached her on a sand bar off the old community of Pardoville, Ontario, about 7 miles (11 kms.) west of Blenheim. The crew abandoned ship and used the lights of the then-newly-constructed church at the end of Bloomfield Road, on a bluff above the lake, as guidance in reaching shore, where they warmed themselves around the stove of the Pardo family. That church was only recently (early 2000s) torn down.

Formerly of the Gilchrist fleet, the *Colonial* was owned, at the time of loss, by the Reid Wrecking Company of Sarnia, which immediately dispatched two of their tugs, the *Manistique* and the *James Reid*, to the rescue of their beached property, in which they had invested about $20,000 for a rebuild just two years earlier. However, the winds of November increased two days after the *Colonial* was beached, and the ship was pounded to pieces, her "age and wooden construction being an easy victim to the gale," according to one newspaper. She was 32 years old at the time. Only the ship's anchors were salvaged.

Local divers and researchers Roy Pickering and Tim Roberts, over the winter of 1990-91, studied the various accounts of the *Colonial's* demise and established an approximate location of the wreck. They found it quickly the old-fashioned way -- they towed a diver (Allan King of Leamington) behind the boat. He found the *Colonial* when he slammed into its four-bladed propeller! Lying in 15 to 23 feet of water about 1,200 feet (360 metres) off Lake Erie's bluffs, the *Colonial* is broken up and scattered over a wide area.

SHIP IS BEACHED TO AVOID SINKING

Coal Laden Steamer Colonial Springs Leak in Gale on Lake Erie.

Two tugs of the Reid Wrecking company, the Manistique from Port Huron and the James Reid from Port Colborne, were reported on their way Friday night to the assistance of the wooden steamer Colonial, owned by the Reids, which was beached in Rondeau bay, above Point Pelee, Thursday morning after she sprung a leak in Lake

Above, left: *The steam freighter,* **Colonial.** (COURTESY OF THE ARTIST, PETER RINDLISBACHER)
Above, right: *The loss of the* **Colonial** *was widely reported.* (KOHL-FORSBERG ARCHIVES)
Left: *Roy Pickering and the temporarily-removed bell from this wreck. It was returned to the site, along with a Save Ontario Shipwrecks historic plaque.*
Right: *Wreck co-discoverer Roy Pickering examines the propeller for dings, and the bell is returned.* (PHOTOS BY CRIS KOHL)

64. *Frank E. Vigor*
April 27, 1944   Lake Erie

The **Frank E. Vigor,** *with its length of 418 feet, is one of the largest shipwrecks in Lake Erie. It was launched in 1896 as the* **Sir William Siemens.**   (Kohl-Forsberg Archives)

With the end of World War Two in sight, two different collisions in dense fog involving ships hauling war materials took place on Lake Erie on the night of April 27, 1944. The 455-foot-long freighter, *James H. Reed*, carrying iron ore, sank in U.S. waters at the eastern end of the lake after colliding with the propeller, *Ashcroft*, with the loss of 12 lives from the *Reed*, and the 418-foot-long freighter, *Frank E. Vigor,* sank in Canadian waters with its sulphur cargo, but no lives lost, after colliding with the propeller, *Philip Minch*.

The *Frank E. Vigor* (418'3" x 48'2" x 23'9") rolled over and sank in 90 feet (27 metres) of water near the middle of Lake Erie, south of Erieau, Ontario.

Despite the overturned steel hull of the *Vigor* being uninteresting to divers, the rudder and the propeller offer a welcome break from the monotony of seeing endless, smooth steel hull. A deck crane lies about 100 feet to the right of the bow, at one end of the spilled sulphur cargo. In the 1980s, Ohio divers dynamited a small opening in the wreck's stern area, but shipwreck penetration diving is for the specially-trained, experienced, and prepared.

Left: *The separate collisions that sank the* **James Reed** *and the* **Frank E. Vigor** *received wide media coverage, despite the fact that the war was still going on.*   (Kohl-Forsberg Archives)
Right: *Exploring the stern area of this immense, upside-down wreck, a diver examines the bottom of the* **Frank E. Vigor's** *rudder.*   (Photo by Cris Kohl)

65. *LITTLE WISSAHICKON*

JULY 10, 1896   LAKE ERIE

At noon on a hot, summer day, July 10, 1896, two tired sailors left the steamer, ***Tuscarora***, after she docked at the foot of Detroit's First Street. They were both quite fortunate fellows, happy to have reached solid land. Their ship, the ***Little Wissahickon***, had sunk from under them 10 hours earlier in the middle of the night near the middle of the lake.

The two men spent six hours being tossed about on their frail life raft before being sighted and rescued by the ***Tuscarora***. Two other sailors were picked up by the ***T. G. Lester***. The captain, the cook, and another sailor, less fortunate, perished in the sinking.

The 27-year-old ***Little Wissahickon*** left Buffalo, New York, in tow of the propeller, ***James P. Donaldson***, on Thursday, July 9, 1896. The ambitious, powerful ***Donaldson*** was towing three other schooner-barges as well: the ***A. W. Wright***, the ***James L. Ketchum***, and, finally, the ***T. G. Lester***. All five ships were loaded with coal cargoes.

The three-masted, 376-ton schooner-barge, ***Little Wissahickon*** (146′4″ x 29′4″ x 12′), launched as the ***Edward Keane*** in 1869 at Marine City, Michigan, and given its second (and final) name in 1882, sprang a leak that night in 1896 as the weather worsened, and, despite the crew struggling at the pumps to stay afloat, the ship sank at 2 a.m.

The wreck of the ***Little Wissahickon*** sits upright and intact in 80 feet (24 metres) of water, with the ship's wheel at the stern and two anchors and a windlass at the bow. The ship's bell, originally removed by Ohio divers and exhibited in a scuba dive shop there, was returned to its shipwreck bolted to a concrete block. Because this shipwreck lies in Canada, Canadian authorities had encouraged the bell's return.

Left: *The* Little Wissahickon *resembled the schooner,* Onondaga, *lost in Lake Ontario in 1907.* (KOHL-FORSBERG ARCHIVES) **Right:** *A diver examines the ship's wheel on the* Little Wissahickon. (PHOTO BY CRIS KOHL)

The schooner-barge, *Little Wissahickon*

ARTWORK BY CRIS KOHL, © SEAWOLF COMMUNICATIONS, INC.

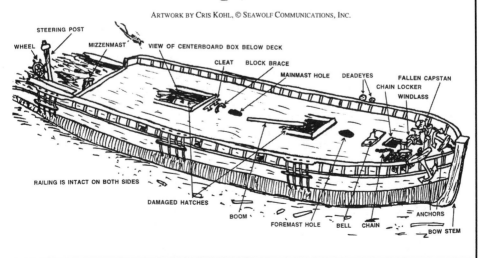

66. NEW BRUNSWICK

AUGUST 26, 1858   LAKE ERIE

Left: *The* New Brunswick *resembled this vessel, the* Detroit, *formerly the* Mary Battle, *which was built by the same builder as the* New Brunswick, *namely Louis Shickluna, at St. Catharines, Ontario. The* Detroit *sank in Lake Michigan near Summer Island after hitting a reef on April 11, 1858.* (KOHL-FORSBERG ARCHIVES)

The three-masted barque, *New Brunswick* (128'8" x 22'6" x 10'7"), built by Louis Shickluna at St. Catharines in 1847, carried a valuable cargo of black walnut and oak lumber when the ship foundered in a storm near Wheatley, Ontario, on August 26, 1858.

Certainly there were strong elements of drama and tragedy in the sinking of this vessel: how the captain and crew took to the rigging when their vessel sank in shallow water during a severe storm, and how, by morning, only five of the nine remained aloft, the others having succumbed to the forces of nature during the long night. However, it was that load of black walnut that had sensationalists spinning tales for years, and every year, the value of the cargo seemed to increase! Several expeditions sought to recover this lumber.

On July 23, 1980, diver/researcher Mike Dilts, working with wreck hunter Jim Kennard, found the wreck of the *New Brunswick*. Mike had purchased the salvage rights from a lady who had inherited them -- she was the great-great-great grand-daughter of the captain who had owned the ship. After intense archaeological survey work was completed (which yielded numerous artifacts clearly dating from the 1850s), Mike started salvaging the cargo. He recovered about 700 cubic feet of heavy, oak timbers from the site, but his sale of the wood was slower than anticipated. So Mike turned slabs of this *New Brunswick* shipwreck cargo oak into bases for clocks, barometers, and pen-holders, which he sold to the public as shipwreck souvenirs. But there was no trace of the more valuable black walnut -- apparently local residents, on the ice with grappling hooks in the 1850s, had recovered that treasure during the first winter that the *New Brunswick* lay on the bottom.

After the wreck was located in 1980, most of the artifacts were removed from the site. The largest of the three bow anchors, for example, was raised, conserved, and donated to the City of St. Catharines, which set it up as a memorial to Louis Shickluna, the famous Canadian shipwright who had built, among many other vessels, the *New Brunswick*.

67. *Kent*

August 12, 1845   Lake Erie

Left: *The* Kent *promoted itself with advertising handbills, called broadsheets, like this one from 1845. This drawing of the steamer appears to be realistic, rather than generic.* (Ontario Archives)
Right: *The anchor outside the Fisheries Building in the harbour at Wheatley, Ontario, was snagged in Captain Norman Omstead's commercial fishing net on November 30, 1961. Hand-forged and wooden-stocked, it is believed to have come from the* Kent. (Photo by Cris Kohl)

Somewhere off the east side of Point Pelee lies this historic shipwreck.

The steamer, *Kent* (122' x 20' x 7'), built by Duncan McGregor of Chatham, Canada West, and launched on June 19, 1841, was commissioned by the American manufacturer and shipbuilder living in Chatham, H. S. Larned. Mocked by Chatham historian Victor Lauriston as being "one of the more pretentious Chatham-built boats plying the lakes," the *Kent* was described early in her career by the Chatham *Journal*, on April 16, 1842, as having "exquisite taste and elegance displayed in her internal arrangements,...making her indeed a credit to the town of Chatham...." The 122-ton *Kent* was powered by a 45-horse-power steam engine which turned twin paddlewheels near midship. Her construction cost, calculated at about $40,000, was considered an enormous sum at the time.

The *Kent* usually ran on the Detroit-Buffalo route, and occasionally the Windsor-Detroit-Amherstburg run. On the night of August 12, 1845, the *Kent* sank in a collision with another steamer, the *London*, off Point Pelee, with the loss of at least eight lives from the *Kent*. The ship reportedly sank in about 11 fathoms (66 feet, or 20 metres) of Lake Erie water. The upbound *London* and the downbound *Kent* had sighted each other at about 3 a.m. while about six miles (10 kms.) apart. For unknown reasons, the *Kent* attempted to pass the *London* on the wrong side by cutting across the latter's bow. The *London* sliced into the *Kent* just ahead of the latter's wheelhouse, and she began to sink. The *London*, not seriously damaged, tried to tow the *Kent* for about five hours into shallower waters while the *Kent* sank deeper and grew heavier. Most of the 75 or so people on the *Kent* were taken aboard the *London*, but they left behind their personal belongings. The rumour that $65,000 (1845 value) of currency in gold and silver in the *Kent's* captain's quarters soon arose. The *Kent* was owned by William and Walter Eberts, Chatham businessmen.

This early steamship will be a significant discovery when it is found.

68. *WILLIS*

NOVEMBER 11, 1872   LAKE ERIE

Collisions were common nautical maladies in the relatively small and overcrowded Great Lakes. The three-masted schooner, *Willis* (131'7" x 27'9" x 9'), sank within ten minutes after a collision with the bark, *Elizabeth Jones*, at about 1:45 a.m., on Monday, November 11, 1872, about 15 miles (24 kms.) off the Canadian shore east of Point Pelee. The *Willis* was built only a few months earlier at Manitowoc, Wisconsin.

The *Willis* was sailing into the night downbound with 17,250 bushels of barley from Chicago to Buffalo. The bark, *Elizabeth Jones*, was heading from Buffalo to Chicago fully loaded with coal. The two ships saw each other's lights while still a fair distance away, yet last-minute misjudgements caused the bow of the *Jones* to slice into the *Willis'* port side. The *Jones* received mere scratches compared to the *Willis*, which started to settle within two minutes and sank in about ten. The *Willis'* crew launched their lifeboat and rowed in the darkness to the safety of the *Elizabeth Jones*, which transported them to Detroit. Once there, both captains denounced the accuracy of the other's lights and sailing directions. The ensuing court case lasted 13 years before being resolved in favour of the *Willis*.

Within two days of this sinking, a steam vessel crashed into the *Willis'* mizzenmast, breaking it off. Her other two masts came down shortly thereafter.

The wreck of the *Willis* was located in the 1960s by Michael Schoger, a hardhat diver working on submerged gas wells in western Lake Erie. An Ohio diver found the *Willis'* tonnage numbers (245.28) carved into the rear hatch combing, confirming identification.

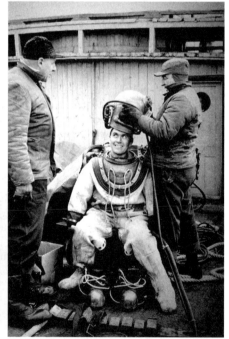

Left, top: *The wreck of the* Willis, *which sank in a collision with another ship in 1872, is the best-preserved shipwreck in the Pelee area.*   (COURTESY OF ARTIST PETER RINDLISBACHER)
Left, bottom: *Deadeyes, blocks, & other nautical components on the* Willis. (PHOTO BY CRIS KOHL)
Right: *Gas company commercial diver, Mike Schoger, in the 1960s and 1970s, found several shipwrecks east of Pelee, including the* Willis, *in his line of work.*   (COURTESY OF MICHAEL SCHOGER)

69. *CONEMAUGH*

NOVEMBER 24, 1906   LAKE ERIE

The wooden propeller named the *Conemaugh* (251'3" x 36' x 15'2") is the closest shipwreck to Point Pelee, lying about 400 feet (121 metres) off its western shore in about 20 feet (6 metres) of water.

The *Conemaugh*, sister ship to the *Lycoming* (see page 84), was built at Bay City, Michigan, in 1880. On November 24, 1906, a violent storm beached the *Conemaugh* just off Point Pelee with such smashing force that three of her four propeller blades broke off. Fortunately, the entire crew was rescued by the daring men at the Point Pelee Lifesaving Station. Over a period of six days, salvage teams could work only a total of 22 hours due to bad weather, but they recovered 799 cases of dry goods (each case weighing 700 pounds!), 1,000 packages of canned goods, and 130 bags of oyster shells. Winter set in quickly and, by spring, any hopes of salvaging the vessel were pounded to pieces just like the ship.

The shifting, underwater sands cover and uncover this shipwreck in unpredictable ways, just like the sandy "point" on land grows and shrinks and twists around differently in certain years; it grew by 400 feet (121 metres) overnight during a storm on the Labour Day weekend in 1968! Some years, scuba divers can see the entire wreck clearly, while, in other years, only the top of the large boiler can be found.

Years ago, a local scuba diver recovered the *Conemaugh's* capstan and donated it to Point Pelee National Park., which put it on outdoor display. Unfortunately, the capstan was not properly conserved, and it soon became a broken pile of rust, especially after vandals rolled it around the concession stand.

Top, left: *Point Pelee National Park erected a historic marker to the* **Conemaugh** *on shore.*
Top, right: *This aerial photo of Point Pelee shows the location of the* **Conemaugh** *shipwreck.*
Bottom, left and right: *Showing the impact of the zebra mussel invasion of the Great Lakes, these "before and after" pictures of the* **Conemaugh's** *propeller hub, shot from the same angle, were taken in June 1987, and July 1888, exactly 13 months apart.*   (ALL PHOTOS ARE BY CRIS KOHL)

70. CLARION

DECEMBER 8, 1909   LAKE ERIE

Left: *The* Clarion *looked strong and elegant, even while under construction on the stocks at Erie, PA.* (KOHL-FORSBERG ARCHIVES) Right: *The* Clarion *moves slowly into the harbour at Erie, PA.* (FROM A GLASS PLATE NEGATIVE IN THE KOHL-FORSBERG ARCHIVES) Below, right: *Headlines told the fate of the* Clarion. (KOHL-FORSBERG ARCHIVES)

Storms spring up unpredictably on Lake Erie, the shallowest of the Great Lakes. They get their worst in November and December; in the darkness of night, the terrors double; add a burning ship, they triple.

On the evening of December 8, 1909, while bound from Chicago to Erie, PA, with a load of flour, glucose, and general merchandise (and to lay up there for the winter), the *Clarion* (240'9" x 36'1" x 15'5") encountered fierce winds, normal for this time of year, as she began rounding Point Pelee. Usually this would not have been a problem, but smoke emanating from a cargo hold at 7 p.m. indicated that something was quite amiss.

The *Clarion* was about one mile north of the Southeast Shoal Light Ship off Point Pelee. The First Mate, overcome by smoke, died in the hatchway while trying to extinguish the fire. A west-southwest gale was blowing, and flames quickly leaped out of control to the superstructure, dividing the crew into two groups. The bunch on the bow, including the captain, lost hope in saving the ship and launched one of the lifeboats. The ship's oiler perished when the violent waves swept him away from the lifeboat which he was attempting to bail. Thirteen unlucky souls left the flaming *Clarion* in this lifeboat. They were never seen again.

TWO PERISH AND 13 ARE SET ADRIFT

Burning of Steamer Clarion May Cost Lives of Fifteen Men.

Six of Crew Are Saved From Disaster Upon Lake Erie.

Mate Frozen to Death and Captain and Twelve Men Are Missing.

Cleveland, Ohio, Dec. 9.—Two men lost their lives and the fate of thirteen others is unknown, as the result of the burning of the steamer Clarion, near Point Pelee, in Lake Erie, early today. Six members of the crew were taken from the Clarion by the steamer L. C. Hanna and brought here.
Without stopping long enough to

The Clarion *was built of a composite (combination) of iron and wood. Here, wood decking has burned off, but the steel frames remain.*   (VIDEO FREEZE-FRAMES BY CRIS KOHL)

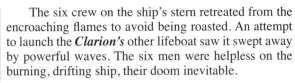

The Leonard C. Hanna *brushed up against the flaming* Clarion, *in this* MARINE REVIEW *drawing, Jan. 1910.*

The Hanna *succeeded in removing 5 of the 6 men left on board the* Clarion. WIDE WORLD MAGAZINE, MARCH 1911

The Hanna *made a second attempt to rescue the last man left on the* Clarion. WIDE WORLD MAGAZINE, MARCH 1911

The six sailors rescued by Anderson on the Hanna; *the last man saved stands front and centre.*
(ABOVE: KOHL-FORSBERG ARCHIVES)

The six crew on the ship's stern retreated from the encroaching flames to avoid being roasted. An attempt to launch the *Clarion's* other lifeboat saw it swept away by powerful waves. The six men were helpless on the burning, drifting ship, their doom inevitable.

One passing ship, the *Josiah C. Munro*, failed to effect a rescue when it ran aground.

Miraculously, the 524-foot steamer, *Leonard C. Hanna,* downbound with ore, with Captain Matthew Anderson at the helm, sighted the burning *Clarion* in the fog. In a daring and dangerous maneuver, Anderson positioned the *Hanna* on a course close enough to just brush up against the blazing *Clarion's* bobbing stern. Five of the six men on board the doomed ship were able to jump aboard the *Hanna*. The sixth man, advanced in years and benumbed by the cold, had hesitated to leap from the ice-covered, rolling deck. He threw his hands up in despair as the *Hanna* drew away with his five companions.

Captain Anderson, with calm judgment and nerves of steel, resolved to try again to rescue that sole life left aboard the death ship. He turned the *Hanna* around in the smallest possible circle, and, again in the howling gale and churning seas, passed under the *Clarion's* stern to within one foot of the ship, and the last man jumped to the waiting arms of Anderson's men, who quickly hauled him aboard. The blazing ship then drifted off into the night and eventually sank.

Captain Anderson was celebrated by the press all across the Great Lakes, with praising headlines like, "Heroes That Brave the Perils of the Lakes."

The *Clarion* was valued at $125,000, and her cargo at $150,000, but the appalling forfeiture of 15 lives overshadowed those losses. Only two bodies were ever recovered. The storm that sank the *Clarion* also sank the *Marquette & Bessemer No. 2* (see pages 78-79.)

The *Clarion's* stern is almost totally intact and can be penetrated, but the bow half has completely collapsed onto the lake floor. The huge, four-bladed propeller and the rudder remain impressively in place. Identification was verified when Roy Pickering found a spoon below deck with the *Clarion's* name engraved on it.

Roy Pickering explores the Clarion's *nooks and crannies, even below deck inside the shipwreck. Snagged commercial fishing nets make the wreck dangerous.* (VIDEO FREEZE-FRAMES BY CRIS KOHL)

71. *TASMANIA*

OCTOBER 20, 1905   LAKE ERIE

The 1871 James Couch *(renamed* Tasmania *in 1890) at Chicago.*

The immense Tasmania *in harbour ice, probably at Cleveland.*

The Tasmania *in 1903, having been reduced to a tow-barge. Note the anchors and the donkey engine.* (THE ABOVE THREE IMAGES ARE FROM THE KOHL-FORSBERG ARCHIVES)

The large, wooden schooner, *Tasmania* (221' x 35' x 16'), originally named the *James Couch* when she was launched on April 22, 1871, at Port Huron, Michigan, was the largest schooner on the Great Lakes at the time.

During the 1870s and 1880s, the *James Couch* was owned in Chicago, but in 1890, the ship was purchased by the Corrigan Brothers of Cleveland, who rebuilt the vessel as a schooner-barge, meaning it would be fully-loaded with some bulk cargo and towed behind a steam-powered ship. They also renamed it *Tasmania*.

In a very violent and wide-ranging storm that sank more than a dozen ships, and damaged many others, the *Tasmania* foundered three miles south of the Southeast Shoal Light off Point Pelee at 5 a.m. on Friday, October 20, 1905, with the loss of all eight people on board.

The *Tasmania*, which was reduced to being a schooner-barge in her final years, and another schooner-barge named the *Ashland,* were towed by the propeller, *Bulgaria*, with cargoes of iron ore from Escanaba, Michigan, bound for Cleveland, Ohio, at the time of the foundering during that storm. The other vessels survived.

The *Buffalo Evening News*, on October 22, 1905, gave details of the sinking:

The boats were on their way to Cleveland from Escanaba, ore laden. The *Bulgaria* led, behind her was the *Ashland*, and next the *Tasmania*.

The storm came up so suddenly as to find the crew unprepared. The darkness of night hung over the lake. The wind rose with fearful suddenness, howling and sweeping around the boats. The lake became mountainous. The boats were tossed about at the will of the storm. It looked for a time as if all would be lost.

The *Ashland* was lost to view of the *Bulgaria*. Those on board the *Ashland* could dimly see the *Tasmania*. One moment she rode toward it on great waves; another moment she receded [sic] in the trough of the sea. On board the *Ashland*, they were keeping from being washed into the sea only by clinging to objects on deck. It was seen that the line to the *Ashland* must be cut. One of the crew made his way to the stern. With a knife, he reached down and severed the line. The end of it dropped away out of sight. That was the last the crew of the *Ashland* saw of the other boat [the *Tasmania*]. It seemed that she sank at once.

The *Marine Review* of October 26, 1905, gave a description of the shipwreck:

The wreck of the schooner *Tasmania*...was visited on Sunday, Oct. 22, by United States Assistant Engineer Wm.

T. Blunt, on the United States tug *Spear*. The vessel lies on an even keel in 38.5 feet of water, headed west three-quarters south... three miles from Southeast Shoal lightship,...eight miles from Pelee island lighthouse. Both masts with their rigging are standing and may be easily seen several miles away. The mainmast is shattered at its cross head. Proper angles were taken so that the vessel can be found readily if the surface marks are destroyed. The 18-ft. ensign was found floating attached to its halyards--a mute and touching witness of the tragedy it was raised to avert, in a last, silent appeal for help. The flag was cut away to be returned to its owners.

The Tasmania *anchor, stolen from the wreck site in 1987, was publicly displayed in Kingsville for a short time after its 1989 return.*

Considered a menace to navigation, the wreck of the *Tasmania,* in only 40 feet of water, was dynamited in July 1906.

Today, the *Tasmania's* large, timber remains and iron ore cargo are scattered on a sand and rock bottom. The site exhibits many mounds of iron ore, part of the original cargo, as well as a small donkey boiler used for cargo handling. But the most impressive sights are the ship's two, huge, wooden-stock anchors.

The Can. Coast Guard ship, Kenoki, *returned the anchor to its wreck on June 3, 1989.*

In the late summer of 1987, Leamington diver/historian Allan King, being very familiar with many of the shipwrecks in the Point Pelee area, was surprised to find a freshly-cut, steel, anchor chain link at the *Tasmania's* bow. Looking around the wreck, he quickly realized that one of the gigantic anchors was missing! Subsequent investigations by a number of people, particularly *Toledo Blade* journalist, Natalie Parsons, uncovered the fact that the anchor had been stolen by Ohio divers utilizing two boats, a hacksaw to cut through the chain, and airlift bags. Unfazed at having crossed an international border with stolen goods from an historic site in another country, these divers, upon request from the Windsor chapter of Save Ontario Shipwrecks, refused to return the anchor to the site. At that point, U. S. Customs officials and other law enforcement agents swooped down on the storage site and confiscated the anchor, as well as the boats used to acquire it, thereby beginning, for the culprits, legal headaches that lasted for years.

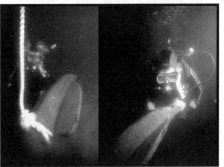

Diver Art Vermette releases the anchor's line after it was placed perfectly off the bow.

The divers had failed to report their importation of an historic artifact into the USA.

The *Tasmania's* anchor was returned to its shipwreck on June 3, 1989, by the Canadian Coast Guard cutter, *Kenoki*.

Art Vermette reads the inscription on one of the two, historic markers from Save Ontario Shipwrecks (S.O.S.), placed next to the Tasmania with the return of the anchor.

(ALL OF THE ABOVE PHOTOS ARE BY CRIS KOHL)

72. NORTHERN INDIANA

JULY 17, 1856   LAKE ERIE

The **Northern Indiana** *was one of several luxury passenger steamships plying Lake Erie in the 1850s.* (COURTESY OF THE ARTIST, PETER RINDLISBACHER)

The three scenes above represent some of the destruction and chaos on board the **Northern Indiana** *when the ship burned off Point Pelee in 1856* (FROM FRANK LESLIE'S ILLUSTRATED WEEKLY, AUGUST 2, 1856, IN THE KOHL-FORSBERG ARCHIVES)

A large, luxury, sidewheel steamer named the **Northern Indiana** (300′6″ x 36′10″ x 13′8″) sank with tragic results just off the tip of Point Pelee, and, ironicallly, that dangerous point of land had absolutely nothing to do with the sinking!

Early scuba divers on this unidentified, shallow shipwreck, which was found in 1984, located several 12-inch pipes that resembled modern pipe casings, so they nicknamed the wreck, "The Drill Barge."

Later speculation added the possibility that this ship may have been a sandsucker due to the presence of steel wheels connected by an axle, hinting at a device for moving sandsucker hoses.

The presence of a huge boiler, plus a smaller one, prompted a revised nickname, "The Point Pelee Steamer."

A capstan with a brass plate, naming "Oswego, New York" as the place of production, proved interesting, but did little to advance the cause of shipwreck identification.

Finally, in the summer of 1996, a small, metal item, identified as a luggage tag, was found by diver Brian Roffel, with evidence that finally yielded this shipwreck's actual name (see photo, next page.)

The **Northern Indiana**, built at Buffalo, New York, was launched on March 3, 1852, not making her maiden voyage until June 1, 1852, after her interior was completed. Three weeks later, the **Northern Indiana** collided with the schooner, **Plymouth**, off Cleveland, sinking the sailing vessel. A few weeks after that, the steamer broke both of her arches and disabled her engine in a severe gale. This ship had a very challenging first year!

She was still considered a young vessel when she met her demise on July 17, 1856, on a day so calm with smooth seas and such a light wind that the looming disaster seemed totally unlikely. A fire broke out below deck on the ship, which reportedly carried 104 passengers and 43 crew, as it steamed past Point Pelee. Spreading quickly to the main deck, the flames drove the crew from the engine room, thwarting the captain's command to stop the engine.

The nearby steamers, *Mississippi* and *Republic,* immediately raced to the rescue when they saw the smoke billowing from the *Northern Indiana*, but had difficulty catching up with the out-of-control vessel.

The scene on board the burning ship was chaotic. One journalist wrote the next day that, "the frantic shrieks of women, the cries of children, the struggles of men to save those near and dear to them, were indescribably appalling."

The press reported personal tragedies. One man on board the burning vessel was placed in the horrible position of having choose which one of his family he would save, his wife or his four-year-old son; "the little fellow sank, probably to rise no more. The mother and father were saved." One woman lost her husband, both of her parents, and both of her children, in other words, her entire family, in this tragic accident.

Initial estimates of loss of life amounted to 56, but later figures of a more reliable nature generally indicate 28 lives lost. Since the "trip sheet" on the vessel was not saved, and it was not yet a requirement to keep one at the port of departure, there was no way of ascertaining precisely how many people were on board the *Northern Indiana* at the time of her loss.

The loss of life, however, was definitely staggering, but, had the steamer not been an hour behind schedule, the losses might have been greater. The rescuing steamers would have been much farther away when their assistance was needed.

Bodies from the wreck of the *Northern Indiana* washed ashore for weeks, locally and as far away as Port Burwell, 90 miles (145 kms.) away. Newspapers, in tryng to be helpful with the identifications, described the bodies and the contents of their pockets as completely as possible. For example, one badly burned body of a man wore "black pantaloons" containing two keys, a knife, a steamboat ticket from Buffalo to Toledo marked "D. Miller" and two, three-dollar bills.

Some good also emerged from the ashes. A man and a woman, survivors who met through this disaster, were married shortly afterward. The tugboat, *Queen*, that took them from Detroit to Sarnia, sank in Lake St. Clair, leaving them struggling in the water for two hours before being rescued. It is hoped that their marriage sailed on a less rocky course than their sea travels.

The **Northern Indiana** *rests in relatively shallow water (25 feet, or 7.5 metres) very close to the point at Point Pelee.*

A zebra-mussel-encrusted ventilation grill lies in the vast debris field.

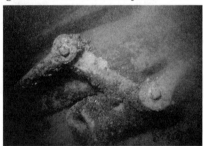

Pieces of the large, vintage steam engine and the walking beam from the **Northern Indiana** *can be found on site.*

In 1996, scuba diver Brian Roffel found a metal luggage tag that proved the identity of this shipwreck: it read "M.S. & N.I. RR" -- the Michigan Southern and Northern Indiana Railroad, which owned the **Northern Indiana.**

(ALL PHOTOS ON THIS PAGE ARE BY CRIS KOHL)

73. MAYFLOWER

NOVEMBER 20, 1854   LAKE ERIE

This photograph of the Mayflower *is generally credited as being the oldest picture of a Great Lakes shipwreck. Taken in late 1851 five miles below Conneaut, Ohio, when the ship ran aground there, this was not the* Mayflower's *final loss, as the ship was recovered and worked on Lake Erie for another three years after this particular stranding.* (KOHL-FORSBERG ARCHIVES)

The double-decked, side paddlewheel steamer, the *Mayflower* (283'2" x 35'7" x 13'9"), launched at Detroit on November 16, 1848, with the interior finished in time for the 1849 season, was a luxury vessel used for the influx of immigrants travelling between Buffalo and Detroit. It was the first steamer of the Michigan Central Railroad Company. Her official enrollment documents listed the ship's name as *"Mayflower,"* despite the fact that the name in large letters on the ship itself, as well as on all of her china, appeared as two words: *"May Flower."* The enrollment name, without the space, is deemed the official one.

Her launch provided a spectacle for thousands, according to this press account:

...At five minutes before the appointed time, the noble vessel gradually started from the stocks, and gracefully glided into the water, amid the shouts of the thousands of spectators present. The docks and every place where a good chance to see could be found, was crowded with ladies and gentlemen; and the steamer *Canada*, with a perfect moving throng of the young and fashionable, was lying off in the river, as if proud of welcoming her competitor....

...The *Mayflower* was neat and appropriately decorated with flags and the national standard, that fluttered in the air as the music from the band and the shouts of the multitude cheered her on the swift course, to the waters of the majestic Detroit river. She's now afloat, and may she ever be as punctual in her trips as in her first start. Success to the *Mayflower*.

The first-class *Mayflower* provided 85 comfortable staterooms that could accommodate 300 passengers, with an additional 12, luxuriously-appointed "bridal chambers" for

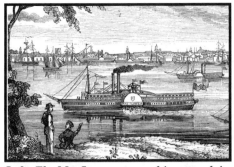 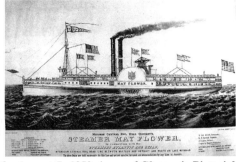

Left: *The* Mayflower *appeared in artwork in the August 7, 1852, issue of* Gleason's Pictorial Drawing Room Companion; *the background location is Detroit.*
Right: *A detailed, 1850s lithograph of the* Mayflower. (BOTH ITEMS: KOHL-FORSBERG ARCHIVES)

honeymooners. In addition, the ship provided less luxurious accommodations in steerage for another 300. The *Mayflower,* like the *Atlantic* (see pages 72-73), provided a daily service between Detroit and Buffalo. In fact, the *Mayflower* set a speed record of 17 hours between those cities.

On the foggy night of November 20, 1854, the steamer stranded on rocks at Grubb's Reef, and before the vessel could be recovered, it began to break up, soon becoming a total loss. All on board were rescued. The *Mayflower* was stripped of her furnishings, such as doors and china, and all other loose items, such as anchors and rigging, almost

immediately, and her machinery was recovered in 1855 for use in a mill at Wyandotte, Michigan. Years later, much of the cargo of railroad iron was reportedly salvaged.

The *Mayflower* was one of several, elegant, passenger sidewheel steamers built in the 1840s-1850s to carry passengers from one end of Lake Erie to the other prior to the construction of a railroad. Others included the *Northern Indiana* (see pages 96-97), the *America* (see page 100), and the *Atlantic* (see pages 72-73).

The luxury steamer, Mayflower, *like most of the other vessels transporting passengers across Lake Erie, offered its passengers the use of ship's china made in Europe.* (PHOTOS BY CRIS KOHL)

74. *America*

APRIL 5, 1854   LAKE ERIE

The New, Swift and Magnificent Steam Packet

AMERICA

CAPTAIN D. HOWE.

Above: *The elegant steamer,* America, *as depicted in an 1850s advertising flyer.* (KOHL-FORSBERG ARCHIVES)
Right: *The 1833 Pelee Island Lighthouse, restored in the year 2000, stands within 200 metres (630 feet) of the 1854* America *shipwreck.* (PHOTO BY CRIS KOHL & JOAN FORSBERG)

The 1,083-ton, wooden, sidewheel, passenger steamer, *America* (240'2" x 34'2" x 13'8"), was built in 1847 at Port Huron. She spent most of her first season, in 1848, operating between Buffalo and Milwaukee-Chicago. The Milwaukee Sentinel newspaper wrote this about the *America* on May 8, 1848:

> **The new and splendid steamer *America* made her 'first appearance' in our port on Saturday last. She arrived from Buffalo about 11 a.m. with a full cargo. The *America* is a first class steamer, spacious, swift and elegant. Her saloon is a pattern of taste and neatness....**

Despite this initial praise, the *America*, like most early vessels operating under steam pressure, experienced difficulties, including tragedies. On July 31, 1850, while off Erie, Pennsylvania, one of her steam pipes burst, killing eight passengers, a pair of engineers, and one fireman, and severely scalded more than 30 others. On July 12, 1852, the *America* collided with the propeller, *City of Oswego*, sinking that ship with the loss of 15 lives.

Finally, on April 5, 1854, the *America*, bound from Cleveland to Detroit in the middle of the night, was placed under the command of the First Mate, who decided to alter his course slightly to "correct" the one spelled out by the Captain. Upon seeing the light of the old Pelee Island Lighthouse on the island's north side quickly approaching, the Mate rethought his course, but it was too late. The *America* stranded hard and fast on a rock bottom close to the lighthouse. The winds picked up, the captain, crew, and passengers were removed by other ships, and, by April 9, 1854, the ship was so badly pounded that she could not be saved. To this day, the *America,* completely broken up and with most of her equipment and machinery having been salvaged, lies in a maximum of 15 feet (4.5 metres) of water. The *America's* boiler, which was not recovered, rises close to the water's surface.

75. GEORGE STONE

OCTOBER 13, 1909   LAKE ERIE

The large, wooden propeller, *George Stone* (270' x 40' x 19'1"), was built by F. W. Wheeler & Company of West Bay City, Michigan, in 1893, and launched on June 20th of that year.

Sixteen years later, on October 13, 1909, the vessel, loaded with coal from Ashtabula, Ohio, headed for Racine, Wisconsin, stranded in the Pelee Passage on Grubb Reef and broke to a complete loss. A fire that began in the pilot house from an overturned, lighted oil lamp after the vessel struck was subdued by waves and spray that dashed over the ship.

Controversy arose when a lifesaving crew was absent at the time a lifeboat with eight men in it capsized near shore, and six lives, including the captain, were lost when, after the *Stone* began to break up, they tried to reach the nearest land, Point Pelee, four miles away. The *F.M. Osborne* later removed the 10 crew members who had remained on the wreck, taking them to Detroit. In all, 12 lives, from a total of 18, were saved from the *Stone*.

The (Windsor) *Evening Record* of October 15, 1909, reported the matter thusly:

"If the life saving crew had been at the station, Capt. Howell of the steamer *Stone* could certainly have been saved."

Capt. William Grubb, keeper of the Grubb Reef light, thus puts the responsibility on the Point Pelee life saving crew for the loss of at least one life.

"I drove to the home of Norris Atkins, the captain of the volunteer crew, early in the morning," he continued. "I pointed to the *Stone* on the reef and said, 'Do you see that barge there?'

"'She isn't flying any distress signal, and her whistle isn't blowing,' Atkins replied. I exclaimed, 'Good heavens, man, you don't expect her to sound her whistle when she's full of water and her fires out, do you!'

"The crew didn't come to the station. Capt. Howell and Wheelsman Connors and Second Mate Hindle came ashore within a quarter of a mile of the lifesaving station. If even one had been on the spit, he could have saved Capt. Howell by throwing him a line.

"Between the time that I drove to Atkins' house and my arrival home again, the lifeboat had left the *Stone*. I did not know of this, and stood on the roof of my house with my glass watching the steamer *Osborne* take the rest of the crew off safely."

Located on the south edge of Grubb Reef, this shipwreck site contains the huge, wooden hull, complete with the boiler, propeller, steam engine, and chain. There is plenty of lumber from the ship and piles of burned wood. The rudder lies flat on the reef in shallower water. There are no windlass and no capstan at this site, which was salvaged shortly after the *George Stone* was wrecked.

Left: *Six lives were lost when the* George Stone *stranded off Pelee.*   (KOHL-FORSBERG ARCHIVES)
Right: *A diver examines a porthole opening on the* George Stone.   (PHOTO BY CRIS KOHL)

76. *Maumee Valley*

November 22, 1900 Lake Erie

Above: *The* Maumee Valley *met with disaster off Point Pelee in November 1900.* **Below:** *When a ship was lost with its entire crew, the news usually made headlines across the Great Lakes; this came from Chicago.* (Both: Kohl-Forsberg Archives)

SCHOONER'S CREW OF SEVEN LOST.

Drop from Rigging of the Wrecked Maumee Valley Into Lake Erie.

RESCUERS COME TOO LATE

Tug Goes After Lifeboat, but When It Returns Men Have Disappeared.

SUNK OFF POINT PELEE.

Toledo, O., Nov. 27.—It is believed here the entire crew of the schooner Maumee Valley, which sunk in shallow water on the Point Pelee middle ground, have been lost. There were seven of them, including the officers. The schooner was owned and commanded by Captain Henry Scanlan.
Another of the ill-fated crew was J. Harry Spain of Toledo. The mate was William Smith, formerly of Toledo, but who recently moved to Chicago. He leaves a widow and three children. Captain Scanlon's brother,

The three-masted, 32-year-old schooner named the **Maumee Valley** (126'5" x 25'7" x 11'5"), with a cargo of coal, was stranded and sunk on Middle Ground Shoal off northeast Pelee Island by a severe gale on November 22, 1900.

Over the course of three days, while the seven crew members clung for survival to the ship's rigging in the freezing cold gales, several rescue efforts were made by a tugboat from Amherstburg, the Life Saving boat at Point Pelee being "unfit for service," according to newspapers.

When the weather calmed on the fourth day, no one was left in the rigging; the entire crew had perished before help could reach them, and the ship broke up quickly in place. The bulk cargo carrier, **Maumee Valley,** was launched at Perrysburg, Ohio, on September 6, 1868.

After the tragic loss of the **Maumee Valley** and its crew, which one newspaper claimed "furnished a shipwreck story like those in novels," serious examination was made. A Life Saving station had been established at the southern tip of Pelee Island in 1887, but it was of limited use because nearly all shipping traffic passed north of the island. In the summer of 1899, their lifeboat, already in need of repair, was moved to the lighthouse called the "Dummy Light" on Southeast Shoal off Point Pelee. When the "Dummy Light" burned down eight monthes later, in April 1900, the lifeboat was moved to Point Pelee, where there was no Life Saving Station. Seven months later, when the **Maumee Valley** ran into trouble, that unfit lifeboat proved useless.

The 1900 **Maumee Valley** disaster caused two things to happen. First, a volunteer Life Saving Station was established in 1901 near the tip of Point Pelee. Then, in 1902, a new aid to navigation, named the Pelee Passage Lighthouse, marked the Middle Ground Shoal where the **Maumee Valley** had come to grief. The lighthouse served until 1975, when it was replaced by a much more modern, electronic structure. In 1980, to save the original, historic, 1902 lighthouse, Dean Construction Company dismantled, moved, and reassembled it at a marina in nearby Windsor, Ontario, where it remains a popular landmark to this day.

77. *M. I. Wilcox*

May 8, 1906   Lake Erie

The 377-gross-ton schooner, *M. I. Wilcox* (137' x 27'5" x 12'7"), was staunchly constructed at Toledo, Ohio, in 1868 for the lumber trade, and her standing rigging was made of wire, a very modern amenity at that time. The *Wilcox* had her share of incidents: she went ashore in Lake Michigan's Green Bay in early November 1882, and again at Big Sandy, New York, on Lake Ontario, on August 14, 1901, but was released with only minor damage each time. The vessel's value in 1871 was $21,000; by 1906, it had dropped to a mere $3,500 due to age.

Finally, on May 9, 1906, the (Windsor) *Evening Record* newspaper reported from Colchester that, "A barge with two masts lies sunk off here, one-quarter of a mile from shore. The decks are under water, but there are evidences that the crew escaped. The wreck was apparently an old schooner, bound up with coal....the vessel foundered some time during the night." The crew, after working the pumps for 10 hours, took to the yawl boat and headed for the safety of shore. No lives were lost.

The wreck of the *M. I. Wilcox* was located on July 2, 1990, by Ed Fabok, Joe Drummond, and Lloyd and Betty Kerr, all local scuba divers.

This shipwreck lies in about 25 feet (7.5 metres) of water, 0.4 miles (0.6 km.) off Colchester harbour. The *M. I. Wilcox* was named after Mr. Minot Ignatius Wilcox (April 7, 1829 - November 20, 1905), the president of a ship supply company in Toledo; he passed away in Toledo about six months before his namesake vessel sank not far from Toledo!

Above: *Initial newspaper accounts indicated that the ship sunk off Colchester was a TWO-masted schooner, while the* M. I. Wilcox *carried THREE masts. Likely the mizzen mast collapsed early.* Below: *News in the (Windsor)* Evening Record, *May 10, 1906.*
(Both: Kohl-Forsberg Archives)

CREW ESCAPED BY YAWL BOAT

Sailors on Schooner Wilcox, Sunk Off Colchester, Obliged to Abandon Old Craft

It was the old schooner M. I. Wilcox, built in 1868, which foundered off Colchester. She was bound from Huron to Sandwich with 718 tons of coal for the Pittsburg Coal Co.

After working the pumps for ten hours, the crew took the yawl boat and reached the shore. The crew consisted of Capt. Wm. Somerville, who, with C. C. Baumkart, of Vermillion, O., is the owner of the boat, his daughter, who was cook, Frank Doyle, mate; George Ford, of Chicago

The schooner, M. I. Wilcox, *retains most of its components at the shallow wreck site, including hull planking (with fish!) and rigging deadeyes.* (Photos by Cris Kohl)

78. *N. J. Nessen*

October 22, 1929   Lake Erie

Above: *The* Nessen *was already old in this 1921 photo.* Below: *News of the ship's loss.*   (Both: Kohl-Forsberg Archives)

Above: *The N. J. Nessen, her spine broken by the storm, lay helplessly stranded off Leamington's dock.* Below: *Captain James Grubb led the daring rescue team.*   (Both: Kohl-Forsberg Archives)

A trim, wooden propeller, the 440-gross-ton *H. Louella Worthington* (148'6" x 37' x 11'5"), was launched on July 14, 1880, at Lorain, Ohio, and renamed the *N. J. Nessen* in 1903, after the 13-year-old son of a Chicago lumber businessman, who had purchased the ship for his J. O. Nessen Lumber Company.

This durable vessel had experienced many close calls in her 49 years of hauling mostly lumber on the lakes (including a sinking in 30 feet of water caused by ice in Lake Charlevoix, Michigan, on April 10, 1907, and sinking in shallow water near Meaford, Ontario, on Georgian Bay, with a lumber cargo in 1919, but each time being recovered, repaired, and returned to service). However, her long career ended about 1,500 feet (455 metres) off shore, about half a mile (0.8 km.) east of the Leamington dock on October 22, 1929.

An extremely violent storm forced the *Nessen* to take shelter and anchor off Leamington. But the strong winds out of the northeast suddenly changed direction a full 180 degrees, and the archaic ship, which had been reduced to the lacklustre job of hauling deckloads of scrap metal from Detroit to Cleveland, stranded, broke her spine (or keel), and sank in shallow water in severe southwest gales.

The 13 people on board the battered and wrecked *N. J. Nessen,* nearly all of them from Detroit and Marine City, Michigan, were rescued with difficulty, under the worried gazes of dozens of watchers on shore, in two lifeboat trips made by brawny members of the Point Pelee Life Saving Station, a brave crew operating under the able and courageous leadership of Captain James Grubb, one of the younger members of that locally famous maritime family. The *Nessen's* Captain Bernard Benson, from Marine City, followed the time-honoured tradition of the master of the ship being the last person to leave a doomed vessel.

The Life Saving Station closed shortly thereafter due to lack of business, since modern devices had greatly increased safe navigation on the Great Lakes. The *Nessen* was the Point Pelee Life Savers' final rescue operation before they disbanded.

This violent storm of October 22, 1929, disrupted most of the Great Lakes region, also sinking the railroad car ferry *Milwaukee* on Lake Michigan with the loss of all 52 hands, plus wrecking the steel freighter, *Chicago*, at Lake Superior's Michipicoten Island (see page 183 for that story.)

Most of the scrap iron on the *Nessen's* deck (surprisingly, the ship carried nothing below deck!) was recovered, as were a few items of hardware from the ship (including the reported removal of the boiler), but the vessel was too damaged to be salvaged, and it soon broke up. Her smokestack, however, remained upright and visible above the water for many years afterwards, according to a lady who moved to Canada as a child in 1940 and saw the unusual nautical item.

Robert McCracken offered some space on his farm north of Leamington for the temporary storage of the Nessen's *bow.*

In 1984, during construction of a marina near the Leamington dock, the large bow section of a wooden steamer was accidentally dredged up, along with various other pieces of broken timbers from the shipwreck. A Leamington youngster, watching the dredging, saw something unusual in the saturated sand that was being dumped on shore, and he quickly excavated it -- it was the ship's 70-pound, brass bell! Reportedly his mother telephoned the Leamington mayor about this discovery, and the bell was put on display at the town's public library before being moved to the maritime museum on the second floor of the Leamington Arts Centre (the former Post Office building).

Plans to utilize this wreckage as the visual highlight of a memorial to Great Lakes maritime history did not materialize.

These excavation discoveries rekindled interest in the story of this shipwreck that had occurred more than half a century earlier.

Maritime enthusiast Robert McCracken agreed to store the 20-foot-long, (weighing 17 tons soaking wet), dredged-up, bow section of the *Nessen,* plus heavy engine crank pieces and other nautical components, on his farm at Staples, Ontario, just north of Leamington. Plans were made for creating a public memorial to Great Lakes maritime history at the city marina in Leamington using this large piece of a shipwreck, but these plans have yet to materialize.

Some of the scrap metal the N. J. Nessen was hauling as cargo was dredged up with pieces of the ship's hardware.

Nearly three decades later, and by now in his 80s, Robert McCracken wanted to be rid of the *Nessen*, so, in the spring of 2013, the badly deteriorated wreckage (it had been described by one Leamington official as being "in very fragile condition" in 2011) was moved to yet another nearby farm, where it currently awaits final disposition. An attempt to secure a provincial grant was rejected, and, to date, raising the $75,000 needed to fund the project has not been successful.

Large pieces of the N. J. Nessen's broken, 1880, fore-and-aft compound steam engine were also recovered in 1984 during the dredging at a Leamington marina. (ALL PHOTOS ON THIS PAGE ARE BY CRIS KOHL)

Detroit River

The Detroit River, like the St. Clair River, has been a "bottleneck" to Great Lakes maritime traffic for centuries. Because the river is narrow, contains numerous islands and shoals, and includes a brisk current, navigation is far more dangerous than on the open lakes. Not surprisingly, the result has been shipwrecks. What may come as a surprise is that, of the thousands of times that ships stranded or sank in the Detroit River, more than 95% of them were recovered and returned to service.

However, scuba diving on shipwrecks in these high-traffic, murky waters can be dangerous, and Detroit has long had laws banning swimming and diving in the Detroit River within its city limits; more recently, Windsor enacted similar laws within its city limits. That still leaves a lot of river to explore beyond those two cities.

CANADA'S MOST FAMOUS DETROIT RIVER SHIPWRECKS

The most visible "shipwreck" in the Detroit River is the canaler, Queenston *(261' x 43'3" x 20')* (left; KOHL-FORSBERG ARCHIVES), *formerly the* Lachinedoc, *launched in Sunderland, England, in 1927, and which sailed immediately for service out of Montréal. Decommissioned in 1961, and with its cabins removed, the steel hull was purposely sunk as an extension to the ferry dock on Canada's Bob-lo (formerly Bois Blanc) Island in the Detroit River* (right).   (PHOTO BY CRIS KOHL)

Some Other Shipwrecks on the Canadian side of the Detroit River

INTERNATIONAL -- This 27-gross-ton tug, built at Tonawanda, NY, in 1871, burned to a total loss at Amherstburg, Ontario, on December 8, 1892.

TOPEKA -- This bulk freighter (228'3" x 28' x 19'2"), launched in 1889 at Milwaukee, Wisconsin, sank at Sandwich, Ontario, on August 15, 1916, after colliding with the steamer, *Christopher*. It was dynamited four months later.

MINNIE MORTON -- This 55-foot-long tug did not sink in the Detroit River in 1881 (as indicated in some sources of information), but was swept into Lake Erie from the river by an enormous log raft towed by the tug, ***John Owen*** (later renamed the ***Columbus*** -- see pages 180-181 for its story) before sinking; however, the wreck of the ***Minnie Morton*** was found in Lake Erie and raised in 1886.

79. *JOHN PLANKINTON*

MAY 9, 1917   DETROIT RIVER

Left: *The* John Plankinton *under way in better days.*
Right: *The railroad car ferry named the* **Detroit** *collided with, and sank, the propeller* **John Plankinton** *in the Detroit River in the spring of 1917. Unfortunately, one life was lost.*

The 1,821-gross-ton, wooden, freight propeller, *John Plankinton* (267' x 41' x 23'), launched on April 27, 1889, at West Bay City, Michigan, was named after a Milwaukee resident (1820 - 1891) who had made his fortune in the meat and produce markets.

The *John Plankinton,* at about 9:30 p.m. on May 9, 1917, collided with the railroad car ferry, *Detroit,* on the crowded Detroit River, and sank, with the loss of one life from the *Plankinton,* in 40 feet (12 metres) of water "off Detroit" (as some sources of misinformation state); the ship really sank 780 feet (236 metres) off Windsor, Ontario -- clearly placing it on the Canadian side of the river. Crew members, except for the missing man who presumably drowned, were rescued by the Marine Reporter and the U. S. Mail Boat.

The official "Wreck Report," filled out by the *Plankinton's* Captain John Stansen and today in the National Archives at Chicago, placed the value of the ship at $80,000 (with only $10,000 of insurance coverage!), and its 2,400-ton soft coal cargo, bound from Toledo to Hancock, Michigan, at "about $20,000" (which was fully insured), with the vessel sinking "opposite lower part of Windsor, Detroit River." Despite the "wind light, weather clear," "cross signals by the downbound steamer," namely the *Detroit,* prompted the *Plankinton* to "blow alarm signals and [back] full speed," but to no avail. With its machinery removed, the wreck was flattened by dynamite in July 1917.

This photograph of the wrecked **John Plankinton** *shows the distant Detroit shoreline and a Detroit excursion steamer in the background.*   (ALL IMAGES ON THIS PAGE: KOHL-FORSBERG ARCHIVES)

80. *Tashmoo*

June 18, 1936   Detroit River

The Tashmoo, *launched on December 30, 1899 -- the last ship built on the Great Lakes in the 1800s (compare this to the last ship lost on the Great Lakes in the 1800s on pages 186-187) -- frequently ran between Detroit and the dock at Port Huron.*   (Both: Kohl-Forsberg Archives)

Music danced through the warm night air, as did hundreds of lighthearted people on the wooden floor that glided smoothly across the waters of the Detroit River. They danced on board the popular passenger excursion vessel, the *Tashmoo,* which had just started her 37th season. While many of the passengers thrilled to the music on the ship's decks, others, mostly couples, drifted to the edges so they could lean over the vessel's rails and watch the moonbeams play upon the gently-ruffled waters. It had been an excellent evening, and the *Tashmoo* was returning to Detroit after a 25-mile run down to Sugar Island. It was the night of Thursday, June 18, 1936, and the many people who started their weekend a day early also celebrated the arrival of another enchanting summer on this lively river.

Only Capt. Donald McAlpine and a few of his crew knew that the ship was sinking.

In his greatest trial of seamanship, while his passengers laughed, danced, and caroused, the worried captain raced against time to reach the nearest pier, the Bruner-Mond dock at Amherstburg on the Canadian side of the river about a mile away. He had felt his ship strike something, probably a boulder, and he soon received a report from the engine room that water was gushing in at an alarming rate. Without a word, he arranged for the band to keep playing. Most of the lively crowd of passengers maintained a rhythmic revelry and made merry, none the worse for the people's ignorance of what was happening.

The *Tashmoo's* clocks struck midnight when a small, makeshift gangway was dropped and the passengers, thrilled by this adventure, were all discharged at Amherstburg so that "a quick engine repair" could be made to the ship. Then the *Tashmoo* sank. There had been no panic, no injuries, and no deaths. Capt. McAlpine breathed a deep sigh of relief.

Three trolley cars from nearby Windsor were dispatched to Amherstburg, where they collected 300 of the stranded merrymakers and conveyed them to Windsor, from where they caught busses to Detroit (both the Detroit-Windsor Tunnel and the Ambassador Bridge had been built by this time). Another excursion steamer, the *Columbia,* one of the two Bob-Lo Island Amusement Park boats, picked up the remaining passengers and took them home.

The *Tashmoo,* however, would never sail again. The docked ship eventually settled on the river bottom with her bow and stern lower than her middle, and the pressure broke the ship's back. It would take an estimated $40,000 to raise and recondition the hull of this 37-year-old, wooden ship, with additional cost to refurbish the vessel's interior. The owners opted to dispose of the hull, but not before the pilot house was purchased and removed

The Tashmoo *just barely made it to a dock in Amherstburg, Ontario, and discharged her passengers and crew before she sank in the shallows on June 18, 1936.* (KOHL-FORSBERG ARCHIVES)

for use as a cottage on the Snye Channel near Wallaceburg, Ontario. This cottage burned to a complete loss on June 10, 1951. A suggestion to use the *Tashmoo's* hull as the base of a dancing pavilion at Bob-Lo Island Amusement Park in the Detroit River fell through, and the hull was scrapped. Capt. McAlpine died in Windsor's Grace Hospital on January 1, 1944, after a lengthy illness. The man who had succeeded in saving 1,419 passengers and 120 crew that June night on the Detroit River was remembered by many.

The 1,344-gross-ton steamer, *Tashmoo* (302'9" x 37'6" x 13'6"), was not the largest, nor the fastest, nor the most luxurious of the many Detroit River excursion steamers in the early 1900s, but it was the most popular. Although designed by Detroit's famous Frank E. Kirby to carry 4,000 passengers on day trips, the owning company limited the number to 2,800 for passenger comfort. Even so, between 1900 and 1936, more than 12,000,000 passengers enjoyed traveling on the *Tashmoo*. The ship's day trips from Detroit to Port Huron and back within a 12-hour span were the most popular of the river excursions. The *Tashmoo* regularly made quick and punctual pinpoint stops at ten different resorts in "The Flats" along the scenic St. Clair River to discharge or to collect passengers. While the *Tashmoo* lost, by 45 seconds, a highly-publicized steamboat race with the steamer, *City of Erie,* over a 94-mile course on June 4, 1901, it was the *Tashmoo* that was selected, proudly and amidst great publicity, to carry President Theodore Roosevelt on a nautical sightseeing tour past the city of Detroit's skyline on September 22, 1902.

The Queen of the River, *Tashmoo,* helped create millions of fond memories -- and her story of racing to save the lives of more than 1,500 passengers and crew, while she herself was dying, has become a river epic.

Left: *The* Tashmoo, *as she awaited news of her fate, sank at the Amherstburg dock in 1936.*
Right: *The* Tashmoo's *pilot house, used as a cottage, 1940s.* (BOTH: KOHL-FORSBERG ARCHIVES)

81. MONTROSE

JULY 30, 1962   DETROIT RIVER

The Montrose, *a British, ocean-going vessel visiting the Great Lakes, came close to gaining permanent residency here -- the wrong way!* (COURTESY OF THE PETER VAN DER LINDEN COLLECTION)

Rarely does one have an opportunity to see a shipwreck at relatively close range, from a vantage point accessible by car, with much of the wreck visible above water! That was the tourist attraction that resulted from a collision on the Detroit River one night in 1962.

The 4,993-gross-ton, steel freighter, *Montrose* (421'6" x 58'6" x 35'9"), built in Sunderland, England, by C. Bartram & Sons Ltd. and powered by Swedish diesel engines, was launched on September 23, 1960. The ship's interior was completed by early 1961, when she, owned in Montréal and expressly built for service between the Great Lakes and ports in Spain, North Africa, and the Mediterranean, started her maiden voyage on March 28, 1961, delivering goods around the Great Lakes, e.g. 100 tons of wine and olives to Milwaukee (where she lost a huge anchor that local divers, led by Clark Willick, quickly recovered

The Montrose *lay in the long shadow of the Ambassador Bridge between Detroit, Michigan, and Windsor, Ontario. The tall building in the background is the Penobscot Building, the tallest structure in Detroit in 1962.* (COURTESY OF THE PETER VAN DER LINDEN COLLECTION)

The salvage of the freighter, Montrose, *required a high degree of engineering knowledge and 101 days of work on the Detroit River in 1962.* (KOHL-FORSBERG ARCHIVES)

for her), and loading 3,350 tons of flour at Milwaukee to be taken to Syria.

On July 31, 1962, the *Montrose,* having just returned from across the Atlantic, made her first stop at Detroit to unload some cargo. Pulling out of the Detroit Harbor Terminal dock at 9:30 p.m., when it was already dark, loaded with fine wine and aluminum from France, and with neither vessel seeing each other, the *Montrose* was struck by a cement barge being pushed by the tug, *B. H. Becker*. Holed at the bow, the *Montrose* quickly filled with water, rolled onto her port side, and sank in 45 feet (13.6 metres) of water near the middle of the river. Fortunately, no lives were lost, all 41 crew escaping easily, with Captain Ralph Eyre-Walker, 48, the last to leave his ship over her sloping side at 2:30 a.m.

Frank Becker, the captain of the tug, reportedly quipped that he was the first American to sink a British ship on the Great Lakes since the War of 1812!

Salvage of the *Montrose* commenced in late August 1962. Offshore anchors and pulling tackle gradually positioned the vessel upright. The hole in her side was patched with 73 cubic yards of cement, and the ship was slowly towed towards shore where the water could easily be pumped out and the vessel refloated. This finally happened on November 9, 1962, 101 days after the collision. The initial plan to tow the *Montrose* to Montréal for repairs was changed to having the ship repaired at Lorain, Ohio, on Lake Erie. In April 1963, just before repairs began at Lorain, the wrecked vessel was sold to a company in Haugesund, Norway. On June 1, 1963, renamed the *Concordia Lago*, the repaired ship passed through the Welland Canal on its way out of the Great Lakes to Norway. It never returned.

The *Montrose* gave many people on both sides of the Detroit River several months' worth of amazing shipwreck views, the likes of which will never be seen again.

The Montrose *changed owners and names, becoming the* Concordia Lago *in 1963, and the* Lago *just before being scrapped in Pakistan in 1982.* (COURTESY OF THE PETER VAN DER LINDEN COLLECTION)

The St. Clair River System

The St. Clair River is the heart of the "Bluewater" tourist region, and the water is amazingly clean as it attempts to squeeze itself from broad Lake Huron into the narrow funnel that is this river. It is only about 30 miles downstream, at the wide, multiple fingers of the shallow St. Clair Flats where the river empties itself into Lake St. Clair, that it becomes dirty with suspended sediment. Nonetheless, being considered a "bottleneck" in the navigation of the Great Lakes, this river has been crowded with maritime traffic over the past two centuries that often resulted in shipwrecks. The Thames River, which flows into Lake St. Clair, and thus is part of the St. Clair River system, has also experienced dramatic, and tragic, shipwrecks over the years.

CANADA'S MOST FAMOUS ST. CLAIR RIVER SYSTEM SHIPWRECKS

The *Sidney E. Smith, Jr.* and the Canadian heroes....

At approximately 2:00 A.M. on June 5, 1972, the 532-foot-long steel freighter, *Parker Evans,* collided with the 489-foot-long steel freighter, *Sidney E. Smith, Jr.,* just south (downstream) of the Bluewater Bridge at Port Huron/Point Edward/Sarnia. The quick actions of a local pilot boat captain and his deckhand probably saved many lives in a dramatic rescue.

The 66-year-old, upbound *Smith,* fighting the strong current, had angled too much and caught her bow, the forceful water swinging the ship's nose right into the course of the 64-year-old *Evans,* itself being pushed downstream with great force. The long shriek of steel-on-steel abruptly caught **Capt. Robert Campbell's** attention. He jumped from the pilot office on the Canadian shore and quickly activated his little boat, the *Sally M.* Along with deckhand, **James Chadwick,** he removed 31 of the 34 men on board (the remaining three reached shore safely in the *Smith's* work skiff).

The *Evans,* her bow damaged but not leaking, proceeded to a nearby dock, but the *Smith,* her starboard bow pierced, took on water quickly, settled in 35 feet, and took on a severe list. The bow section hung over a drop-off that was 55 feet deep, and several days later, the ship cracked in half, eventually breaking completely in two. The salvage was longer and costlier than anyone imagined.

Left: *In retirement, Captain Robert Campbell enjoyed the panoramic view of the St. Clair River from his residence in Sarnia.* (1997 PHOTO BY CRIS KOHL)
Right: *The City of Sarnia honored Capt. Campbell by placing a historic marker along the waterfront where the sinking of the* Sidney E. Smith, Jr. *occurred -- a reminder of heroic actions during the last commercial ship sinking in the St. Clair River.* (PHOTO BY CRIS KOHL)

82. THE THAMES RIVER WAR OF 1812 WRECK

SEPTEMBER 1813   THAMES RIVER

The shipwreck found and raised from the Thames River at Chatham, Ontario, in 1901, one of the ships in Proctor's 1813 retreat, may have been the **General Myers.**   (KOHL-FORSBERG ARCHIVES)

Charred and battered remains of an old ship were discovered by two loggers in 1899 in the Thames River at Chatham, Ontario. Investigating this wreck in 12 feet of water, the Superintendent of the Chatham Waterworks declared it to be the schooner, ***General Myers.*** This historic ship was raised in early 1901, removed from the river, and placed on public display in Chatham's Tecumseh Park, starting a long, mudslinging fight with Detroit's chief historian, Clarence Burton, who fought tooth-and-nail, but unsuccessfully, to have that wreck placed in a public park in Detroit as a victory memorial.

Some background information: After the British fleet was defeated in the Battle of Lake Erie on September 10, 1813, British forces in the area fell back. General Henry Proctor abandoned Fort Malden and the captured Fort Detroit, and, with 850 soldiers and 1,000 First Nation allies under Tecumseh, retreated with many bateaux and five larger ships (the schooner ***General Myers***, and the gunboats ***Ellen, Eliza, Mary,*** and ***Miamis***) up the Thames River, heading deep inland into Upper Canada with 3,000 angry Americans in hot pursuit. Proctor burned and/or scuttled three of the five named ships, but the remaining two were captured by the Americans (and were reported lost in Lake St. Clair on their way back to Detroit!) Tecumseh was killed, Proctor was courtmartialed, the War of 1812 ended in late 1814, and the three shipwrecks in the Thames River were forgotten.

However, with no conservation efforts made in Chatham in 1901, the timbers that had been perfectly preserved under water for 88 years began to dry out and disintegrate in the open air. Furniture and collector pieces were cut or carved from the undamaged wood and conserved with furniture oil, but the rest of the wreck was hauled away to the local dump.

Recent research suggests that the raised wreck might have been the ***Miamis*** instead of the ***General Myers***. Two 1813 wrecks remain in the Thames River, although the Americans may have recovered the munitions at the time of sinking, while two more wrecks lie in the mud bottom of Lake St. Clair. All await discovery, conservation, and public exhibition!

Left: *The 1813 shipwreck was displayed in Chatham's Tecumseh Park.* (KOHL-FORSBERG ARCHIVES)

Right: *Artifacts from that War of 1812 shipwreck in the local museum.* (PHOTO BY CRIS KOHL)

83. *VICTORIA*

MAY 23, 1881   THAMES RIVER

Left: *The stern paddlewheeler,* Victoria, *at her dock near the sulphur springs tower on the Thames River, Ontario.*
Above: *The crowded* Victoria *underway on the Thames River, Ontario, as she appeared in England's* The Graphic.
(BOTH IMAGES: KOHL-FORSBERG ARCHIVES)

Many rivers form part of the vast Great Lakes waterways system, and one of them, the Thames River in Ontario, was the site of one of the worst maritime accidents in the history of the lakes. In the late 1800s, just downstream from the city of London, Ontario, was a popular picnic area named Springbank Park along the shores of the Thames River. Several steamboats conveyed residents of London to this nearby park on spring and summer weekends. A small steamboat named the *Victoria* was built and launched in that river in 1880. This double-decked vessel, only 80 feet (24.2 metres) long and 23 feet (7 metres) wide, was named after the long-reigning queen who, by that time, had sat on the throne of England for more than four decades already (with many more years to go.)

The steamer, *Victoria,* joined two other day excursions ships on May 24th, 1881, to help hundreds of people celebrate Queen Victoria's 62nd birthday by transporting them to Springbank Park. The crowds were larger than anticipated in this picnic-perfect weather, and, by the end of that afternoon, when the return traffic became heavy, two of the three

Above and Right: *Artists profusely illustrated many publications with their concepts of the* Victoria *disaster and its immediate aftermath.* (BOTH IMAGES: KOHL-FORSBERG ARCHIVES)

THE UPPER DECK GOING OVERBOARD.

Victoria disaster news appeared in **Harper's Weekly,** *June 18, 1881.* (KOHL-FORSBERG ARCHIVES)

boats were temporarily put out of commission. The pressure was placed on the *Victoria* to get these people back home to London.

Captain Donald Rankin weakly gave in. Licensed to take 400 passengers, the *Victoria* crammed 600 people on board. With the ship sitting dangerously low in the water, many passengers suddenly shifted to one side to watch a rowing race. The resulting list toppled the ship's boiler, breaking several stanchions that supported the upper deck. The topmost deck collapsed onto the lower deck, and the ship began to sink. People were crushed between decks, while others found themselves thrown into 17 feet (5 metres) of water.

An enormous number of people died within the first two minutes, despite assistance from individuals on shore and in small boats. The dismal recovery of bodies occupied the remainder of that evening and all of that night. By 10 p.m., 157 bodies had reportedly been recovered, and they were laid out in the yard near the sulphur springs tower. Huge bonfires were lit along the river's shoreline after dark to offer some light in locating bodies, and also to guide small boats returning to shore with bodies. A gloom fell over the community. All business in London was suspended. The city quickly ran out of coffins, having to bring in many more from neighbouring communities. Funerals occurred non-stop over the next eight days. This tragedy made front-page news all across Canada, as well as in the U.S.A. and in England, where Queen Victoria went into mourning at the loss of so many of her subjects, particularly since they perished while celebrating her birthday.

Tragic reminders remain in London, where many cemetery headstones read, "Drowned by the Foundering of the Steamer *Victoria*" or "Drowned in the Thames Disaster." Springbank Park and the steamers are gone, but the ghosts of the victims still haunt the river.

While the *Victoria* sinking, with 182 lives lost, ranks as the fourth worst maritime disaster in overall Great Lakes history (following the Chicago River's *Eastland* capsizing, Lake Michigan's *Lady Elgin* collision, and Lake Erie's *G. P. Griffith* fire), this tragic event on the Thames River at London, Ontario, in 1881 grimly tops the list of all maritime disasters on the Canadian side of the inland seas. The loss of the *Asia* in Georgian Bay (see pages 162-163) and the burning of the *Noronic* in Toronto harbour (see pages 50-51) rank, respectively, second and third worst in Canada.

While many victims of the **Victoria** *disaster rest in London cemeteries, a historic marker from the Province of Ontario marks the wreck site along the Thames River.* (ALL PHOTOS ARE BY CRIS KOHL)

84. WILLIAM H. WOLF

OCTOBER 20, 1921   ST. CLAIR RIVER

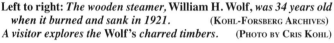

Left to right: *The wooden steamer,* William H. Wolf, *was 34 years old when it burned and sank in 1921.* (KOHL-FORSBERG ARCHIVES)
A visitor explores the Wolf's *charred timbers.* (PHOTO BY CRIS KOHL)

The huge, wooden propeller, *William H. Wolf* (285′5″ x 42′5″ x 18′5″), the largest ore carrier on the Great Lakes at the time, started life catastrophically when three people were killed at her launch in Milwaukee on August 6, 1887. According to one Milwaukee paper:

> A suppressed cry of horror rose from the lips of the 3,000 or more people who witnessed the launch of the mammoth new steamer *William H. Wolf* yesterday afternoon... a staging... gave way and the seventy-five persons upon it were precipitated either upon the dock below or into the river....

Despite that tragic beginning, the *William H. Wolf* worked hard for 34 years on the waters of the Great Lakes, suffering only minor incidents, until the year 1921.

On September 18, 1921, the ship, loaded with coal from Detroit to Houghton, Michigan, sprang a leak on Lake Superior and sank in 22 feet of water at the entrance to the Portage Waterway on the Keweenaw Peninsula. The ship was raised, repaired and quickly returned to service. The Chicago owners decided to load the *Wolf* with pulpwood on Lake Superior, unload that cargo at Port Huron, Michigan, then take the boat to Detroit for early winter layup to give it a rest. The *Wolf* made it to Port Huron, but not to Detroit.

The empty *William H. Wolf* caught on fire at 1:40 a.m. on Thursday, October 20, 1921, on the St. Clair River while passing Sombra, Ontario. The official "Wreck Report" in the National Archives at Chicago, written and signed by Captain John Hanson of the *Wolf*, gave the reason for loss as "Fire from unknown cause," on the "St. Clair River, vessel beached on Canadian shore, just below Woodtick Is." Note: Woodtick Island was later renamed Fawn Island. The crew fought the wind-blown flames, but were forced to launch their lifeboats; 20 of the 22 crew made it to shore, the First Mate and the Wheelsman having died on the *Wolf*. The charred hull sank on an underwater slope, and today lies in 6 to 60 feet (1.8 to 18 m.) of fast-moving water, the *Wolf's* propeller lying in the deepest part.

The William H. Wolf *was reduced to a charred hulk on Oct. 20, 1921.* (KOHL-FORSBERG ARCHIVES)

85. *FONTANA*

AUGUST 3, 1900   ST. CLAIR RIVER

The huge, yet graceful schooner, *Fontana* (231'4" x 39'1" x 17'), built at St. Clair, Michigan, on the shores of the St. Clair River, by Simon Langell in 1888, originally carried four masts, but was soon reduced to two masts when the 1,163-gross-ton vessel was demoted to being a schooner-barge, meaning that she would be towed by a steam-powered vessel while loaded with bulk cargo, rather than sail under her own power.

On the hot night of August 3, 1900, the *Fontana,* while in tow of the steamer, *Kaliyuga*, and loaded with 2,593 tons of iron ore from Presque Isle, Michigan, bound for Cleveland, Ohio, sank in a collision with the schooner-barge, *Santiago,* which was being towed by the steamer, *Appomattox*. This took place right at the point where Lake Huron tries hard to empty itself into the narrow funnel named the St. Clair River. One life was lost, a sailor named John McGregor, who was sleeping below deck on the *Fontana*.

The *Fontana's* location created a severe danger to navigation, and it took weeks of bickering over matters such as jurisdiction (was the wreck in Canada or the U.S.A.? She was, incidentally, just inside the Canadian boundary), and was the ship to be salvaged, or dynamited (she was eventually dynamited), but in the meantime, during all the bickering, the *Fontana* wreck caused the sinking of the schooner, *John B. Martin*, with the loss of four lives. More than two months after the *Fontana* sank, a tug finally pulled her apart, and then the wreck was dynamited to a safe level with 25 feet (7.5 metres) of water over her.

The remains of this once-beautiful schooner lie badly broken (due to the dynamiting and the strong current) at a depth of 60 feet (18 metres) of the fastest-moving water anywhere in the Great Lakes (excluding Niagara). The wreck still features deadeyes along one stretch of railing, but the strong current makes it difficult to stop and examine the details.

This iconic photo of the wrecked Fontana *has appeared on at least two book covers -- and clearly shows the wreck lying on the Canadian side of the St. Clair River.* (KOHL-FORSBERG ARCHIVES)

86. *MONARCH*
JULY 6, 1934   ST. CLAIR RIVER

This rare photo (left) *of the* Monarch *was taken when the tug was still named the* W. H. Simpson. *The loss of four lives in this sinking made front-page news* (above) *on both sides of the border!*
(BOTH: KOHL-FORSBERG ARCHIVES)

On July 6, 1934, the 49-gross-ton, wooden tugboat, the ***Monarch*** (63'3" x 19'1" x 7'7"), launched as the ***W. H. Simpson*** in 1889 at Sheboygan, Wisconsin, sank in 55 feet (16.5 metres) of water while towing the ***C. F. Bielman***, an old, wooden hulk that had been abandoned for a long time in Sarnia Bay, out of the rushing St. Clair River and into the calm, open waters of Lake Huron. While slicing through some of the fastest-moving waters in all of the Great Lakes, a surging wave caught the ***Bielman's*** bow, causing the ship to veer sideways. Attempting to compensate, the ***Monarch*** turned in the opposite direction, but was also caught by the swift current. She was able to regain a level keel, but too much of the fast-rushing water had entered the ***Monarch's*** hull, and the vessel sank, stern first, two minutes later, approximately 200 feet (60 metres) off the Canadian shore.

Some wreckage, including a life jacket, popped to the surface immediately, and four men from the tug, swimming in the river, managed to hold onto this flotsam until they were picked up by two small boats, both operated by marine news reporting agencies.

But four of the eight men on board the ***Monarch*** died in the sinking. The first body to be recovered was that of Captain Richard McDougall, 58. A man who was camping along the shoreline near Marine City, Michigan, discovered the body in the river on the morning of July 10, 1934, four days after the sinking. The body was found in a heavily battered condition, presumably caused by the buffeting it received from the heavy current where the ***Monarch*** sank. The captain, born at Port Lambton, Ontario, but who later resided at Harson's Island and Algonac in Michigan, never lived very far from where he was born, but he was buried, surprisingly, in Detroit's Woodmere Cemetery.

The second body was spotted by two Sarnia fishermen on shore on the evening of Friday, July 13, 1934, close to where the ***Monarch*** sank. Unable to snag the body with their fishing lines, the two anglers eventually contacted one of the marine news reporting boats, which recovered the body of the sailor.

On July 19, 1934, nearly two weeks after the sinking, another body was found, this time about 300 feet (90 metres) off the Sarnia ferry dock. The ferry boat, ***Ariel,*** took the body in tow across the river to Port Huron. Despite being in a fairly advanced stage of decomposition, the body was identified from its various tattoos as being the Monarch's 22-year-old Fireman, Duane Precious. His funeral was held in Goderich, Ontario, and he was buried near his parents in that town's Maitland Cemetery.

The fourth and final body was never found. A hardhat diver from Detroit descended to the wreck on Saturday, July 14, 1934, and, finding the current too strong to do any searching, abandoned any attempts at locating a body inside the wreck. Plans to raise the *Monarch* had been abandoned, as the cost of salvaging the old vessel would have been disproportionate to its value. If, as suspected, the final body, that of the assistant engineer, remained inside the tugboat at the bottom of the St. Clair River, it would have the undisturbed shipwreck as its private mausoleum, with the rushing current providing a steady, soothing sound, disturbed only occasionally by the deep, thumping sounds of a passing freighter.

The old and decrepit hulk of the propeller, *C. F. Bielman*, was eventually towed north from Sarnia, but not to its original destination of Cheboygan, Michigan. This huge, wooden hull became a combination dock and breakwall at the commercial fishing wharf owned by the Purvis family on the southeast side of remote Great Duck Island in northern Lake Huron, 13 miles (20 kms.) south of Manitoulin Island.

Clockwise from lower left: *A diver's exhaust bubbles, flowing horizontally rather than vertically, hint at the strong current. An early, aerial view of the* Monarch *wreck site. Alan Armbruster pulls himself upstream against the current on the* Monarch's *port railing. The* Monarch's *bow points directly into the oncoming, strong current.*
(ALL PHOTOS ARE BY CRIS KOHL)

About 20 years after the loss of the *Monarch*, adventurous individuals using a relatively new invention called "scuba" began exploring the bottom of the St. Clair River. The strong current at that river's mouth ensured that only the daring and the foolhardy would make the challenging descent to the wreck of the *Monarch*.

Since the 1950s, many divers have explored the wreck of the *Monarch*, lying on its starboard side with its bow facing directly into the strong current rushing down from nearby Lake Huron. Some have explored it once and said, "Never again," while others make regular visits to this site. But the tragedy did not end with the loss of four lives when the *Monarch* sank; two scuba divers have died here over the years while challenging the very strong currents in the river at this wreck site.

The underwater, braided steel cable that was used to guide divers from the old Canada Steamship Lines dock to the wreck of the *Monarch* was removed, along with that old dock, when a gambling casino was built there in recent years along the waterfront. Divers must now enter the river far upstream and let the current carry them into the shipwreck, or they have to drop down to the wreck carefully and quickly from a boat on the surface. Either method is exhilarating, and requires swiftwater diving experience. And if the assistant engineer is still on the wreck, either method will disturb his eternal sleep.

87. HAMONIC
JULY 17, 1945   ST. CLAIR RIVER

The impressive **Hamonic** *resembled a classic ocean liner: its elegant furnishings, the best that money could buy in 1909, included polished wood, ornate trim, and carved decorations.*
(KOHL-FORSBERG ARCHIVES)

The luxurious, 5,265-gross-ton passenger steamer, **Hamonic** (349'7" x 50' x 24'), launched at the famous Collingwood, Ontario, shipyards on November 26, 1908, had its interior completed by skilled craftsmen over that winter of 1908-1909. This ship is viewed by many steamship experts as having been one of the finest vessels that ever sailed the Great Lakes. Her immense quadruple expansion steam engine and her half a dozen large, scotch boilers, could produce 6,000 horsepower that propelled the vessel along at a good clip, even when fully loaded. The **Hamonic** spent her 36 years plying the route between Windsor-Sarnia and the Lakehead cities of Fort William and Port Arthur on Lake Superior.

The complete defeat of Germany in the spring of 1945, coupled with the looming conquest of Japan later that summer, provided positive newspaper headlines in numbers not yet seen during World War Two. But then, right at a time when genuine smiles started to appear again on people's faces in Canada and the U.S.A., a homefront disaster struck.

The **Hamonic**, following her established routine, tied up in the darkness very early that Tuesday, July 17, 1945, at the Canada Steamship Lines dock, which was shared with the Canadian National Railway at Point Edward, Ontario, a small, waterfront town right next to Sarnia, to load supplies. On this particular day, 220 passengers, bound for points north, prepared to depart in late afternoon, to return the following Monday.

However, a fire started in a freight shed on the dock when a defective gas engine on a forklift machine backfired, igniting a roaring inferno that would consume a large section of the dockside storage sheds and would leap onto the Great Lakes luxury liner, **Hamonic**. Captain Horace Beaton rushed to the wheelhouse and ordered his ship cut adrift. The engines soon started, and the **Hamonic**, now with power, but ablaze, was driven aground in the shallows of a little cove near Purdy's Fisheries, where most of the people on board were evacuated. Elmer Kleinsmith, of Sarnia, creatively using his coal company crane, hoisted as many as 50 people off the burning **Hamonic** to safety onto the dock at Purdy's.

The manager of a marine reporting agency across the river in Port Huron wrote notes about the fire's progress: "8:23 a.m. -- Smoke was seen in the freight sheds, about 50 feet south of the **Hamonic,** which was lying stern north, moored at the wharf opposite the sheds.... 8:25 a.m. -- Flames shot from the freight sheds towards the **Hamonic**.... 8:35 a.m. -- A freighter, upbound, veered to avoid the **Hamonic**, which had cast off from the wharf and was backing with the current downstream,...." The marine reporters then jumped into their boat and rescued about 55 passengers in four trips to the **Hamonic**. Even with the many areas and methods of rescue, about 100 passengers were treated for burns.

The fire that began on the dock at Point Edward, Ontario, jumped onto the Hamonic, which was tied up at her regular space along that dock. Cut adrift, the ship was rammed into shore a short distance downstream, away from the burning sheds, near Purdy's Fisheries. There, the vessel continued to burn while the passengers and crew were removed. Once an inspection had been made of the cooled-off hulk, it was sold for scrap.

(KOHL-FORSBERG ARCHIVES)

It took some time for anyone to realize that one person had been killed by this fire. James O'Neil, a 44-year-old freight handler employed by the Canada Steamship Lines at its freight shed at Point Edward, was last seen fighting the fire in the shed. When he failed to pick up his pay cheque, it was presumed that he had left the boarding camp set up by the company for its workers; nonetheless, C. S. L. officials requested that local police try to find him. His wallet and identification were then located in his room at the camp. When his body was found by an amateur fisherman off the old ore docks, floating perpendicular in the water, on July 25, 1945, they knew that O'Neil had been a victim of the fire. Many sources of Great Lakes shipwreck information list no lives lost in the burning of the *Hamonic* because O'Neil was, technically, not one of the ship's crew or passengers.

The charred hull was examined; fortunately no bodies were found, and no one from the ship was reported missing. A Windsor, Ontario man purchased the *Hamonic* wreck, towing it to nearby Sandwich on September 10, 1945. He, in turn, sold the hulk to the Steel Company of Canada in Hamilton, Ontario, which scrapped the vessel in June 1946.

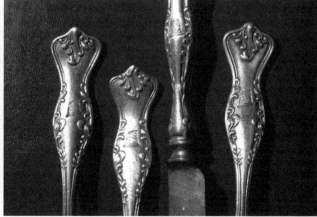

The Hamonic continued to use the fine china and silverware supplied by the Northern Navigation Company, which owned the ship from 1909 until 1913, when it was amalgamated into Canada Steamship LInes. Diver Bill Humphries found these pieces in the St. Clair River where the Hamonic docked, and gave them to co-author Cris Kohl in 1986. Each dining utensil is engraved with the "NNCO" flag representing the ship's first owner. (PHOTOS BY CRIS KOHL)

Lake Huron

Lake Huron, named by the French after their indigenous allies, has the distinction of being the first of the Great Lakes to be seen by Europeans. French explorer Étienne Brûlé first ventured into this enormous body of water via the Ottawa and Mattawa Rivers in 1609 or 1610, followed shortly thereafter by Samuel de Champlain.

Second largest of the five Great Lakes (only Superior is larger), Huron is also considered to be the second "least settled." Again, Lake Superior has the "wildest," or least built up, shoreline of all the Lakes, despite the fact that, surprisingly, it can claim cities larger than any of those on Lake Huron.

Lake Huron's most famous shipwrecks on the Canadian side range from a "fighting sail" vessel from the War of 1812 (today a museum ship), and an exploded tug represented by a "boiler on the beach," to ships that were lost with all hands, such as the *Waubuno* and the *Wexford*, to the schooner that is the most visited shipwreck in all of the Great Lakes, and even further onward to ships still missing, like the enormous *James Carruthers*, the incredibly tragic *Asia* -- and perhaps even explorer La Salle's long-lost *Griffon*!

CANADA'S MOST FAMOUS LAKE HURON SHIPWRECKS

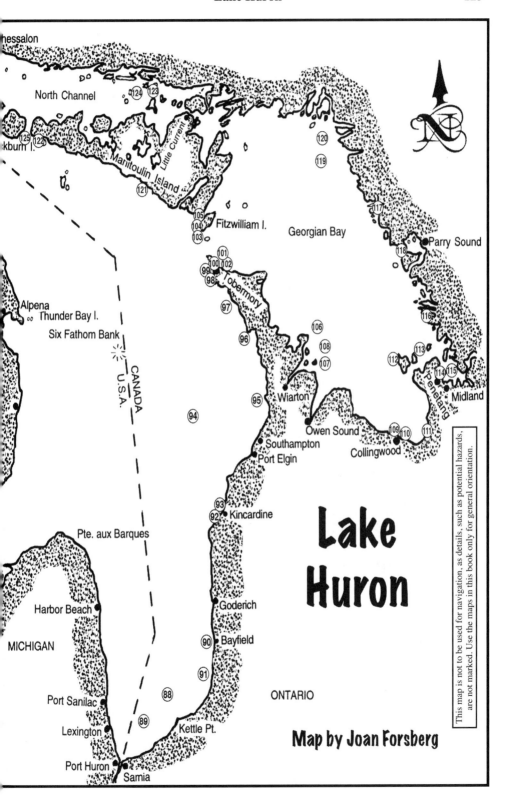

hessalon

North Channel

124 123

kburn I.

125 122

Manitoulin Island

Little Current

121

105
104
103

Fitzwilliam I.

101
100 102
99
98

obermory

97

96

106

108

107

120

119

117

118 Parry Sound

116

112

113

114 115

Penetang

Midland

Alpena
Thunder Bay I.

Six Fathom Bank

CANADA
U.S.A.

95 Wiarton

94

Owen Sound

109
110 111

Southampton
Port Elgin

Collingwood

93
92 Kincardine

Pte. aux Barques

Lake
Huron

Harbor Beach

Goderich

MICHIGAN

90 Bayfield

91

Port Sanilac

88

89

Lexington

Kettle Pt.

ONTARIO

Port Huron

Sarnia

Map by Joan Forsberg

This map is not to be used for navigation, as details, such as potential hazards, are not marked. Use the maps in this book only for general orientation.

88. GHOST FLEET OF THE ST. CLAIR RIVER
1928-1936   LAKE HURON

Early scuba divers in the 1950s were unable to locate any of these vessels that had been researched as shipwrecks in the St. Clair River:

The Yakima, *wrecked in 1905*
(KOHL-FORSBERG ARCHIVES)

The Province, *capsized in 1923*
(MOORE MUSEUM. MOORETOWN, ON)

The Aztec, *burned in 1923*
(KOHL-FORSBERG ARCHIVES)

The Sachem, *sunk in 1928*
(LIBRARY AND ARCHIVES CANADA)

A hundred years ago, ships sank in the St. Clair River, but these wrecks were nowhere to be found when the first scuba divers searched for them after World War II. Of the 250+ ships that sank in the St. Clair River, most were raised and returned to service, but a few dozen remained on the river bottom -- and a few simply disappeared altogether!

Those ships that sank in the river, but mysteriously disappeared from there, are part of "The Ghost Fleet of the St. Clair River."

Starting in the mid-1980s, Cris Kohl researched all of the ships that sank in the St. Clair River, resulting in a 1987 book titled, *Shipwreck Tales: The St. Clair River (to 1900)*. The anticipated follow-up volume, "*(since 1900)*," never materialized, despite 90% of the research for it having been done. Those files were temporarily put aside, while others were picked up.

In the summer of 1993, a team, led by Jim and Pat Stayer, and which included Tim Juhl and Cris Kohl, started finding shipwrecks in lower Lake Huron. They were operating in Canadian waters under Cris' archaeological licence from the Province of Ontario to search for the wreck of the *Wexford* (see pages 128-129). Well into that summer, the searchers knew exactly where the wreck of the *Wexford* was not located; in the process, they had found a small fleet of other shipwrecks, old, wooden vessels difficult to identify. As it turned out, the mid-1980s research done by Cris proved to be invaluable in identifying those shipwrecks.

Numerous Great Lakes maritime history books that had been published by the early 1990s informed us that vessels like the *Yakima,* the *Aztec,* the *Province*, and the *Sachem* all sank in the St. Clair River. That much was certainly documented. However, Cris Kohl's research took each story a giant step further; he found evidence indicating that these shipwrecks had been raised, patched, and towed into Sarnia Bay, this area's "ship's graveyard" or "unwanted vessel dumping ground," in the early 1900s. This same situation existed in numerous other Great Lakes harbours, such as present-day Thunder Bay, Ontario, and Chicago, Il-

Sponsored by
MAYOR MIKE BRADLEY
AND
SARNIA CITY COUNCIL

linois. However, by the late 1920s and 1930s, the many ugly, abandoned hulks of old ships that stuck out above the waters of these harbours began to be viewed as serious eyesores, and money was spent to clean them up. Cris' research gave the names of ships and the exact dates that they were raised and removed from Sarnia Bay, towed far out into Lake Huron, and sunk again -- this time in deep water. Back in those environmentally worry-free days, out of sight meant out of mind.

Jim Stayer videotapes the enormous, wooden hull of the historic steamer, Yakima. (PHOTO BY CRIS KOHL)

In the summer of 1993, the team found the *Yakima*, the *Aztec*, the *Province*, and the *Sachem*, although the latter shipwreck had been located by another party who, despite not being able to identify the wreck, refused to divulge its location. Our search team located it independently and was able to identify it.

These wrecks lie about 11 miles (18 kms.) north-northeast of the Bluewater Bridge at Point Edward-Sarnia, Ontario, in depths between 68 and 78 feet (20.6 to 23.6 metres) of water. Jim Stayer gave them the suitable nickname, "Ghost Fleet of the St. Clair River."

The huge, wooden propeller, *Yakima* (279′ x 40′5″ x 20′6″) built at Cleveland in 1887, was the first commercial ship on the Great Lakes to be built with electric lights. She stranded and burned in the St. Clair River on June 10, 1905, was towed into Sarnia Bay, abandoned, then scuttled in Lake Huron in late 1928.

The search team found the hull of the Province *loaded with the dynamited pieces of the* Aztec. (PHOTO BY CRIS KOHL)

The remains of the steamer, *Aztec* (180′ x 33′3″ x 13′9″; built at Marine City, Michigan, in 1889), and the barge, *Province* (162′ x 40′ x 10′; built at Fort William, Ontario, in 1911), lay rotting in Sarnia Bay until the 1936 clean-up, when the dynamited pieces of the *Aztec* (which had become too embedded in the bay's shoreline to remove in one piece) were placed aboard the refloated hull of the *Province*, and both were scuttled in lower Lake Huron. The *Aztec* had burned at Marine City on November 9, 1923, while the *Province* had capsized in the St. Clair River, with the loss of two lives, on September 28, 1923. Both wrecks were raised, towed to Sarnia Bay, and abandoned. It was easy to identify these two from the many broken timbers of one shipwreck lying inside the hull of another.

Jim examines a metal, lightbulb-protection cage on the wreck of the Sachem. (PHOTO BY CRIS KOHL)

The wooden propeller, *Sachem* (187′ x 33′5″ x 14′8″), constructed at Grand Haven, Michigan, in 1889, burned and sank in the St. Clair River on October 8, 1928. Raised and towed to Sarnia Bay, the ship was scuttled in lower Lake Huron a few weeks later.

Some of the other ships that are part of this "Ghost Fleet," but have not yet been located or identified, are the *Naiad*, the *Majestic*, the *Constitution*, the *John Kilderhouse* and the *Maple Gulf*. Stay tuned!

LIFESTYLES

Finding history on lake floor

Searching for the 'Ghost Fleet' often a mysterious adventure for city diver

Numerous newspapers on both sides of the international border printed articles about the discovery of the "Ghost Fleet" in 1993. (KOHL-FORSBERG ARCHIVES)

89. *GLADSTONE*

1923 AND 1936   LAKE HURON

The old, wooden freighter, *Gladstone* (282' x 40'3" x 23'), built in 1888 at Cleveland, Ohio, and enormous with its 2,181 gross tons of displacement, ended her above-water days in the 1920s and 1930s fending off Lake Huron's waves trying to protect the shoreline. Today, this wreck is a popular shore-access site for scuba divers.

But in the *Gladstone's* early years, she was known as the ship that refused to die.

In 1888, during the *Gladstone's* first season, she collided with the steamer, *T. W. Palmer* in mid-July in the St. Clair River near Stag Island, sending the *Palmer* to drydock in Buffalo for repairs. On June 2, 1892, the *Gladstone's* steering cable failed and the barge, *Marvin E. Selden,* towed by the steamer, *Edward Smith*, collided with her at Port Huron; both vessels were damaged. On Friday, November 20, 1903, the *Gladstone* sank in a collision with the steamer, *Sacramento,* off Lake Erie's Bar Point, but was lightered (that is, she had her grain cargo removed) and was raised and being repaired within a week. In early September 1907, the *Gladstone* spent more than a week stranded off Sandusky, Ohio, on Lake Erie. Regular collisions and strandings were commonplace for the *Gladstone*.

The aging *Gladstone* sank in the early spring of 1919 due to ice in the Pine River at St. Clair, Michigan, where the vessel had wintered. The *Gladstone's* keel was bent and broken, so, although raised and pumped, she never sailed again. In late 1923, the *Gladstone's* stripped hull was sold to Canadian interests, who had the ship carefully towed to Point Edward, and there sunk as a breakwall dock, along with two, old barges, the *A. W. Wright* and the *Arrow*, in front of the Huron Sand and Gravel Company's leased property (which today is waterfront property in Canatera Park). Fire destroyed these ships/docks to the water's edge in 1936. A formal request by two Sarnia men for permission to remove all of the steel and spikes from the *Gladstone* in 1937 was denied on the grounds that it would "impair the usefulness of the wreck as a breakwater."

From the time the ship burned nearly to the water line until the early 1960s, portions of the *Gladstone's* stern and engine could be seen above the water. Reportedly much of the wreck was removed in the winter of 1963, except for the parts that scuba divers can still see today, namely a stern section of the hull and the steam engine amidst wood debris.

Above: *The large, wooden propeller,* Gladstone. *Her twin smokestacks were reduce to one near the end of her career.*   (KOHL-FORSBERG ARCHIVES)

Right: *This 1937 map of Sarnia's Lake Huron shoreline shows where the* Gladstone *and two other vessels were sunk as docks/breakwalls in 1923.*
(LIBRARY AND ARCHIVES CANADA)

90. *Lynda Hindman*

November, 1973   Lake Huron

Tourists gazing down at Lake Huron from their clifftop perch at Pioneer Park in the beautifully restored and carefully maintained historic town of Bayfield, Ontario, often wonder what unspeakable tragedy befell the broken shipwreck that is so visibly sticking out of the shallow waters below them. We have heard many tales, including that this wreck is from the Great Storm of 1913, the worst storm in Great Lakes recorded history, and that all hands on it were lost! The truth, however, is not quite as dramatic as that.

This obvious portion of a shallow shipwreck sticking up high out of Lake Huron's waters at Bayfield, Ontario, adds enormously to deep meditation and dramatic sunsets. (Photos by Cris Kohl)

This "wreck" spent many decades as a very active Great Lakes workhorse. The large, 410-gross-ton *William A. McGonagle* (110' x 28' x 15'3"), built as a fire tug at Lorain, Ohio, in 1908, underwent a series of name and ownership changes in her long history, with her original name lasting the longest of any of them, from the time of launch in 1908 until 1935. That year, her original owner, the Duluth, Missabie & Iron Range Railroad Company, sold her to the Pigeon Timber Company in Canada, which promptly renamed the vessel, *Marguerite W.,* a name it carried until 1953 past two more owners, Lakehead Transportation Company (1937-1947) and Great Lakes Lumber & Shipping Company (1947-1953).

The tug had spent its entire 45-year career working on Lake Superior, but that changed in 1953, when the Hindman Transportation Company of Owen Sound purchased the vessel and moved it to Lake Huron, amending its name twice, first to *Ruth Hindman* in 1953, then to *Lynda Hindman* in 1965. A Bayfield resident bought the old hull for use as a breakwall off his property when the *Hindman* was about to be cut up for scrap in 1973 at Goderich. By error, she was scuttled too far off shore, and subsequent winters broke her up.

Left: *The* **William A. McGonagle,** *although built on Lake Erie in 1908, spent the first 27 years of her long career operating out of Duluth on Lake Superior.* (Kohl-Forsberg Archives)
Right: *Renamed the* **Lynda Hindman** *in 1965 (she had two other names between the first and the last), she became a breakwall, of sorts, in 1973.* (Courtesy of the Peter van der Linden Collection)

91. *WEXFORD*

NOVEMBER 9, 1913   LAKE HURON

The steamer, Wexford, *the oldest of the steel ships lost in the Great Storm of 1913.*
(KOHL-FORSBERG ARCHIVES)

The bodies of unfortunate sailors from the Wexford *washed ashore near St. Joseph, Ontario.*
(KOHL-FORSBERG ARCHIVES)

STEAMER WEXFORD LOST ON HURON WENT DOWN IN SUNDAY'S STORM BODIES WASHED UP ON THE BEACH

The Bodies Bore Life Preservers Marked "Wexford"...Ship Thought To Have Foundered Between Kettle Point and Bayfield.

Goderich, Ont., Nov. 11.—That the steamer Wexford, of the Western Steamship Company, Limited, To-ronto, was lost in the storm of Sunday is without question.

Many newspapers reported the Wexford's *loss.*
(KOHL-FORSBERG ARCHIVES)

The Wexford *was found upright in 75 feet (22.7 metres) of water off Grand Bend, Ontario.*
(COURTESY OF THE ARTIST, ROBERT MCGREEVY)

The 2,104-gross-ton steamer, *Wexford* (250' x 40'1" x 23'7"), one of eight steel freighters that disappeared on Lake Huron with all hands in the Great Storm of November 1913, the worst storm in Great Lakes recorded history, was built by William Doxford & Sons Company in Sunderland, England, in 1883. Just as the *James Carruthers* (see page 132) was the newest of those lost ships, the *Wexford* was the oldest.

The *Wexford*, a typical "canaller" in that her dimensions were just right for the size of the Welland Canal locks at that time, had her original steam engine replaced in 1904 with a triple expansion engine built by the Collingwood Ship Building Company. The *Wexford* operated under that name from 1883 until 1898, when she was purchased by N. Dubuisson of Dunkirk, France, who changed her name to *Elise*. In 1903, the *Elise* was again purchased by a British firm, and her original name was restored.

On November 9, 1913, hauling 96,000 bushels of wheat from Fort William, Ontario, on Lake Superior, to Goderich, Ontario, on Lake Huron, the *Wexford* foundered with the loss of all hands. Her whistles blowing frantically (heard by people on shore at Goderich) as the strong winds, huge waves, and blinding snowstorm prevented the ship from entering the dangerously narrow harbour at Goderich, she desperately proceeded south in a futile attempt to reach the safety of the St. Clair River.

When the storm subsided somewhat, farmer Robert Trumbull, living between the Ontario communities of St. Joseph and Grand Bend on the lower Lake Huron shore, went to the pebbly beach along his property to assess any damage, and, to his shock, he found the frozen body of a dead man in a pleading-for-help posture. An immediate search located two more bodies and a broken lifeboat. All three of the bodies wore cork-and-canvas life preservers bearing the name, *Wexford*.

More bodies from the *Wexford* were later found washed ashore. The ship reportedly carried a crew of 18, and two 24-year-old cousins from Goderich named Murdoch and Donald McDonald were hitching a ride home, so a total of 20 lives were lost when the *Wexford* sank.

Cris Kohl first wrote about the *Wexford* in his 1985 book, *Dive Southwestern Ontario!* In early 1990, he teamed up with Michigan shipwreck hunters Jim and Pat Stayer, Tim Juhl, and Gary Biniecki to search for the *Wexford*. Annually for seven years, Cris applied, on behalf of the team, for the archaeological licence (free, but entailing considerable paperwork) mandatory for doing any shipwreck hunting in Ontario waters. The team researched extensively and searched sporadically, met a lot of people who had also searched for the *Wexford* (all without benefit of any licence), spoke with commercial fishermen and Canadian Coast Guard personnel, walked the shore of the old Trumbull farm, but failed to find the wreck. They searched off Grand Bend, but began their search in 80 feet (24 metres) of water and went deeper, presuming that if the *Wexford* were any shallower, it would have been found already. We now know that this was not the case.

When it seemed as though everyone had stopped searching for the *Wexford*, someone found her -- accidentally. In mid-August 2000, a retiree named Don Chalmers, while fishing off Grand Bend, saw, on his inexpensive fish finder, that he had drifted over a large object rising about 20 feet off the 75-foot-deep bottom. Noting the location coordinates, Don told diving friends about his find, they explored the wreck -- and it turned out to be the *Wexford*!

The upright *Wexford* was a unique shipwreck discovery -- it was the only one from that storm located to date that was NOT upside-down (which attested to the storm's powerful violence.) Although the pilothouse and smokestack had washed away, the site features brass portholes, their glass still intact, large, open hatches, machinery, hoses, cups, plates, and many other fascinating artifacts inside the wreck.

Roy Pickering from Erieau, Ontario, studies the open hatches as he glides over the deck.

Inside the **Wexford's** *immense cargo holds lie ladders and pieces of the ship's superstructure.*

The **Wexford** *has so many openings that exits can almost always be seen from inside the wreck, making slight penetration relatively safe.*

Many interesting artifacts from the **Wexford** *lie embedded in the silt inside the shipwreck.*
(ALL PHOTOS ARE BY CRIS KOHL)

92. *ERIE BELLE*

NOVEMBER 21, 1883   LAKE HURON

The steamship, Erie Belle, *exploded off Kincardine with tragic results.*   (KOHL-FORSBERG ARCHIVES)

A massive, contorted mound of thick, broken steel interrupts an otherwise idyllic shoreline of white, sandy beach about two miles (3 kms.) south of Kincardine, Ontario. This out-of-place object is the most visible thing left of the wooden steamer, *Erie Belle* (120'5" x 20'5" x 9'1"), after that ship exploded on November 21, 1883. A mid-November storm had stranded the schooner, *J. N. Carter*, at this location, and the powerful *Erie Belle,* dispatched from its home port of Windsor, Ontario, and attempting to free the ship, pushed its steam engine to the limit. The resulting boiler explosion blew the ship into little pieces and killed two engineers and two firemen from the crew of twelve. The survivors were pulled out of the freezing water by the volunteer lifeboat crew from Kincardine. One deckhand was blinded, the cook was severely scalded, and another survivor reportedly became mentally unbalanced and died a few years later.

The stranded *J. N. Carter*, pulled free by another tug in 1884, enjoyed ten more years of life before being wrecked off the southwest shore of Manitoulin Island in northern Lake Huron on September 15, 1894, at a dangerous location today called Carter Rock.

Built as the *Hector* in Cleveland, Ohio, in 1862, by Peck & Masters, this ship was sold to Canadian interests in 1879 and was renamed the *Erie Belle*, operating among the ports of Windsor, Leamington, and Pelee Island. The vessel had been rebuilt by the Jenkins Brothers in Windsor in 1882. Today it serves as a reminder of our extensive, maritime history.

The Erie Belle *left a long-lasting reminder of its existence: its boiler lies in the open on the sandy beach at Kincardine; a historic marker recalls its story.* (PHOTOS BY CRIS KOHL AND JOAN FORSBERG)

93. *ANN MARIA*

OCTOBER 7, 1902   LAKE HURON

The ship was wrecked while attempting to enter Kincardine harbour.   (KOHL-FORSBERG ARCHIVES)

Unimaginably violent waves crashed on shore at Kincardine, Ontario, close to where the schooner, *Ann Maria,* had stranded and was breaking up at 10 p.m. on October 7, 1902. Her six-man crew clung desperately to the rigging while a rescue team was quickly assembled on shore. Four local men, bobbing in a large rowboat, struggled to reach the wreck and, despite wild waves pounding over her, removed the crew. When starting for shore, the rescue boat was dashed by a giant wave, spilling its human cargo. Only three rescuers and two crew made it back to the stricken schooner. By 2 a.m., the seas calmed down enough for a second boat to rescue these five. But four sailors and one rescuer had drowned.

The oak-hulled *Ann Maria* (131′2″ x 26′3″ x 11′3″), constructed at Conneaut, Ohio, in 1864, and named after the teenage daughter of Capt. Marshall Capron, the builder, was carrying coal from Cleveland to Kincardine at the time of loss.

BRAVE MEN OF KINCARDINE, ONT., PRESENTED WITH GOLD MEDALS

President Roosevelt Recognizes the Heroism of Hardy Canadians Who Nearly Lost Their Lives In Saving Crew of American Schooner Last Fall.

Chicago, April 15.—A dispatch to the Record-Herald from Kincardine, Ont., says: Before President Roosevelt left Washington for his Western trip, he took the first step in a kindly act of international courtesy which was completed here last night. Eight gold medals, given in recognition of their bravery in saving the lives of the crew of an American schooner, were presented to attempt a rescue. Four men entered a small boat, and after great exertion took the crew aboard. Just as the boat started to return a wave filled the rowboat and its occupants were thrown into the water. Then followed a long, hard struggle with the storm. William Ferguson, one of the rescuing party, and four of the schooner's crew were lost. Thomas, John and Walter McGraw, the remaining rescuers, succeeded in regaining

Left: *The* Ann Maria *wreck attracted shore crowds.* **Right:** *On April 14, 1903, President Theodore Roosevelt performed an international courtesy when he presented gold medals to "the eight principals in the rescue" of the crew of this American schooner.* (BOTH: KOHL-FORSBERG ARCHIVES)

94. JAMES CARRUTHERS

NOVEMBER 9, 1913   LAKE HURON

The steel freighter, *James Carruthers* (550' x 58'2" x 26'7"), the largest of the eight ships in Lake Huron that was lost with all hands in the Great Storm of 1913, the worst storm in Great Lakes recorded history, is the final one of the eight still awaiting discovery. However, it could rest far off shore near the middle of the lake southwest of the Bruce Peninsula's Cape Hurd, in the deep trench called the Manitoulin Basin, where depths reach 750 feet (227 metres) -- or it could lie in 102 feet (31 metres) of water on the shelf right next to that deepest part of Lake Huron.

Just as the *Wexford* (see pages 128-129) was the oldest ship to disappear with all hands on Lake Huron in that storm, the *James Carruthers* was the youngest. Like the *Wexford*, she sailed under Canadian registry. The *Carruthers*, the largest ship ever built in Canada at that point in time, lasted less than six months on the lakes after being launched on May 22, 1913, at the Collingwood Ship Building Company yards. Near the end of June, with her interior work completed, the *Carruthers* proceeded on her maiden voyage. This enormous, 7,862-gross-ton vessel was powered by a single triple expansion engine and three Scotch boilers that could generate 2,400 horsepower.

This impressive, new vessel foundered in that storm on November 9, 1913, loaded with 370,000 bushels of wheat (valued at $400,000 and insured for $350,000), from Fort William on Lake Superior, bound for Port Colborne on Lake Erie (the ship itself was insured for $400,900). Various sources have given the number of lives lost as between 22 and 24, with many of the bodies washing ashore at Southampton and points north of there. The *James Carruthers'* career ranks as one of the shortest in Great Lakes maritime history.

The launch of Canada's largest freighter at the time, the **James Carruthers,** *at Collingwood. The ship was lost with all hands within six months.*   (COLLINGWOOD MUSEUM COLLECTION, X974.539.1.)

Sponsored by the **COLLINGWOOD MUSEUM**
45 St. Paul Street, Collingwood, ON L9Y 3P1
Tel: 705-445-4811   museum@collingwood.ca   www.collingwood.ca/museum
Conserving and promoting Collingwood's heritage and the legacy of the Huron Institute since 1966

95. GENERAL HUNTER
1816   LAKE HURON

General Hunter *off Fort Malden, where it was built.* (COURTESY OF THE ARTIST, PETER RINDLISBACHER)

A man taking his customary morning stroll along the Lake Huron shoreline at South-ampton, Ontario, in late April 2001, saw something he had never seen before -- a dozen, curved timber tips, well-worn and blackened, poking through the sand in a straight line. Winter weather, coupled with low lake levels, had altered the beach structure, and the location of a shipwreck, lost for nearly two centuries, was revealed.

Archaeologist Kenneth Cassavoy investigated the site. This led to an excavation, beginning on May 10, 2004, of this shipwreck. Regimental military buttons and a small cannon were among the many clues found on the wreck. Research by historians Patrick Folkes, Stan McLellan, and Leslie Currie pointed to this ship being a vessel named the *Hunter*.

The British, 93-ton, two-masted schooner known originally as **H.M.S.** *General Hunter* (54' x 18' x 8'), designed by William Bell from Scotland and constructed in 1805-1806 at Amherstburg, Upper Canada (later Canada West, and much later, Ontario) as a ten-gun ship of the Royal Navy, was similar to the schooner, **H.M.S.** *Hope*, which was wrecked in the Detour Passage of northern Lake Huron on October 4, 1805, and which, through coincidence, the *General Hunter* essentially replaced.

In the War of 1812, the *General Hunter*, converted to a brig rig, took part in the Battle of Lake Erie on September 10, 1813, and was captured by American forces, who shortened the name of the ship simply to *Hunter* to remove any connection to the British military. Sold to private interests (allegedly to a fur trader at St. Joseph, Michigan) after the war, the *Hunter,* on August 1, 1816, sailed from Detroit to Fort Mackinac with government supplies, arriving there on August 14th. The cargo was quickly unloaded, and the *Hunter* left on the return leg of its trip the very next day. The ship encountered bad weather on August 17th, predominantly a particularly heavy wind, that blew the *Hunter* onto a Lake Huron wilderness shoreline at about midnight on August 19, 1816. The ship was wrecked, but all on board survived by climbing down a fallen mast to the beach. The captain, six sailors, the cook, and two children who were passengers took a week to reach Detroit, their original destination, approximately 160 miles (260 kms.) to the south, in their open yawl boat.

The remains of this shipwreck, once completely studied and surveyed, were again covered with sand to preserve it, with beachgoers again getting tanned while unknowingly lying atop a cultural resource. The Bruce County Museum in Southampton displays numerous interesting items from the *Hunter* that were recovered and properly conserved.

96. *EXPLORER*

NOVEMBER, 1867 AND SEPTEMBER 4, 1883   LAKE HURON

A CAPTAIN'S CRIME.

Discovery and Raising of the Schooner Explorer After Five Years' Mystery.

A Terrible Crime Brought to Light by the Successful Operations of the Wreckers.

The Vessel Sunk for the Insurance, and the Crew Foully Murdered.

The unknown sunken schooner which Captain Jex's wrecking expedition went to has been raised, and proves to be the schooner Explorer, which went down several years ago. With the recovery of the vessel the particulars of a great crime came out. It is not often that mysterious "disasters" can be so fully explained. Late in October, 1867, the Explorer was fitted out at Chatham, Ont., with a stock of goods to trade with the Indians around Georgian Bay

Left: *It was not until the wreck of the schooner, Explorer, was found and raised that the realization that a serious crime had been committed surfaced.*
Above: *The schooner,* Explorer, *was built at Chatham, Canada West, in 1866 expressly for Captain John Waddell, a longtime, respected resident. The ship in the above photo, the* Una, *was similar in appearance to the* Explorer.   (BOTH: KOHL-FORSBERG ARCHIVES)

On a bitterly cold day in November 1867, a gaunt, unshaven man, more dead than alive from starvation and exposure, clutched at his single oar and slowly propelled his yawl boat into the harbour at Wiarton, Ontario. A crowd gathered, the local newspaper later writing that "assistance was required to enable him to be removed from the boat to the tavern." There, he told a tragic tale: how he was the master of a small schooner, the *Explorer,* how his two crewmembers had been crushed to death below deck when they attempted to stabilize the cargo of shifting whiskey barrels after the ship struck a rocky shoal near Tobermory in harsh weather, how he could barely free the yawl boat in time to save himself after waves pulled the vessel into deep water, how it had taken him 11 days to reach Wiarton with little food.... The man, Captain John Waddell, returned to Goderich to recuperate.

Over the next three years, Waddell made several trips of an undisclosed nature in a small boat to the western Bruce Peninsula area. On one such trip north, on July 20, 1870, Waddell's boat capsized and he drowned. His body was buried at Goderich.

In 1876, a Tobermory fisherman accidentally found the sunken, but intact-looking, *Explorer.* When the schooner was raised in 1881, shocking discoveries were made. The ship had been stripped of everything, including cargo, and loaded with rocks. The bodies of the two crew members were found locked below deck, and auger holes had been drilled into the hull. The general conclusion was that Waddell had his crew unload the cargo and hide it along the shore before he made them incapacitatingly inebriated. Then Waddell locked them below deck, drilled holes in the boat, and jumped into the yawl boat before the ship sank. Waddell, formerly the Sheriff of the Western District of Upper Canada when he lived in Chatham, even collected the vessel's insurance money. Those mysterious trips to the wilderness shoreline were likely to pick up portions of the hidden cargo.

The *Explorer* (48' x 16' x 5'6"), repaired and sold, sank with the loss of all four lives on board in a storm on Sept. 4, 1883, near Stokes Bay, Ontario, just south of where the vessel sank the first time. This time, however, the *Explorer* was not raised from the dead.

97. *AFRICA* AND *SEVERN*

OCTOBER 7, 1895   LAKE HURON

Above: *The white propeller,* Africa, *safely at dock in an unidentified harbour.*

Right: *When a ship failed to reach port, and no word of it having reached some safe harbour was heard, then newspaper headlines began to ask, "Are They All Lost?" Such was the case with the propeller,* Africa.
(BOTH: KOHL-FORSBERG ARCHIVES)

ARE THEY ALL LOST?

CANADIAN STEAMER AFRICA FOUNDERS ON LAKE HURON,

REPORTS INDICATE THAT ELEVEN SOULS ARE GONE.

A SLIGHT HOPE THAT THEY MAY HAVE ESCAPED.

Her Boats and Life Preservers Found on Loyal Island.

Stokes Bay, Ont., October 9.—Reports indicate that the steamer Africa, of Owen Sound, is lost with all on board. Following is a complete list of her crew: Capt. H. P. Larsen, Toronto; Mate William Anderson, Owen Sound; Chief Engineer Hay

On October 5, 1895, the 482-ton, wooden steamer, *Africa* (148' x 26' x 13'), built in 1873 at Kingston, Ontario, towing the schooner-barge, *Severn* (151' x 27'5" x 12'7"), constructed at Welland, Ontario, in 1872, both vessels heavily loaded with coal, departed Ashtabula, Ohio, bound for Owen Sound, Ontario. Two days later, a "heavy northwester" caught the ships southwest of Tobermory, 15 to 20 miles from the Cove Island Light.

Seeing that the storm was increasing in severity, with conditions on the wild, choppy waters getting worse, and realizing that the ships stood a better chance at survival by not being tethered to each other, the *Africa* released its tow, the *Severn*. One newspaper wrote:

> ...The *Severn* ran before the gale under bare poles [meaning no sails were raised], and finally fetched up on the beach five miles north of Loyal [sic; should be Lyal] Island. Nothing could save her from the fury of the gale, to which she was fully exposed, and she became a total loss. The crew were saved by some fishermen after being in the rigging 20 hours....

The *Severn* stranded on a shoal off Bradley Harbour, near Stokes Bay, Ontario.

The *Africa*, when last seen by the *Severn's* crew, "was rolling heavily and suddenly disappeared from view." A few days later, an *Africa* crewmember's body was found on the rocky beach at the Lyal Island Light. A smashed lifeboat and life-preservers were also located, but there was no trace of the ship or her other ten crewmembers. Two bodies washed up the following summer, one near Stokes Bay, the other at Sauble Beach.

Divers have explored the wreck of the *Severn*, reportedly lying in about 30 feet (9 metres) of water near Stokes Bay, but the steamer, *Africa's*, location, despite vague references to any number of rocky shoals where it supposedly sank, is still wrapped in mystery.

98. SWEEPSTAKES

SEPTEMBER 1885   LAKE HURON

The twin-masted schooner, **Azov,** *very closely resembled the* **Sweepstakes;** *both ships were built by the same builder at the same place, one year apart.*   (KOHL-FORSBERG ARCHIVES)

The *Sweepstakes* is the most visited shipwreck in all of the Great Lakes due to her intactness and accessibility. Sitting upright in only 20 feet (6 metres) of cold, fresh, clear water, this wreck is like an old friend to many visitors, and a valued commodity among this site's numerous stakeholders. Awed boaters, for decades, have slowed down when passing over this wreck; kayakers glide silently over her rare remains; glassbottom boats give tourists unforgettable views of a unique item from the distant past; snorkelers adventurously fin past her railings and other wooden features; scuba divers examine, up close, the wreck's exterior features, and even descend into her holds; and surrounding cottage owners enjoy a spectacular view of a scenic, historic shipwreck every day from their balconies.

The 218-ton, twin-masted schooner, *Sweepstakes* (119' x 22'8" x 10'1"), built at what was called Wellington Square, but is now called Burlington, Ontario, by John and Melancthon Simpson in 1867, was launched on September 24, 1867, when Canada, as a country, was less than three months old.

After two decades of hauling a variety of bulk cargoes, stranding in a number of different locations, and colliding with a few other ships (with minor damage), the *Sweepstakes* was stranded and seriously damaged at Cove Island, a few miles north of Tobermory, on August 23, 1885, but was pulled off and towed by the tug, *Jessie,* to Big Tub Harbour at Tobermory on September 3, 1885. The schooner sank, possibly with a snapped keel, before

The SWEEPSTAKES

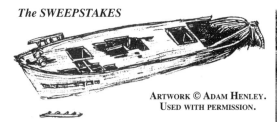

ARTWORK © ADAM HENLEY.
USED WITH PERMISSION.

repairs could be made, and she has rested in that spot for over 130 years now. Her coal cargo, plus some rigging and fittings, such as anchors, chains, and masts, were salvaged before the rest of the schooner was abandoned in place.

The *Sweepstakes* was a stout, little workhorse, carrying a variety of cargoes such as 24,000 bushels of wheat, 356 tons of coal, or, on one trip, 1,000 telegraph poles. By late 1883, George Stewart of Moore Township (south of Sarnia, Ontario) became her sole -- and final -- owner.

The *Sweepstakes*, one of the best-preserved, 1800s Great Lakes schooners to be found, is the most popular divesite in Fathom Five National Marine Park, the first underwater park in the Great Lakes, and the first in all of Canada, for that matter! Access to this shipwreck is determined by time slots that the park has assigned to each of the stake-holding groups. Scuba divers can freely explore the exterior of the wreck during their allocated times, but they can no longer swim below deck from one end of the wreck to the other; the below-deck area is fenced off because trapped divers' bubbles were corroding the undersides of the wooden deck.

Ice and waves have tried to flatten the *Sweepstakes*, but the end of Big Tub harbour is naturally protected from wind, and ice does not move at all in that quiet inlet, melting instead in place every spring, and hence, doing no damage to the wreck. Scuba divers also have not let the *Sweepstakes* collapse. In the late 1970s, the first sets of steel rods were attached to the wreck's sides below deck. More bracing was added in recent years.

Of great diver interest are the bow's intact, starboard railing, the windlass on the deck, the Roman numeral draft markings running down the bow stem, the mast holes, and the centreboard box.

This is one shipwreck not to be missed!

The schooner, Sweepstakes, *lying in shallow water at the end of a protected bay, is clearly visible from a boat on the water's surface.*

This model of the Sweepstakes, *built by Stan McClellan, is displayed at the Fathom Five National Park Museum.*

Joan Forsberg examines the Sweepstake's *huge windlass; its chains were removed during salvage in 1885.*

A diver points out the Roman numeral depth markings on the Sweepstake's bow.
(ALL PHOTOS ARE BY CRIS KOHL)

99. CITY OF GRAND RAPIDS

OCTOBER 29, 1910   LAKE HURON

Left: *The doubled-decked* City of Grand Rapids *burned in 1907.*   (KOHL-FORSBERG ARCHIVES)
Right: *The remains of this wooden steamboat, since the fire destroyed it well over a century ago, rest near shore in Big Tub Harbour's shallow waters at Tobermory.*   (PHOTO BY CRIS KOHL)

The 336-gross-ton, wooden propeller named the ***City of Grand Rapids*** (125′6″ x 26′4″ x 9′3″) was built at Grand Haven, Michigan, by Duncan Robertson in 1879. Her original 1879 steam engine was replaced by a new one in 1904. The 28-year-old ship was sold to Canadian interests early in 1907, but the vessel saw only brief service with them. On October 29, 1907, while tied up at a dock in Tobermory's Big Tub Harbour, the ***City of Grand Rapids*** mysteriously caught on fire and burned to a total loss. The circumstances surrounding this fire's origins remain suspicious.

The wreck of the ***City of Grand Rapids*** is located about 100 feet (30 metres) off the starboard bow of the schooner, ***Sweepstakes*** (see pages 136-137).

The port side of the ***City of Grand Rapids*** rises close to the surface, and even protrudes in years of low water. The charred, mostly-buried hull lies filled with burned deck and superstructure debris. Portions of the boiler and the engine remain in place, while the propeller and the rudder are part of an outdoor display at the Tobermory and St. Edmunds Township Museum just south of Tobermory.

Parts of the City of Grand Rapids' *steam engine and boiler box remain readily identifiable at this shallow shipwreck site.*   (PHOTOS BY CRIS KOHL)

100. *FOREST CITY*

JUNE 5, 1904   LAKE HURON

The **Forest City,** *with the pilot house forward.*   (KOHL-FORSBERG ARCHIVES)

The **Forest City** *ran hard aground on Bear's Rump Island on June 5, 1904.*   (KOHL-FORSBERG ARCHIVES)

The FOREST CITY

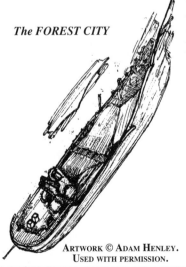

ARTWORK © ADAM HENLEY.
USED WITH PERMISSION.

Of the known shipwreck sites at Tobermory, one of the deepest is a very historic, steam-powered, wooden freighter -- but this ship started its life as a massive, three-masted sailing vessel!

In Cleveland in 1869, a shipbuilder named Elihu M. Peck designed and built a revolutionary style of freighter that could easily handle bulk cargoes of iron ore. His trendsetting ship would be the design-of-choice for Great Lakes freighters for the next century. Visually, the most revolutionary aspect was Peck's positioning of the pilot house right on the bow of the steamship, as far forward as possible, and the engine as far aft as it could be placed, to allow for maximum cargo space in midship. He named this vessel the *R.J. Hackett*. This new ship design was an instant success, and in 1870, only a year later, in order to transport twice as much cargo with only one steamship, Peck built a towable companion for the *Hackett*, an engine-less, schooner-rigged, near-replica with three masts, and named it the *Forest City*.

The 740-ton schooner, *Forest City* (213'7" x 33'5" x 21'3"), launched on May 7, 1870, was given her own steam engine two years later, converting the ship into a near-duplicate of the historic *R. J. Hackett*. This makes the *Forest City* one of the first two freighters in the world built in this new design. After their success, many shipbuilders across the inland seas constructed hundreds of ships copying that pattern.

For decades, the *Forest City* hauled bulk cargoes around the Great Lakes, with a normal number of mal-functions, groundings, and collisions. But on June 5, 1904, in heavy fog, the big propeller ran hard aground on rocky Bear's Rump Island. The crew was rescued by the local tug, *Joe Milton,* only a week before the *Milton* burned to a total loss at Papoose Island in Georgian Bay. Salvagers stripped the *Forest City* just before the hull slid down an underwater slope into deep water. Today, the *Forest City* still rests on that steep slope. The wreck starts at a depth of 60 feet (18 metres) at the broken-up bow, and descends to 150 feet (45 metres), where the rounded, wooden stern and propeller remain amazingly intact.

Sponsored by **DIVERS DEN**
3 Bay Street, Tobermory, ON N0H 2R0
Telephone: (519) 596-2363   Email: info@diversden.ca   Web: www.diversden.ca
Celebrating 50 Years "Divers Serving Divers Since 1967"

101. *ARABIA*

OCTOBER 5, 1884   LAKE HURON

The Arabia, *with its keel length of 134 feet (40.6 metres), resembled this schooner, the* H.C. Winslow, *(above), which was built in the same year and the same region as the* Arabia.

In early 1876, the Arabia *was converted from a barque, or bark* (left), *to a schooner rig* (right).

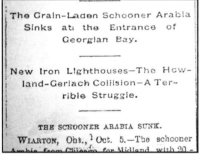

The Grain-Laden Schooner Arabia Sinks at the Entrance of Georgian Bay.

New Iron Lighthouses—The Howland-Gerlach Collision—A Terrible Struggle.

THE SCHOONER ARABIA SUNK.

WIARTON, Ont., Oct. 5.—The schooner Arabia from Chicago for Midland with 20 .

No lives were lost when the Arabia *succumbed to her leaking condition on October 5, 1884.* (ALL OF THE ABOVE: KOHL-FORSBERG ARCHIVES)

The ARABIA

ARTWORK © ADAM HENLEY. USED WITH PERMISSION.

The bark-turned-schooner, *Arabia*, is the most intact shipwreck in the Tobermory area, which is itself famous as the place where the first underwater park in the Great Lakes, indeed, in all of Canada, was established in 1972, a park created largely to protect the newly-found *Arabia*.

The 309-ton *Arabia* departed Chicago on her final voyage on Wednesday, October 1, 1884, heading to Midland, Ontario, in the southern corner of Georgian Bay, with 20,000 bushels of corn. Captain Henry Douville sailed his ship up Lake Michigan, through the Straits of Mackinac, and towards Tobermory across Lake Huron. On Saturday, October 4, 1884, while still about 70 miles (113 kms.) west of Tobermory, violent storm conditions developed. Waves battered the *Arabia* repeatedly with savage intensity. Before long, the ship began leaking badly. After several hours of strenuous pumping, the weary crew realized the hopelessness of the situation, and, after passing the Cove Island Lighthouse, their vessel began to sink. At about 3 a.m., Sunday, October 5, 1884, Captain Douville gave the order to launch the yawl boat and abandon ship. The *Arabia* sank in deep, icy water off Echo Island just after the last man scrambled onto the yawl boat.

The *Arabia's* crew bobbed around in these tempestuous conditions until just after sunrise, when a passing tugboat rescued them and transported them to Wiarton, Ontario.

The three-masted *Arabia* (131' x 26' x 12'), was built by George Thurston (who constructed 24 vessels between 1842 and 1869) at Kingston, Canada West (later Ontario) and launched on Tuesday, April 26, 1853. The *Arabia* spent her first year sailing on Lake Ontario routes, but in 1854, made the big crossing from the Great Lakes to Glasgow in the British Isles, loaded with 14,000 bushels of wheat and 500 barrels of flour. The canals in the St. Lawrence River had been improved by 1848, the beginning of large cargo movements between Canada and Great Britain, and the *Arabia* was one of the first Great Lakes vessels to cross the Atlantic Ocean with a cargo for Britain. The *Arabia* returned to the Great Lakes the following year, hauling a cargo of goods from Britain directly to Chicago, becoming the very first vessel to do so (fully two years before the *Madeira Pet* was incorrectly lauded, as it is to this day, as being the first ship to accomplish this!)

For nearly 90 years, the final resting place of the historic *Arabia* remained a mystery, other than the general concensus that it was somewhere off Echo Island north of Tobermory. The area's commercial fishermen knew that the wreck was nearby, because they were bringing in catches of corn-stuffed fish. Finally, late in 1971, Tobermory Captain Albert Smith pinpointed the wreck. Stan McClellan, of the Ontario Ministry of Natural Resources (and a Past President of the Ontario Underwater Council), directed the first investigation, which resulted in the wreck being definitely identified as the *Arabia*.

The *Arabia's* hull, lying north-to-south, is split fore and aft along the keel, with the sides intact, but leaning. The huge rudder lies flat near the ship's wheel and steering gear. Deadeyes still appear in place along the railing, particularly on the port side. There is a cooking stove near the stern, plus a door, a table, and a centreboard winch. The afterdeck, separated from the hull, rests against the starboard quarter. The three masts have all collapsed and are located alongside the wreck. A capstan hangs under the decking next to the centreboard box, or well. At the bow is the magnificent bowsprit, intact and aiming slightly upwards as if yearning for the surface, resplendent with its hanging chains. Catheads and wooden-stock anchors on both port and starboard sides, a large windlass with a pawl bitt, a samson post, and a pump complete the list of interesting artifacts at the bow.

The *Arabia* is in such excellent shape because the wreck sits in freezing, fresh, often dark water 102 to 117 feet (31 to 35.5 metres) deep, an icewater showpiece, and one of Canada's most famous shipwrecks. Numerous *Arabia* artifacts are on display at the Fathom Five National Marine Park museum.

While the historic wreck of the *Arabia* was instrumental in the establishment of the underwater park at Tobermory, and while it is the best-preserved shipwreck in the region, it also has a dark claim to fame: more scuba divers, a total of ten, have died on this shipwreck than on any other wreck in all of the Great Lakes, which is truly ironic in light of the fact that no lives were lost when the ship sank in 1884. Every precaution must be utilized on this cold, deep dive.

Specially-conserved artifacts from the Arabia, *such as an ornamental piece of wooden scrollwork from a cabin, and a jug, appear in a display case in the park museum at Tobermory.*

Roy Pickering examines a row of deadeyes, part of a ship's running rigging, on the port rail of the schooner, Arabia.

Both of the Arabia's *bow anchors remain in place, in the traditional locations and positions typical on 19th-century ships.*

The Arabia's *wheel and steering mechanism have shifted off the decking.*
(ALL PHOTOS ARE BY CRIS KOHL)

102. *NIAGARA II*

MAY 15, 1999   LAKE HURON

The Niagara II, *May 15, 1999, near Tobermory.*

The first of three explosions to sink this ship.

The third explosion completed the job.

"They're just not making shipwrecks like they used to!"

We sometimes utter those words, with tongues firmly planted in cheeks, when we start the description of a ship that was purposely sunk. Of course, we are fortunate that very few ships and lives are being lost nowadays, thanks in large part to modern, electronic aids to navigation. But with recent increased interest in wreck diving, many of our natural, historic shipwreck sites are in danger of deterioration due to over-visitation. To take pressure off these older shipwrecks, new ones have been created for the express purpose of establishing new scuba dive sites. These relatively new vessels still look like ships, so they have become popular alternatives for divers.

On May 15, 1999, several miles to the east of Tobermory, the 700-ton freighter and sand dredge named the *Niagara II* (182'6" x 35'3" x 13'), was scuttled (purposely sunk), -- complete with exciting dynamite flame bursts! -- to create another shipwreck scuba dive site in the popular Tobermory area. This vessel had to be sunk, technically, outside the boundaries of Fathom Five National Marine Park because, reportedly, of official opposition to this planned sinking by the park. To accomplish their mission, several people formed the Tobermory Maritime Association in 1997 under the enthusiastic guidance of President Susan Garlock, found and purchased this available ship in 1998, and spent over 1,000 hours cleaning her up before she was authorized to be scuttled just outside the park boundary.

Left: *The sinking ship tilted onto her starboard side somewhat, but, fortunately, landed upright on the lake bottom. Observers could breathe a sigh of relief!*
(THE IMAGES ON THIS PAGE: KOHL-FORSBERG ARCHIVES; PHOTOGRAPHER UNKNOWN))

Sponsored by **DIVERS DEN**
3 Bay Street, Tobermory, ON N0H 2R0
Telephone: (519) 596-2363   Email: info@diversden.ca   Web: www.diversden.ca
Celebrating 50 Years "Divers Serving Divers Since 1967"

Canadian authorities allowed the use of explosives to sink this ship -- unlike the three vessels purposely sunk off Chicago in Lake Michigan in recent times: the **"Holly Barge"** on May 6, 2000, *The Straits of Mackinac* ferry on April 10, 2003, and the former U.S. Coast Guard rumrunner-chasing cutter, the *Buccaneer*, on June 18, 2010. Opening each ship's below-deck seacocks and allowing it to sink slowly was the only scuttling method allowed for these vessels.

Divers swim around the stern rail of the Niagara II. *The very bottom of the wreck meets the lake bottom at a depth of 98 feet.*

The *Niagara II,* a steel ship built by the Furness Shipbuilding Company in England and launched at Haverton Hill-on-Tees in 1930 as the *Rideaulite*, bore five different names in the course of her 67-year career: after *Rideaulite, Imperial Lachine,* 1947-1954; *Niagara,* 1954-1969; *W. M. Edington*, 1969-1984; and her final name, *Niagara II*, 1984-1999. This vessel, owned by Imperial Oil for her first 24 years, was converted to a self-unloading sandsucker at the Toronto Dry Dock Company in 1954, when she was renamed the *Niagara.* At that time, the ship was owned by Holden Sand & Gravel in Montréal. On March 1, 1965, an explosion in the engine room killed two people and injured one at Whitby, Ontario.

All of the Niagara II's *railings, dorades (air intake vents), tanks, and other deck hardware remain in place.*

In 1972, a diesel engine replaced the ship's original triple expansion steam engine which, in 1977, was placed in Toronto's Upper Canada Marine Museum. In 1990, her diesel engine was removed and she was utilized as a towed barge. In 1997, the ship was taken to Port Maitland for scrapping, but fate diverted this vessel from the scrapper's torch and aimed it at a more useful, pleasurable purpose.

Joan Forsberg glides across the Niagara II's *bow deck just behind the large, steel windlass, at a depth of about 70 feet.*

This is a magnificent site, with enough places to explore on this vessel to occupy a half a dozen dives. Many railings and passageways guide the diver along, at whatever depth level the diver chooses. All doors and hatch coverings have been removed, and access/egress holes have been cut, for diver safety. A steel "ship's wheel" was fashioned and attached to the *Niagara II* just prior to the sinking, and it remains a focal point in the pilot house on the ship's stern.

Right: *Leaving the bow and heading up the ascent line back to the surface.*
(THE IMAGES ON THIS PAGE ARE BY CRIS KOHL))

103. *CITY OF CLEVELAND*

SEPTEMBER 15, 1901   LAKE HURON

The four-masted propeller, City of Cleveland, *was salvaged after this 1889 sinking -- but she looked very similar in 1901 off Perseverance Island!* (KOHL-FORSBERG ARCHIVES). *Chains and cables fell across part of the propulsion system on the* City of Cleveland.   (PHOTO BY CRIS KOHL)

Winter arrived early in late 1901 when, at 4 a.m. on Sunday, September 15, a blinding snowstorm and southwest gale forced the large, twin-decked, four-masted propeller, *City of Cleveland* (255'7" x 39'5" x 18'4"), heavily loaded with 3,200 tons of iron ore from Lake Superior's Michipicoten, bound for the blast furnaces of Midland, Ontario, off course and onto the rocks of Little Perseverance Island, near Fitzwilliam Island, about 18 miles (29 kms.) north of Tobermory. The ship settled in 30 feet (9 metres) of water, while the crew rowed to the safety of the island. Four days later, with the small quantity of food they had being rationed to one piece of bread a day per man, the small propeller, *Hiram R. Dixon,* rescued them and took them to South Baymouth. Having lost all their possessions, the crew hired a tug to return them to the wreck in hopes of recovering personal items, but the ship was already under water. A steamer took the crew to Killarney, and another took them to Sault Ste. Marie, from whence they returned to their homes. A Detroit hardhat diver hoped to recover the ship the following year, but a winter on the rocks totally wrecked her.

The 1,609-gross-ton *City of Cleveland* was built by Thomas Quayle's Sons at Cleveland, Ohio, and launched on June 17, 1882.

Left: *The immense and upright fore 'n aft steam engine from the* City of Cleveland, *standing on spindly legs, is a highlight of this site.*

Right: *With the silhouette of the tall steam engine behind him, a diver examines a portion of the propulsion system on the* City of Cleveland.
(BOTH PHOTOS BY CRIS KOHL)

104. *S. D. HUNGERFORD*

NOVEMBER 26, 1883   LAKE HURON

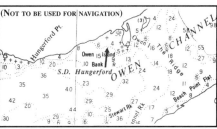

The 137-foot-long Samana *(ex-*Dane; *wrecked in Lake Erie in 1892) was very similar in appearance to the 137-foot-long* **S. D. Hungerford**, *wrecked along southeastern Manitoulin Island in 1883.*
(KOHL-FORSBERG ARCHIVES)

This story is the closest tale we have in the Great Lakes to *Robinson Crusoe*.

On Sunday, November 25, 1883, the tug, *Gladiator,* towing four lumber-laden schooners, including the 267-gross-ton *S. D. Hungerford* (137' x 26' x 11', built at Stoney Creek, NY, in 1866), cleared Tobermory heading for Buffalo. When the tug encountered mechanical difficulties during a severe gale, it abandoned its tows. All but one were soon accounted for; a search for the *Hungerford* and her crew of six (Captain William Moore of Buffalo, the ship's mate, a female cook, and three sailors) failed to find anything. Concerns grew. Families of the crew hoped daily for word of their loved ones' survival. But no word came. Ten days later, on Dec. 5, 1883, a Buffalo newspaper wrote about the *Hungerford* that she "has not been heard from since the tow broke up, and is given up as lost." With that, the crew's families went into mourning. For six households, it would be a very sad Christmas.

But on December 21, 1883, several newspapers printed a telegram they had received:

> The schooner *S. D. Hungerford,* of Buffalo, left Tobermoray [sic] **Nov. 25,** ...wind northeast, weather fine; at 3 p.m. the tug got disabled...; we made all sail and continued on our voyage till 9 p.m. when the wind freshened, blowing hard from south-southeast; shortened sail and discovered the vessel leaking very fast;... commenced throwing the deck-load overboard. The heavy sea breaking over the stern swept away the boat and wheel house; binnacle gone, and no compass to steer by.
>
> **Nov. 26, 2 p.m. --** Wind veered to west, with snow, blowing a hurricane; six feet of water in hold; 4 p.m., weather cleared off; saw Manitoulin; ran under southeast sound and let go anchor; pumped her next day and got all ready for sea; came on gale from southwest, vessel dragged anchors ashore. We lived on the island nineteen days in a tent, short of provisions; left on Sunday, 16th inst., in an old fishing boat for Tobermoray [sic], and arrived the same evening all right. I wish you to give my kind regards to the people of Canada for their kindness to us in our trouble.
>
> **-- William Moore, Master, and crew, six all told.**

For six households, it turned out to be a very happy Christmas.

The *Hungerford* had anchored off what was later named Hungerford Point in her honour; winds dragged the schooner east. The captain and his crew safely reached Owen Island, off southeast Manitoulin Island. Their ship sank just west of that island.

105. *GARGANTUA*

DECEMBER 6, 1952   LAKE HURON

The **Gargantua,** *formerly the* **Seafarer,** *worked out of Sault Ste. Marie, Ontario, for 25 years.*
(KOHL-FORSBERG ARCHIVES)

Above and Below*: Until recently, a visitor could see more of the large tug,* Gargantua, *above water than scuba divers could see below. This eyesore shipwreck, never popular with local cottage owners, lost what was left of her superstructure in a mysterious, 1971 fire. But the decking was stable enough to walk upon in 1986 when co-author Cris Kohl visited for the first time. Today, as the wreck settles lower and lower, Mother Nature, with plant growth and a beaver den inside the hull, is taking over.* (PHOTOS BY SCOTT PARENT)

At Cabot Head near the tip of the Bruce Peninsula, a shipwreck, partially above water, rests in the northwest corner of the small, somewhat protected, circular harbour called Wingfield Basin, just west of the scenic, 1896 Cabot Head Lighthouse.

Launched in 1919 as the *Seafarer* by the S.C. McLouth Shipyard at Marine City, Michigan, for use on oceans by the U.S. Shipping Board, this heavy-duty, wooden tug saw the contract for its construction cancelled because World War One had ended and the ship was no longer needed by the government. The McLouth yard scrambled to rid itself of this war-surplus hull. Finally, in 1923, the Toronto Dry Dock Company purchased it and finished its construction at Chippawa, Ontario, renaming it *Gargantua* (130' x 32'1" x 15'4"). The Lake Superior Paper Company, Ltd., of the Canadian Soo, bought the finished tug and operated it in the log raft business until 1948. After a Soo layup, the *Gargantua* was purchased in 1949 by an owner who took it to Thessalon, in Lake Huron's North Channel, where the ship sat idle for three more years.

With the decision to convert it into a barge, the *Gargantua* was towed to Collingwood for the removal of its cabins, pilothouse, and machinery. Once stripped, and while being towed back to Thessalon by the tug, *Mac,* on December 5-6, 1952, a storm forced them to seek shelter in Wingfield Basin, where the *Gargantua* was scuttled to avoid her destruction on the rocky shoreline. Plans to raise the ship failed, but her registry was not closed until 1967.

Hardly remembered today is the fact that the *Gargantua* rescued most of the crew of the large steamer, *Orinoco,* when that ship sank in Lake Superior at Montréal Island in 1924 (read story on page 177).

Sponsored by **FRIENDS OF CABOT HEAD LIGHTHOUSE**
806 Cabot Head Road, Miller Lake, Ontario N0H 1Z0
Tel.: (519) 795-7780   Email: info@cabothead.ca   www.cabothead.ca
Discover Cabot Head Lighthouse

106. *J. H. JONES*

NOVEMBER 22, 1906   LAKE HURON

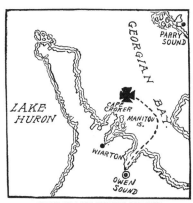

Above: *The tugboat,* J. H. Jones, *built at Goderich, Ontario, in 1888, sank with all hands in Georgian Bay in 1906.*
Right: *One newspaper "pinpointed" the wreck's location, but it has yet to be found.*   (BOTH: KOHL-FORSBERG ARCHIVES)

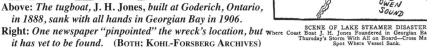

SCENE OF LAKE STEAMER DISASTER.
Where Coast Boat J. H. Jones Foundered in Georgian Bay During Last Thursday's Storm With All on Board—Cross Marks Spot Where Vessel Sank.

The 152-ton, wooden steamer, *J. H. Jones* (107′ x 21′4″ x 10′), was constructed at Goderich, Ontario, and launched on Aprl 24, 1888, by Henry Marlton. The ship's namesake, Jasper Huff Jones, was a Detroit businessman who vacationed in the Port Elgin - Wiarton, Ontario area, and who invested in Marlton's shipyard at Goderich. The 70-year-old Jones died at Port Elgin on September 10, 1893, but Marlton had honoured his investor five years earlier by building this ship and naming it after him.

The *Jones* began life as a single-cylinder, steam-driven fishing tug, and had one serious encounter in the middle of its career. On September 7, 1898, the *J. H. Jones* sank in about 33 feet (10 metres) of water in the North Channel after a collision with the passenger and freight steamer, *Pacific,* but she was raised on October 17, 1898, and towed to Owen Sound for repairs. The *J. H. Jones'* final conversion was to a passenger and package freighter combination at Owen Sound in 1901.

The final, tragic moments in the life of the steamer, *J. H. Jones*, came on November 22, 1906. The vessel departed Owen Sound at 10 a.m. that day with 17 passengers, a crew of 13 (most of them from Wiarton), and a full load of freight. The *Jones* planned to run to Lion's Head and Tobermory, stopping to collect boxes of fish from a number of fishing stations along that route. But she disappeared in a fierce storm off Cape Croker with the loss of all hands. Part of the ship's cabin, a life boat, and two unidentified bodies were found by First Nation Canadians on the north shore of Christian Island. The *Jones*, which regularly plied the waters between Owen Sound, Wiarton, and Manitoulin Island. was commanded by Captain Crawford, a highly-experienced, freshwater navigator. The ship was owned by the Crawford Tug Company of Wiarton at the time of loss.

Seven years after the loss, the Great Storm of 1913 (the worst Great Lakes storm in recorded history) struck the lakes. The strong winds and waves washed ashore three barrels of coal oil, a tub of lard with *"J. H. Jones"* written on it, a bale of cotton, and blankets. Yet the *Jones* remains one of Lake Huron's still-to-be-located mystery wrecks to this day.

Sponsored by **FRIENDS OF CABOT HEAD LIGHTHOUSE**
806 Cabot Head Road, Miller Lake, Ontario N0H 1Z0
Tel.: (519) 795-7780   Email: info@cabothead.ca   www.cabothead.ca
Become a Friend of Cabot Head Lighthouse. See website to join

107. *MANASOO*

SEPTEMBER 15, 1928   LAKE HURON

A tragic, relatively modern, steel shipwreck lies in deep water somewhere off Griffith Island near Wiarton in southern Georgian Bay.

The 529-gross-ton, passenger-and-freight steamship, *Manasoo* (178'4" x 24'1" x 16'3", after being lengthened by 23 feet at Collingwood in 1905), launched by the William Hamilton Company as the *Macassa* in Glasgow, Scotland, in 1888, sailed across the Atlantic Ocean that spring, arriving at the dock of its new owner, the Hamilton Steamboat Company of Hamilton, Ontario, on June 7th that year. This vessel enjoyed a long, 40-year career on the Great Lakes, operating mostly among western Lake Ontario ports -- until her final year, providing a classic example of the bad luck that will plague a vessel, according to sailors' superstition, after its name has been changed.

Disaster struck the *Macassa* after its new owner, the Owen Sound Transportation Company, had the vessel rebuilt by the Toronto Dry Dock Company in early 1928 as a combination passenger and cattle carrier, changed its location from Lake Ontario to Lake Huron to operate on the Owen Sound-Soo route, and renamed it the *Manasoo* (which combined Manitoulin Island and the Soo, reflecting its chief harbour stops). The ship left Owen Sound for its first run on this new route on April 22, 1928, and was on its way to having a very successful season -- until September 15, 1928.

The *Manasoo* departed Manitowaning on Manitoulin Island on September 14, 1928, operating with a crew of 17 and carrying four passengers and 116 head of cattle. During the night, heavy seas arose, and when the restless cattle reportedly shifted to one side of the ship at 2 a.m., the vessel listed and rolled over in the strong gales. Five survivors (the captain, three sailors, and one passenger) drifted on a life raft for 60 hours before being rescued by the passing steamer, *Manitoba*. Sixteen human lives and all the cattle perished.

This ship sank in an area with depths as great as 300 feet (90 metres), that being the main reason that this shipwreck has not yet been located.

Above: *The steamer,* Manasoo, *of solid, steel construction, sank during heavy weather in late 1928; humans and livestock died.*
Right: *Such heavy loss of life came as a shock in the late 1920s, a time when the public felt that modern technology had conquered nature. And for survivors to be drifting on a raft for nearly three days in lower Georgian Bay was simply unimaginable in this "modern era."*   (BOTH: KOHL-FORSBERG ARCHIVES)

16 BELIEVED LOST WHEN SHIP SINKS

5 on Raft Picked Up After 60 Hours by Lake Steamer.

Owen Sound, Ont., Sept. 17.— (A.P.)—Sixteen men were believed to have lost their lives when the passenger and cargo steamer Manasoo foundered in a heavy sea off Griffith's island Saturday night. Word of the sinking was brought tonight by the steamer Manitoba, which picked up five survivors from a life raft.

The Manasoo carried a crew of 17 and was said to have had four passengers. Captain John McKay, First Officer Osborn Long, Purser Arthur Middlebro, Roy Fox, an oller, and B. Wallace of Oil Springs, Ont., a passenger, were rescued.

Man Dies on Raft.

A sixth man, Chief Engineer Tom McCutcheon, had been on the raft, but died from exposure. He had

108. *JANE MILLER*

NOVEMBER 26, 1881   LAKE HURON

Somewhere off the mouth of Colpoy's Bay, near Wiarton, Ontario, lies the tragic wreck of a small, coastal steamer.

The 210-gross-ton, wooden propeller, *Jane Miller* (78′ x 18′ x 7′6″), was a common and welcomed sight transporting cargo and passengers among the numerous, small ports of Georgian Bay and the North Channel.

But on November 26, 1881, the *Jane Miller* departed Meaford, Ontario, bound for Wiarton, 40 miles (65 kms.) away, with 28 people (reportedly 27 men and 1 woman) on board and a cargo of general freight. She had previously taken heavy cargo on board at Owen Sound. The little ship, last seen at Big Bay wood dock three miles (5 kms.) west of Meaford, pushed right into the eye of a vicious gale, and was never seen again. There were no survivors, and no body was ever recovered.

The main theory for the sinking is that the vessel had taken on too much cargo that the crew had simply piled up on the deck rather than properly stowed below for the short crossing to Wiarton, raising the vessel's centre of gravity and making the ship top-heavy. When no body was ever found, it was surmised that, due to the bad weather, all 28 people were inside the *Jane Miller*, with all doors and hatches secured as tightly as possible, and that they not only went down with the ship, but remained on board after drowning.

It is presumed that the ship sank off Colpoy's Bay in deep water; one account gives the ship's approximate location as being 0.5 miles (0.8 kilometre) off Spencer's Wharf, which is 3 miles, or 4.6 kms., east of Wiarton, in water 35 fathoms (210 feet, or 63 metres) deep. Some wreckage found on the western side of nearby White Cloud Island, including several oars, some pieces of freight, the flagstaff, and a few caps that belonged to the crew, would suggest that this location is probably correct. Unfortunately there are deep crevices in the limestone lake bottom here, and the ship could have landed in one of those.

The wooden propeller, *Jane Miller*, had been constructed by James Miller at Crop's shipyard at Little Current, Ontario, in 1879. Miller named his new vessel after his wife.

Left, top: *The small propeller,* Jane Miller, *was only two years old when she sank with all hands in Georgian Bay in 1881.*

Right: *This advertisement for the* Jane Miller, *printed in the* Manitoulin Expositor *newspaper on June 5, 1880, listed 15 of the ship's stops on her Georgian Bay-North Channel route.* (BOTH OF THE ABOVE: KOHL-FORSBERG ARCHIVES)

Left, bottom: *A historic marker east of Wiarton, commemorating the "Loss of the* Jane Miller," *overlooks the waters where the ship presumably sank.* (PHOTO BY CRIS KOHL)

THE NEW STEAMER

JANE MILLER

WILL LEAVE

COLLINGWOOD

Every FRiDAY after arrival of noon train for the

MANITOULIN ISLAND,

CALLING AT

Meaford, Owen Sound, Killarney,

MANITOWANING

Sheguiandah, Little Current, Mudge Bay, Spanish River, Gore Bay,

COCKBURN and BARRIE ISLANDS,

Shishiwaning, Meldrum Bay, Thessalon River and

BRUCE MINES.

On her return trip she will call at all the above ports, arriving in Collingwood in time to connect with morning trains for Toronto and Hamilton.

Freight and passengers carried at the very lowest rates.

109. *MARY WARD*

NOVEMBER 24, 1872   LAKE HURON

A drawing of the 139-foot-long steamer,
Mary Ward.
(LIBRARY AND ARCHIVES CANADA)

A geographic feature off Craigleith,
Ontario, was named after this ship-
wreck: the **Mary Ward** *Ledges.*

Joan Forsberg reads the historic
marker in Craigleith Provincial Park
that relates the **Mary Ward's** *story.*

Mary Ward *artifacts on display in the*
Craigleith Station Heritage Museum.
(THE ABOVE TWO PHOTOS ARE BY CRIS KOHL)

On Nottawasaga Island, approximately three miles out of Collingwood, Ontario, and marking its harbour entrance, is an aging lighthouse, one of six lights, all of the same "imperial" design, that were built on Georgian Bay in the late 1850s. This one is being restored by an ambitious group of volunteers.

Despite the presence of this lighthouse, a propeller-driven steamship became a victim of the dangerous shoals in this area in 1872.

Lying between a series of shallow, rocky ledges just off the small, waterfront community of Craigleith, Ontario, are the engine, propeller, frames, and much broken wreckage from a vessel named the *Mary Ward.* Today, companies in Collingwood take snorkelers to this shallow site, where exploring this shipwreck in a maximum of 10 feet (three metres) of water is an enjoyable pastime for adults and children alike.

The *Mary Ward* (139' x 25'6" x 11'6"), when launched at Montréal in 1864, was named the *North,* a name it carried for only three years until a fire heavily damaged the ship on the St. Clair River in November 1867. This vessel was originally constructed at a cost of $28,000, but the burnt-out hull and machinery, as it still lay in the St. Clair River shallows where the ship had met with this 1867 accident, were purchased eight months later for only $1,500.

The raising and rebuilding of this ship, surprisingly, took two years, but, like the mythical phoenix, rising from the ashes of the old steamer *North* was the new steamer renamed the *Mary Ward*.

Three years later, in late November 1872, the ship's owner in Sarnia sold the vessel to a group of new owners in Collingwood -- and they wanted the *Mary Ward* laid up for the winter in her new home port on Georgian Bay.

On her way to Collingwood so late in the shipping season, the *Mary Ward* stopped in Tobermory to pick up a few passengers. Despite the fact that it was late November on the Great Lakes, the weather was surprisingly calm and clear as the *Ward* neared Collingwood.

It remains unclear exactly how the *Mary Ward* ended up so far off course that she ran aground in shallow, rocky ledges just two miles (three kms.) off Craigleith, so close to her final destination.

Three possible explanations have been given: the first was a claim that the captain was using a homemade navigation device that proved to be very inaccurate. The second was that the captain mistook a light on shore for the Nottawasaga Lighthouse, and it caused him to steer the ship off course. The third was that, when the vessel left the port of Owen Sound after a brief stopover, there was considerable celebrating going on in the cabins because this was the ship's final run of the season, influencing the crew to pay a little less attention than usual to the business of navigation.

Joan Forsberg snorkels over a portion of the Ward's *engine and propulsion system.*

After the accident, one passenger recounted his experiences when the *Mary Ward* first struck the rocky ledges:

> ...There was no confusion and all seemed to take the matter lightly, since they were near land and it was so calm. I can remember standing out to the stern after she had struck, looking up at the stars and feeling on my face the gentle, warm south-west breeze.... I could hear them singing in the cabin....

Two blades of the original four on the Mary Ward's *propeller remain visible.*

One of the *Ward's* owners, with one of the passengers, rowed a small boat to the shore at Craigleith and walked to nearby Collingwood to obtain a tugboat for assistance. But the weather took a serious turn for the worse before the tugboat could pull the *Mary Ward* off the reef, and alarm spread among those remaining on the stranded vessel.

A second lifeboat left the *Mary Ward* and, struggling, reached shore safely, but the third lifeboat capsized, with the result that all eight men in it were drowned. The celebrations had definitely ended by this time.

The massive construction of the ship's keel can be appreciated at this open site.

A tugboat later, with great difficulty, rescued those left behind on board the *Mary Ward*, but the ship was totally destroyed by the gales of late November.

This historic shipwreck is one of the most interesting, as well as one of the most accessible today, anywhere in the Great Lakes.

Braided steel rigging is snagged onto the Mary Ward's *bottom hull frames.*
(THE ABOVE PHOTOS ARE BY CRIS KOHL)

110. BALTIC (EX-FRANCES SMITH)

SEPTEMBER 5, 1896   LAKE HURON

Above: *The sidewheel steamer,* **Frances Smith,** *was the first steamship built at Owen Sound. She was launched on April 30, 1867, during Canada's Confederation year.*
Right: *The* **Frances Smith** *changed owners in 1888, and was renamed the* **Baltic,** *shown here at Owen Sound in about 1890.*   (BOTH IMAGES: KOHL-FORSBERG ARCHIVES)

The paddlewheel steamer named the *Baltic* was more famous under her former name, the *Frances Smith*, so this shipwreck is listed here under both names.

The first steamship built at Owen Sound, Canada West (which was renamed Ontario just a few weeks after the *Smith* was launched on April 30, 1867), the "palace steamer" *Frances Smith* (181′8″ x 27′9″ x 11′9″) was constructed by noted shipbuilder, Melancthon Simpson, over the winter of 1866-1867.

Owned by Captain William Smith, the new ship was christened by his 11-year-old daughter, Cornelia, and named after his wife, Frances. Built to replace Smith's 1854 steamer, *Clifton* (which was converted to a barge in 1866 that was eventually abandoned, reportedly at Tobermory in 1900), whose engine the *Smith* received, along with the engine from the 1839 steamer, *Gildersleeve* (which had been abandoned at Garden Island near Kingston, on Lake Ontario), the new vessel initially operated between Owen Sound and Collingwood.

This *Frances Smith* was the most luxurious ship to sail from any Canadian port on the upper Great Lakes, setting the standard for speed, comfort, accommodations, and quality service on Georgian Bay and, beginning in 1874, Lake Superior. But this exceptional vessel did experience a rocky start. In November 1868, little more than a year after she was launched, the *Frances Smith* was stranded over the winter at Byng Inlet, Ontario, not being released and repaired until May 1869.

In 1888, the *Smith* was sold to the Great Northern Transit Company, which rebuilt the ship at Collingwood at a cost of $36,000, and renamed her the *Baltic*, running her on the Collingwood-Soo-Mackinac route. In 1893, her route became the Collingwood-to-Chicago run, transporting thousands of people to and from the immensely popular World's Fair in the Windy City. This was the ship's swan song, as she did not run again after that.

Laid up at Collingwood, the *Baltic* caught on fire in the middle of the night on September 5, 1896, at her dock under mysterious circumstances (the $15,000 insurance policy on an old ship that hadn't moved in three years raised many eyebrows; a legal fight took it all the way to the Supreme Court, with the insurance companies ultimately winning.) Later, with her machinery removed, the burned-out hull was towed out of the harbour, with the hopes that it would sink. Instead, it drifted ashore on a remote section of beach at One Tree Island. For years, those decaying timbers served as a reminder of Georgian Bay's Golden Age of excursion steamers.

111. *NANCY*

AUGUST 14, 1814   LAKE HURON

Left: *The twin-masted* Nancy, *under full sail on Lake Huron.*
(ART BY GEORGE CUTHBERTSON)
Above: *The* Nancy *wreck was excavated from its island in the Nottawasaga River in the mid-1920s.*   (KOHL-FORSBERG ARCHIVES)

The only museum on the Canadian side of the Great Lakes entirely dedicated to shipwrecks, or, in this case, a single shipwreck, is situated on Nancy Island in the Nottawasaga River at Wasaga Beach, Ontario. A fabulous museum houses this historic wreck today!

The two-masted schooner, *Nancy* (79' x 23'), built by the North West fur trading company at Detroit in 1789, served the British forces as **H. M. S.** *Nancy* in the War of 1812, as a supply ship (food, clothing, armaments) for their garrison at Mackinac Island.

But the *Nancy* became trapped in the Nottawasaga River by three American ships named the *Tigress*, the *Niagara*, and the *Scorpion*, and, after a seven-hour battle on August 14, 1814, and aware that they were greatly outnumbered, the British set their vessel on fire and allowed it to sink. Eventually, this British force, using their rowboats, captured the *Tigress* and the *Scorpion* at Mackinac Island! The War of 1812 ended later that year, and, with time, an increasingly larger island formed around the river wreck of the *Nancy*.

On July 1, 1911, noted Canadian maritime historian, C. H. J. Snider, located the *Nancy's* hull, but it was not until 1927, through the efforts of Dr. F. J. Conboy, that the wreck was excavated. On August 14, 1928, exactly 114 years after the *Nancy's* demise, the Nancy Museum opened, displaying these significant timbers to the public for the first time.

This 1930s postcard shows the Nancy's *timbers in the museum; they remain the same today, but the museum structure has improved greatly.*   (KOHL-FORSBERG ARCHIVES, AND PHOTO BY CRIS KOHL)

Sponsored by **The Friends of Nancy Island Historic Site and Wasaga Beach Park,**
119 Mosley St., Wasaga Beach, Ontario L9Z 2X1   www.wasagabeachpark.com
705-429-2516 (summer: 705-429-2728)   Email: nancyisland@wasagabeachpark.com
Visit the only War of 1812 "fighting sail" shipwreck museum in the Great Lakes!

112. *MAPLEDAWN*

NOVEMBER 30, 1924   LAKE HURON

The bow half of the **Mapledawn** *was approximately 30 years newer than the ship's stern half, having replaced the original bow half that sank in Lake Ontario in late 1918 when that part of the* **Manola** *was being towed across the lake.*
(BOTH IMAGES: KOHL-FORSBERG ARCHIVES)

The MAPLEDAWN

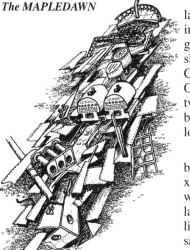

ARTWORK © ADAM HENLEY.
USED WITH PERMISSION.

The steel freighter, *Mapledawn*, was originally launched as the steel freighter, *Manola* (see page 37), in 1890 in Cleveland, Ohio. Purchased by the U.S. government in 1918 for ocean use in World War I, the ship had to be cut in half to get it through the Welland Canal, to be re-assembled on the other side of Lake Ontario. As cruel fate and harsh irony would have it, two things happened after the ship was cut in two: the bow half sank in a storm on Lake Ontario with the loss of all 11 lives, and World War I ended.

The stern half of the *Manola* had a new bow half built onto it, and was renamed the *Mapledawn* (349'1" x 40'2" x 21'3"), but this ship was wrecked in shallow water in 10 to 30 feet (3 to 9 metres) on Christian Island during a snowstorm on November 30, 1924. No lives were lost. Much of this shipwreck's steel was salvaged in 1942 for use in the war effort -- so the ship that failed to make it into World War I ended up serving in World War II!

Left: *A diver glides past shallow, broken* **Mapledawn** *steel.*
Below: *The* **Mapledawn's** *photogenic boiler gets attention.*
(BOTH PHOTOS ARE BY CRIS KOHL)

113. *THOMAS CRANAGE*

SEPTEMBER 25, 1911   LAKE HURON

At the time of launch in 1893, with an audience of more than 10,000 people in attendance, the Thomas Cranage *was the world's largest, wooden propeller.*   (KOHL-FORSBERG ARCHIVES)

The 2,219-gross-ton ***Thomas Cranage*** (305' x 43' x 20'7"), was proudly launched on July 29, 1893, by her builder, James Davidson, at West Bay City, Michigan. Named after banker/businessman/transportation mogul Thomas Cranage (1834-1911), this vessel outlived her namesake by six months. Partly due to its massive size, this ship experienced more collisions and strandings than usual in an 18-year career.

On the calm morning of September 25, 1911, while on a run from Duluth, Minnesota, to Tiffin, Ontario, with a cargo of wheat, the ***Thomas Cranage*** struck Watcher's Reef, five miles northeast of Hope Island, lower Georgian Bay, not far from the ship's intended destination. The stranding of this important vessel in favourable weather conditions called into question the captain's navigation skills, attention focus, and sobriety. Recovery of the grain cargo was made by the tug, ***Gargantua*** (see page 146.) Salvage attempts to recover the ship proved futile and were abandoned about two weeks after the stranding; the huge ship broke to pieces in the early fall storms.

The broken remains of the ***Thomas Cranage***, lying in 10 to 30 feet (3 to 9 metres) of water, include the impressive triple expansion engine, the steel-reinforced rudder, and much planking. The scotch boilers and the propeller were salvaged at the time of loss.

CRANAGE HITS REEF; MAY GO TO PIECES

Bay City Steamer, Grain Laden, is Reported Out Six Feet Forward Near Tiffin, Ont.

Special to The Free Press.
Bay City, Mich., September 25.—The steamer Thomas Cranage, owned by the Cranage Steamship company, of this city, carrying grain from Duluth to Tiffin, Ont., ran on a reef outside Tiffin harbor, Georgian Bay, this morning, and is believed to be in danger of going to pieces. Her bow is six feet out.

Manager S. P. Cranage of the company, has sent a wrecking outfit from Midland, Ont., to the relief of the steamer with instructions to report if she is too far gone to make it worth while repairing her. Owing to the distance her bow is out, it is believed she is probably in bad shape. The steamer is commanded by Capt. L. H. Powell, of Ashtabula, O. She is a wooden vessel, 3,300 tons capacity and is 325 feet long. She was built in the Davidson yards, this city, in 1894.

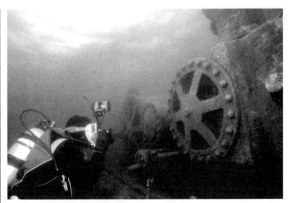

Left: *News of the* Cranage's *stranding in 1911 hinted at her dangerous situation.*   (KOHL-FORSBERG ARCHIVES)
Above: *Although broken up, the wreck of the* **Thomas Cranage** *features significant, identifiable parts, such as the triple expansion steam engine.* (PHOTO BY CRIS KOHL)

114. TECUMSETH

1828   LAKE HURON

Although constructed just after the end of the War of 1812, the vessel, *Tecumseth*, is quite historic.

This 76-foot-long, two-masted schooner named the **H.M.S.** *Tecumseth*, built in 1815 at Chippawa, Upper Canada (later Ontario), on the upper Niagara River, was acquired by the British in 1817 just after the War of 1812, and stationed at Penetanguishene.

While docked "in ordinary" (meaing that it was no longer being used), the ship sank due to hull failure in 1828.

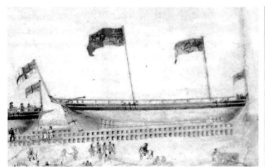 

Left: *A contemporary drawing of the* **Tecumseth** *under construction.*   (KOHL-FORSBERG ARCHIVES)
Right: *Prior to 2014, when the* **Tecumseth** *was moved into an indoor, climate-controlled setting, the wreck was housed outdoors under a simple roof.*   (PHOTO BY CRIS KOHL)

More than a century later, in 1953, these shipwreck remains were raised and placed on the open shoreline, where they stayed for about ten years before being moved under a large, protective roof. Finally, in 2014, 61 years after this shipwreck was raised, these ancient, delicate hull timbers were carefully moved into a modern, climate-controlled building, named the **H.M.S.** *Tecumseth* Centre, on the grounds of Discovery Harbour museum/village at Penetanguishene, Ontario.

The **H.M.S.** *Tecumseth* Centre is unique in Canada, and serves as a vibrant visitor area to permanently showcase the story of this 19th-century site, the Penetanguishene Naval Establishment, and its ties with the War of 1812, and the history of the town of Penetanguishene.

Artifacts on display in the Centre include the Tecumseth's original deck lights, coins from that era, a powder flask, glass embedded in the deck that served as skylights for below deck, compasses, an anchor, a carronade, and a rum bottle and flask. Historical figures associated with this site and/or this shipwreck are also examined, such as British hydrographer Henry Bayfield, Captain Samuel Roberts, and Chief Tecumseh.

The **H.M.S.** *Tecumseth's* sister ship, the **H.M.S.** *Newash*, similarly abandoned in the 1820s, has not been raised from the harbor.

115. WAWINET

SEPTEMBER 21, 1942   LAKE HURON

The 68-gross-ton, yacht named the *Wawinet* (87' x 12'5" x 7'5") -- also spelled *Wa-Wi-Net* and *Wawanet* -- built in 1904 at Toronto's Polson Iron Works and, after being owned for decades by William McKenzie of Toronto, was purchased by Bertrand Corbeau of Penetanguishene in 1938, became one of Georgian Bay's most tragic maritime accidents.

Above: The wreck of the private yacht, Wawinet, *was one of Georgian Bay's worst accidents.*

On Monday evening, at about 10 p.m., September 21, 1942, the *Wawinet*, which had started her trip at 4 p.m., was returning from Honey Harbour to Penetanguishene with Corbeau and colleagues from the Midland Foundry and Machine Company, of which Bertrand was the plant superintendent. The company had just completed a war-time contract ahead of schedule, and Corbeau invited the workers onto his yacht in celebration. Reportedly 42 of the 45 workers at the Midland Foundry accepted the invitation. It was the first day of autumn, yet the weather was mild: no wind, no sea running, and no clouds.

The *Wawinet*, powered by twin Rolls Royce engines of recent vintage, had had her ballast recently removed for increased speed, and also had her original, small, round portholes replaced by large, rectangular ones. Corbeau, at the helm, suddenly swerved to avoid a sandbar off Beausoleil Island and the ship heeled over. Her lower windows were, unfortunately, open, and the vessel filled and sank in 25 feet (7.5 metres) of water within two minutes, with 25 of the 42 people on board, including Corbeau, losing their lives in the ensuing panic. The water was warmer than the air, so the survivors easily swam to nearby Beausoleil Island. Five men jumped into one of the two small rowboats that the *Wawinet* towed, and paddled it towards the island, wading to shore once they could touch bottom. Elmer Shaw from Toronto, the owner of the Midland Foundry plant, was among the survivors. Bodies washed ashore on Beausoleil Island and Present Island, which are about one mile (1.6 kms.) apart; the *Wawinet* sank midway between those two islands. Only three bodies, including Corbeau's, were recovered initially, with another 13 found subsequently.

Bert Corbeau, Midland, Drowned.

Bert Corbeau, former NHL star with the Montréal Canadiens, owned the Wawinet *-- and died on it.*

Free Press Herald

25 DROWN MONDAY NIGHT

17 Survive When Boat Founders Off Beausoleil Island

BAY'S WORST TRAGEDY HITS MIDLAND AND PENETANG
Dread Disaster Strikes in Darkness At Midland Foundry Staff Cruise

DICK BELL, JACK CORBEAU, JAMES GREAVES ARE LOST FROM S.S. COLLINGWOOD

Nearly all of the victims lived in Penetanguishene and Midland, so much anguish was felt in those communities over this enormous tragedy.

The Midland, Ontario, newspaper announced the tragic accident on September 23, 1942. (ALL IMAGES: KOHL-FORSBERG ARCHIVES)

116. WAUBUNO

NOVEMBER 22, 1879   LAKE HURON

TERRIBLE DISASTER.

Wreck of Str. 'Waubuno' on Georgian Bay.

24 PERSONS MISSING.

THE PROPRIETOR OF THE "NORTH STAR" ON BOARD.

The Georgian Bay Transportation Co.'s Steamer "Waubuno" left Collingwood at 4 a.m. on Saturday morning last for Parry-Sound. At ten a. m. the Steamer " Magnettawan " also left for this place and arrived here at noon on Monday, having laid up at the Christian Islands till the weather grew less furious. She reported having seen nothing of the " Waubuno." Accordingly the tug "Mittie" Grew" was despatched in search of her, and returned the same night, reporting that they

Above: *The steamer,* Waubuno, *disappeared on Georgian Bay with all hands in late 1879.*
Right: *Initial reports underestimated the number of people on the ship.*   (BOTH IMAGES: KOHL-FORSBERG ARCHIVES)

The 185-gross-ton, wooden, sidewheel steamer, *Waubuno* (135' x 18'3" x 7'), built by John Simpson at Port Robinson, Canada West (later Ontario) in 1865, enjoyed 14 years of service on Georgian Bay before becoming a mystery shipwreck.

On November 22, 1879, the ship left Collingwood with passengers and freight heading for Parry Sound. Another vessel saw the heavily-laden *Waubuno* pass north on the protected east side of Christian Island, while, later, a logging crew on shore near the Moon River heard the vessel's whistle sounding distress signals in a blinding snowstorm. Then she simply disappeared with all 30 people on board. The following spring, her washed-up hull was located, but no bodies were ever found.

In the late 1950s, adventurous, early scuba divers explored an area two and a half miles west of the *Waubuno's* hull, around an outcropping named Burkett Rock, where they found, in depths up to 50 feet (15 metres), the *Waubuno's* missing pieces: the anchors, chain, paddlewheel, walking beam, windlass, rudder, and other, smaller parts. It was surmised that this location is where the *Waubuno* capsized in the storm. The hull itself lies in shallow water (maximum depth is 15 feet, or 4.5 metres) in an inlet on the southern tip of Bradden Island, just north of Wreck Island, halfway between the Musquash River to the south and Parry Sound, Ontario, to the north. At this shallow depth, it is easier to simply snorkel this shipwreck, rather than scuba dive it.

Left: *A diver descends to the bow of the* Waubuno's *wooden hull.*
Right: *The frames of the* Waubuno's *hull are clearly defined.*   (BOTH PHOTOS ARE BY CRIS KOHL)

117. *Metamora*

September 29, 1907   Lake Huron

Left: *The steamer,* Metamora, *underway.* (LIBRARY AND ARCHIVES CANADA)
Right: *The* Metamora *after the fire.* (KOHL-FORSBERG ARCHIVES)

Located at the east end of Nadeau Island, about 700 feet (210 metres) west of Turning Island, near the community of Shawanaga, the 239-gross-ton, wooden tug, *Metamora* (115' x 39'3" x 10'8"), was built by Peck & Masters at Cleveland in 1864 during the U. S. Civil War. The ship was sold to Canadian interests the following year (in a reversal of the usual situation in Great Lakes maritime history in which Canadian entrepreneurs, desperate for hulls to haul cargoes, became convenient buyers of old, obsolete, but inexpensive U.S. vessels that had seen better days), and served on the Canadian side of the Great Lakes until her demise. Armour plating and cannons became part of her equipment in 1866 when she was used in the defense of the Great Lakes against the Fenians, fanatical Irish nationalists attacking from the northern United States in efforts to take Canada hostage to secure Ireland's independence from Great Britain.

Later, back in civilian use and hauling both freight and passengers on Georgian Bay at the turn of the 19th century, the *Metamora* burned to a complete loss 25 miles (40 kms.) from Parry Sound while outbound from Midland, Ontario, to Byng Inlet on September 29, 1907, with no loss of life, the crew escaping to the nearest island.

Since this ship burned, there is not much left intact. The stern section is the most alluring, since it contains the rudder, steam engine, and propeller. The maximum depth here is 16 feet (5 metres). The boiler, which protrudes above the water, serves as the base for a navigational daymark for boaters.

Above: *The* Metamora's *boiler marks the site.*
Right: *The* Metamora's *four-bladed propeller remains upright and readily identifiable just below the surface.* (BOTH PHOTOS ARE BY CRIS KOHL)

118. *ATLANTIC (EX-MANITOULIN)*
MAY 18, 1882 AND NOVEMBER 10, 1903   LAKE HURON

Above: *The propeller,* **Atlantic,** *was built on the hull of a burned ship.*
Below: *Despite no loss of life, headlines were made when the* **Atlantic** *sank.*
(BOTH IMAGES: KOHL-FORSBERG ARCHIVES)

Steamer Atlantic Burned.

The steamer Atlantic was burned to the water's edge about nine o'clock on Tuesday morning about fourteen miles from Parry Sound. The crew escaped in the boats and reached Parry Sound in safety although a heavy gale was blowing. The Atlantic was on a special trip from Collingwood to Byng Inlet, part of her cargo consisting of 140 barrels of coal oil and five tons of hay. The origin of the fire is not yet stated but in a short time after it broke out the whole

The ATLANTIC

ARTWORK © ADAM HENLEY.
USED WITH PERMISSION.

Flames fanned by the fierce gale of Tuesday, November 10, 1903, destroyed, for the second and last time, the combination passenger/package freight steamer, *Atlantic* (147' x 30' x 11'), on the eastern edge of Georgian Bay.

In the *Atlantic's* first incineration, she was named the *Manitoulin*. About 20 people lost their lives on May 18, 1882, off Shoal Point in Manitowaning Bay, eastern Manitoulin Island in northern Lake Huron. Her relatively new hull (the *Manitoulin* was only two years old when she burned) was deemed salvageable, and the vessel was rebuilt at Owen Sound and renamed the *Atlantic*. This steamship *Atlantic* is not to be confused with the controversial steamer, *Atlantic*, which lies off Long Point in Lake Erie. Read that story on pages 72-73.

For 20 years, this new *Atlantic* served the northern Georgian Bay communities well, while flying the flag of the Northern Navigation Company.

In her demise on Tuesday, November 10, 1903, the *Atlantic*, enroute from Collingwood, Ontario, to Byng Inlet in the northern part of Georgian Bay, struggled to stay afloat in a powerful storm, her hull leaking badly, slowly steamed her way into the lee of the Pancake Islands in an attempt to reach the safe harbour of Parry Sound, Ontario. The engineers left the engine room and headed for the lifeboats, a sure sign that something was amiss. The ship might have succeeded in reaching her haven had fire not broken out in the hay stored in the forward hold. The furious, autumn winds whipped the flames along the entire length of the steamship in mere minutes. Miraculously, the passengers and crew all escaped safely in the lifeboats and rowed away from the conflagration. A passing tug picked them up.

The 706-ton ship was built originally by John Simpson in 1880 at Owen Sound, Ontario, for the Great Northern Transit Company. Shortly after her rebuild in 1882, a "sister ship" was constructed at Owen Sound named the *Pacific*, which burned to a complete loss at Collingwood in 1898.

Easily located are the *Atlantic's* propeller and its huge rudder lying in less than 10 feet (3 metres) of water on the western edge of the Spruce Rocks, south of Spruce Island, several miles west of Parry Sound, Ontario.

The ship's superstructure totally burned off or caved in on the hull and, lying there on a steep slope with the stern in the shallows and the bow in deeper water, the seascape of tangled debris that includes chains, a capstan, gears, boiler, engine, and other machinery proves irresistible to visiting scuba divers. The steam engine is the original one that was placed in the *Manitoulin* in 1880, and was restored for the *Atlantic* when it came out in 1883.

A snowmobile, probably lost through the melting ice at the end of a winter season, sits upright on the lake bottom right off the *Atlantic's* bow. Its operator, fortunately, is not nearby.

Launching an inflatable boat from the beautiful, nearby Killbear Provincial Park has worked well for many scuba divers visiting the *Atlantic*.

Use caution when boating in this area. There are reasons for this region being called the "30,000 Islands." These waters are incredibly island-, islet-, rock-, and reef-strewn, so people operating boats will need to know what they are doing, plus they will have to use plenty of caution. The scenery on the water here, while incredibly beautiful, is very hazardous to navigation.

Scuba divers stand on the Spruce Rocks, south of Spruce Island, on the edge of the slope upon which the **Atlantic** *lies.*

The large rudder, with its steering post, lies flat on the rocky reef in the shallows along the edge of the Atlantic's *steep slope.*

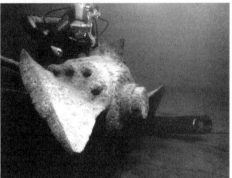

Two of the four steel propeller blades broke off when the Atlantic *struck the hard granite of this reef.*

Left: *Joan Forsberg fins past the wooden frames of the hull heading down the slopng wreck of the* Atlantic.
(ALL PHOTOS ARE BY CRIS KOHL)

119. *ASIA*

SEPTEMBER 14, 1882   LAKE HURON

The **Asia,** *short to fit into the locks of the Welland Canal and heavily built to handle much cargo and many passengers, proved to be top-heavy. Its location, somewhere in Georgian Bay between Collingwood and the French River, covers a lot of liquid real estate.* (KOHL-FORSBERG ARCHIVES)

The worst single ship disaster on all of Lake Huron happened in 1882 when a Canadian ship sank in a violent storm somewhere in Georgian Bay west or southwest of the French River. Sought for more than 130 years, the wreck of the *Asia* has not yet been found.

The 662-ton *Asia* was a wooden, passenger and package freight propeller (136'9" x 23'7" x 11'4") built at the Melancthon Simpson Shipyard in St. Catharines, Ontario, in

FEARFUL LOSS OF LIFE.

The Steamer Asia With One Hundred Passengers Lost on Lake Huron.

The Boat Encounters a Terrific Storm, Which Sinks Her in Twenty Minutes.

During the Storm the Small Boats All Go Down and Only Two Lives Are Saved.

Graphic Description of the Wreck as Told by One of the Surviving Passengers.

After a Night of Suffering on the Beach They Are Saved by an Indian.

COLLINGWOOD, Ont., Sept. 17.—D. A. Tinkis and Christy Ann Morrison, supposed to be the only survivors of the wreck of the steamer Asia have arrived

Left: *Newspapers across the Great Lakes reported the tragic loss of so many lives on the* **Asia** *in the multiple-headline-style of the times.* (KOHL-FORSBERG ARCHIVES)

Right: *After a First Nation member helped the two survivors reach Parry Sound, Duncan Tinkiss wrote a detailed description of what had happened.*
(COURTESY OF THE PARRY SOUND PUBLIC LIBRARY)

THE PARRY SOUND LUMBER CO.
Parry Sound, Ont.,

Mr. Tinkis makes the following statement. I went on board the Asia at Owen Sound about midnight on Wednesday, in company with Mr J.H. Tinkis and A.B. Gallanger, both of Manitowaning. The Steamer was crowded, all the Staterooms being full and many passengers lying on Sofas and other cabin floor, all went well until about Eleven on Thursday morning when the Storm struck. I was in my berth at the time, my Uncle Mr J.H. Tinkis jumped up and said the boat was doomed. Wishes and chains soon

The **Manitoulin Expositor** reported the tragedy of the *Asia* in 1882 as breaking news: this newspaper is still reporting the news as Northern Ontario's oldest paper. We are published in Little Current, Manitoulin Island. www.manitoulin.ca
Visit our website for a full selection of Manitoulin Island-related books for sale.

Left: *Captain John Savage was the experienced and capable master of the* Asia, *and he nearly survived the sinking of his ship. Unfortunately, he failed to return to the metallic lifeboat after one of its capsizings.* (KOHL-FORSBERG ARCHIVES)

Right: *The recovered body of Capt. Savage was interred in the Maitland Cemetery at Goderich, Ontario.*
(PHOTO BY CRIS KOHL)

1873. This vessel, built with a length under 140' that would allow her to fit into the then-small-locks of the Welland Canal, mainly plied the waters between Sarnia and Windsor, Ontario, and Duluth, Minnesota, on Lake Superior in her early years. In 1882, however, the *Asia* was chartered by the Great Northern Transit Company as a temporary replacement for the steamer, *Manitoulin*, which had burned earlier near Manitowaning (and which later was raised, rebuilt, renamed the *Atlantic,* and returned to service -- see pages 160-161.)

On September 14, 1882, the *Asia*, bound from Collingwood to the French River, foundered in a severe storm, the top-heavy design of this vessel not making her very manageable in heavy seas. She carried heavy cargo on her main deck and below, numerous horses, plus 123 passengers and crew, only two of whom survived. These two young passengers, Duncan A. Tinkiss and Miss Christy Ann Morrison, both 17 years old, related their experiences. When the storm broke out at about 11 a.m., panic seized the passengers as the vessel slowly foundered. As many as possible climbed to the uppermost "hurricane deck," which made the ship even more unmanagable due to her heightened centre of gravity. Three overcrowded lifeboats were shoved off, but Tinkiss left the one he was in initially and swam to the metallic lifeboat that contained Capt. John Savage, the mate, Miss Morrison, and others. The lifeboat rolled several times, and each time, fewer people managed to return to it. The two, young survivors were the only ones remaining when the boat drifted ashore about 20 miles (32 kms.) from the site of the *Asia's* sinking. Many bodies were recovered, including Capt. Savage. The *Asia* reportedly was licensed to carry 40 passengers, although permission to carry 150 had been applied for. The ship operators apparently assumed that they would receive permission for the change, and jumped the gun, with catastrophic results. This tragedy hastened the hydrographic survey of Georgian Bay made in the mid-1880s, but many pioneer families along Georgian Bay sadly lost a member or a friend.

Left: *Upon reaching civilization after her harrowing* Asia *experience, survivor Christy Ann Morrison was talked into posing for this pretentious studio photo.*
Right: *From 1882 to 1932, Christy Morrison, later Mrs. Albert Fleming (she reportedly had rejected Tinkiss' marriage proposal), did not talk about that wreck, finally breaking her silence after 50 years.* (BOTH: KOHL-FORSBERG ARCHIVES)

120. *C. C. Martin* and *Albatross*

August 21, 1911   Lake Huron

Left: *The 71-foot-long tug,* C. C. Martin, *resembled this tug, the 70-foot-long* Erastus Day.
Right: *The* C. C. Martin *towed this 136-foot-long barge, the* Albatross. *Both ships were lost.*
(Both Images: Kohl-Forsberg Archives)

On August 21, 1911, two vessels, the five-year-old tug, *C. C. Martin*, towing the 40-year-old barge, *Albatross* (136'6" x 26'3" x 11'9"), towards the French River, met with disaster!

In darkness at 11 p.m., during a storm, the aging barge began to sink from a sudden leak. All seven people on the barge (two men, three women, and two infants, the women and children dressed only in night clothes) somehow made it into their crowded yawl boat before the barge sank. Meanwhile, the lights had gone out on the tug, and it was lost from view, but, before long, the seven from the *Albatross* found the tug's yawl boat adrift, secured it, and balanced their numbers between the two, 13-foot-long boats. They reached the French River Light 36 hours later.

However, the tug, *Martin*, its captain, his wife, and eight sailors, were missing. The first body from the *Martin* was found in remarkably good condition 17 days after the sinking. Near the body was a raft, and further searching recovered two more bodies, all of them located on shoals at Black Bill Island, quite a distance south of the place where the tug and barge had gone down. Two more bodies from the *Martin* were located on September 20th, making a total of five. No others were found. The raft, made up of doors from the *Martin*, suggested that the tug, which had lost its yawl boat in the storm, did not sink immediately, giving the crew time to build this raft. What happened after that is a mystery. But a horrifying fact is that the five recovered bodies had not drowned or died from exposure -- they had all starved to death.

MARINE

TEN ARE LOST; NINE SAVED

Steamer C. C. Martin Believed
to Have Gone Down
With All Hands.

Crew of Barge Albatross
Reaches Lighthouse
Near Midland.

Midland, Ont., Aug. 25.—The steamer C. C. Martin of Midland, with a crew of ten, was probably lost in the storm on Georgian bay Monday night. The barge Albatross, in tow of the Martin, sank during the storm, but her crew reached

Left: *Many newspapers across the Great Lakes spread the tragic news on August 25, 1911.*

Right: *The carefully-crafted raft, consisting of six doors, a flagpole, rope, and spikes, had not been built in haste.*

(Both: Kohl-Forsberg Archives)

121. *SIMCOE*
NOVEMBER 24, 1880   LAKE HURON

Above: *The 136-foot-long* Simcoe, *formerly the* Mary A. Robertson, *resembled the 135-foot-long* Northern Belle.
Right: *The story of the* Simcoe's *loss became known in detail, as there were a few survivors who were able to supply information.*
(BOTH ITEMS: KOHL-FORSBERG ARCHIVES)

THE SIMCOE.

Foundered During a Gale November 24.

ARRIVAL OF FIVE SURVIVORS AT OWEN SOUND.

The Story of the Wreck, and Its Results.

The Fires Put Out by the Waves, Rendering the Steamer Unmanageable.

Five Men Secure a Boat, but Are Unable to Aid Their Shipmates.

TWELVE LIVES LOST—NAMES OF THE VICTIMS.

FIVE SURVIVORS.

OWEN SOUND, November 29.—The steamer Manitoulin arrived to-night from Manitoulin Island, and brought J. A. G. Persons, first mate, Jno. Nesbit, first engineer, Robert McEneeny, wheelsman, Mat Nobles, fireman, and P. Croft, deck hand, of the steamer Simcoe, which foundered on the 24th inst.

On November 26, 1880, a grim report emerged from Lake Huron:

> ...The propeller *Canada*, of the Chicago Line, passed the wreck of the propeller *Simcoe* off Michael's Bay. Her pilot house and part of her cabin works were out of the water, but nothing was seen of the crew, and it is supposed they have gone down with her." The *Simcoe* left Chicago a week ago to-day, with cargo of grain, pork, and corn meal, for this port [Collingwood], and is now three days overdue....

Several days later, five survivors from the crew of 17 who had been on board the *Simcoe* provided details of the loss. The *Simcoe* left Chicago on November 19, 1880, with 19,000 bushels of corn and some general freight, and immediately encountered bad weather, which only grew worse when the ship reached Lake Huron. On the morning of the 24th, while off Providence Bay on southern Manitoulin Island, heavy seas broke through the engine room, putting out the boiler fires. Now unmanageable, the ship continued to take on water while helpless in the trough of the sea until noon, when the hull became submerged. Her upper works were forced away, carrying the lifeboats with them. Five men succeeded in releasing one of the lifeboats and got into it, but were unable to reach the others clinging to the upper works of the steamer. Then the rest of the ship disappeared under the waves, taking the crew with it. The five men in the lifeboat then made for Providence Bay, a distance of about 20 miles. From there, they were taken by wagon to Manitowaning, from whence they took the steamer, *Manitoulin,* to Owen Sound.

The 378-gross-ton, wooden propeller, *Simcoe* (140' x 26'2" x 11'), was built by Hyslop & Ronald and launched at Chatham, Ontario, in 1872 as the *Mary R. Robertson*. Fire destroyed the ship at Byng Inlet on July 29, 1878, but she was rebuilt and renamed *Simcoe*.

Eighteen days prior to the *Simcoe's* loss, another propeller, the *Zealand*, built in the same place by the same builder of the same size and close to the same year as the *Simcoe*, disappeared with all hands on Lake Ontario. For this story, turn to page 44. The similarities in these two tragic sinkings, particularly the fact that both lost steamships had been rebuilt from burnt, sunken hulls, caught critics' attentions, resulting in their damning words.

122. *JOYLAND*

1926   LAKE HURON

The **William A. Haskell,** *launched on Thursday, April 10, 1884, and renamed the* **Joyland** *in 1916, was a large, propeller-driven, wooden steamer with twin boilers and twin smokestacks.*

The **W.A. Haskell,** *under construction, was drawn by Seth Arca Whipple (1855-1901).*

The **Joyland** *was stranded for years on Manitoulin Island before burning.* (ABOVE IMAGES: KOHL-FORSBERG ARCHIVES)

A **Joyland** *boiler on shore marks this shipwreck's location; the wreck lies nearby.* (PHOTO BY CRIS KOHL)

Manitoulin Island in Canada's northern Lake Huron exudes an old-fashioned, humble pioneer spirit that belies its reputation as the largest, freshwater island in the world. Forests and farm fields roll for hours as one drives across this sparsely-populated outpost in Canada's most populated province.

A large shipwreck lies in clean, shallow water (in a maximum depth of 15 feet, or 4.5 metres) at the western end of Manitoulin Island at Burnt Island, which is today not an island, but a peninsula connected to the main shore by a gravel road.

Built as the wooden steamer, *William A. Haskell* (250'5" x 37' x 14'3"), at Detroit by the Detroit Dry Dock Company in 1884, she carried package freight from Ogdensburg on the St. Lawrence River to the Great Lakes ports of Milwaukee and Chicago for most of her life. This ship was conscientiously constructed with the enlarged Welland Canal in mind. Rebuilt between 1875 and 1887, this new canal allowed vessels up to 262 feet (80 metres) to bypass Niagara Falls between Lake Erie and Lake Ontario.

Canadian interests, namely the Montréal Transportation Company, purchased the *William A. Haskell* on March 12, 1916, and renamed her *Joyland*; as such, the ship carried mostly wheat or barley cargoes at Montréal. On April 27, 1922, weighed down by a full load of corn, she ran aground on Little Round Island in the St. Lawrence River near Clayton, New York, after snapping her transmission line between the wheel and the rudder. The underwriters gloomily declared the *Joyland* a total loss, but she was released and rebuilt at Port Dalhousie, Ontario, where the vessel was converted to a sandsucker in 1924, close to the end of her long career.

The *Joyland's* ultimate demise is neither dramatic nor particularly historic. The tired, old steamer simply ran aground at Manitoulin Island in 1926, and, although the Fox Island Sand & Gravel Company purchased the vessel from the underwriters in hopes of restoring her to service, she remained aground. In the autumn of 1930, her huge, wooden superstructure caught fire and everything of wood above the waterline was destroyed, putting an end to salvage hopes. There ensued some accusations and controversy over this ship having been purposely burned for the insurance money. The *Joyland* was over 40 years of age when she stopped operating -- certainly a respectable age for a wooden steamer.

There is an unconfirmed story that a man suffered a head injury on the *Joyland*, and that he died on Burnt Island as a result, but it is not known if this took place before or after the vessel was abandoned there.

"My father removed one of the *Joyland's* boilers in 1934. It's rusting away on the shore now," revealed George Purvis (in a 1994 interview with Cris Kohl), the head of the commercial fishing family which first set up its operations at Burnt Island in the 1880s. That boiler acts as an above water guide to this site today.

Numerous items of interest await visiting snorklers and scuba divers at this shallow shipwreck site. Lying about 100 feet (30 metres) offshore and perpendicular to it, with the bow pointing towards the shore, the *Joyland's* sights include an enormous, upright, four-bladed propeller, the second boiler which is still on the shipwreck, a massive, wooden hull, a multitude of spikes and bolts, as well as a prop shaft and related equipment. Large sandsucking scoops that trailed off the stern of the ship in her latter years of service as a sandsucker remain conspicuous at the site.

When you arrive at this relatively remote site and take a casual stroll around the area, you will feel that there is something pioneer-like, nostalgic, and indeed, even romantic, about the place.

Defeated iron bolts take hollow aim at the water that they can no longer foil; seaweeds wave at the old hull.

The large, four-bladed propeller attracts visitor Joan Forsberg to this part of the Joyland *shipwreck.*

Heavy engine components remain at the Joyland *site.*

Joan Forsberg examines the boiler that is left on the wreck of the the Joyland.
(ABOVE PHOTOS ARE BY CRIS KOHL)

123. NORTH WIND

JULY 1, 1926   LAKE HURON

Above: *The nimble* **North Wind** *steams past a docked vessel in the harbour of Gladstone, Michigan.*
Right: *The* **Manitoulin Expositor** *newspaper at Little Current, Ontario, was the nearest, and the first, newspaper to report the* **North Wind's** *loss.*   (BOTH: KOHL-FORSBERG ARCHIVES)

LAKE CREW RESCUED AS BOAT SINKS

Steamer North Wind Had Clevelanders Aboard.

The Cleveland steamer North Wind, carrying a crew of more than twenty, struck and sank in 100 feet of water at Robinson shoal, Georgian bay, yesterday, according to dispatches.

The crew, many of its members Clevelanders, was taken off and landed safely at Little Current.

The North Wind was bound from Little Current to Fort William, Ont., carrying grain. She was in

By the summer of 1926, the steel propeller, *North Wind* (299′5″ x 40′8″ x 21′6″), was the only vessel remaining on the Great Lakes from the fleet of six, mighty, sister ships launched for the Northern Steamship Company in 1888-1889. The *North Star* had been the first to disappear from sight, sinking in Lake Huron after a collisiion with her sister ship, the *Northern Queen*, on November 25, 1908. The *Northern Queen* was sold for saltwater use in 1917 and was scrapped there in 1925. The *Northern Light* was also sold for saltwater use in 1917, sinking off the Florida Keys on November 8, 1930. The *Northern King* and the *Northern Wave* were both sold for saltwater use in 1917, and both were scrapped there in early 1926.

This lonely, aging sister, the *North Wind*, launched at Cleveland on Tuesday, July 31, 1888, did not have too long to wait before joining her siblings. On Thursday, July 1, 1926, with a cargo of grain from Fort William, Ontario, bound for Little Current, she stranded on Robertson Rock, near Clapperton Island in Lake Huron's North Channel, and slid into deep water within two hours. No lives were lost when the crew took to the lifeboats and rowed to the nearby town of Little Current, where an enterprising crewmember sold one of the lifeboats to a local resident, and then promptly disappeared with the cash!

The *North Wind* saw six years of service (1917-1923) on the Atlantic Ocean out of Boston. The 299-foot-long ship had been cut in half for transit through the Welland Canal's 260-foot locks in 1917, and again for her return to the Great Lakes in 1923.

The *North Wind's* name is faint on the bow, with two anchors and an anchor winch at the bow. Portholes exist at depths of 80 and 100 feet; a spare four-bladed propeller rests on the deck at 110 feet. The wheelhouse is missing, blown off when the ship sank. The interior of this wreck is in excellent condition, experienced by specially-trained, prepared divers.

Sponsored by **THE PORT OF LITTLE CURRENT**
14 Water Street East, PO Box 608, Little Current, ON, P0P 1K0
Telephone: (705) 368-3500   Web: townofnemi.on.ca
Come Home to the Island -- Where memories are made!

124. EMMA E. THOMPSON

MAY 28, 1914   LAKE HURON

The east side of uninhabited Innes Island features a rarity in this rocky part of the Great Lakes: a sandy beach. About a quarter of a mile off this sandy beach on the northeast side just below Hesson Point, in about 30 feet (9 metres) of clear, fresh water, the shipwreck named the *Emma E. Thompson* has rested for more than a century.

Named by a Michigan lumber businessman after his mother, who lived from 1809 to 1891, this wooden steamer (125'9" x 27'6" x 12'8") was launched in 1875 at Saginaw, Michigan. Her high-pressure, non-condensing steam engine could produce 380 horsepower to move her cargoes of lumber and coal at a respectable speed.

In the spring of 1914, dark clouds on the horizon threatened a world still at peace for a few more weeks before the outbreak of World War I. Meanwhile, dark clouds literally forced the *Emma E. Thompson,* en route from French River, Ontario, to Manistee, Michigan, to seek shelter from a storm behind Innes Island.

Unfortunately, while the steamer lay at peaceful anchor, she caught fire and burned to the water's edge on Thursday, May 28, 1914, in the wee hours of early morning. Between four and five o'clock, one of the crew discovered flames raging near the boiler house. By the time the remainder of the crew was roused to fight the fire, that section of the amidships was ablaze. Those people sleeping in the vessel's stern were just barely able to reach the lifeboat in the forward part of the steamer, so quickly did the flames gain headway.

Captain James Maddock (also the ship's owner) saw to it that no lives were lost among the eleven on board at the time, but he knew that it had been a close call. As the yawl boat pulled away, the entire steamer burst into a mass of flames from bow to stern. At that early morning hour, the captain of the passing passenger steamer, *Germanic,* noticed the lurid glare of smoke in the sky, and sped to the scene, picking up the people in the yawl boat. and transporting them safely to Owen Sound.

The *Emma E. Thompson* was located by commercial diver, Richard Hammond, of Little Current, in 1992. Despite having burned, this wreck offers many fascinating sites to see, including the steam engine, the boiler, tools, 1914 rope, pumps, bow chains, and anchors.

The 39-year-old wooden steamer, Emma E. Thompson, *was valued at only $7,000 at the time of loss.*

Barge Burned

The barge, Emma E. Thomson, was burned to the water's edge on Thursday morning last. She was going from French River to Lake Michigan and was compelled to anchor at Ennis Island on Wednesday afternoon as the sea was heavy. At 5 o'clock next morning she was discovered to be on fire. The crew

The Manitoulin Expositor *newspaper reported the loss of the* Emma E. Thompson. (BOTH OF THE ABOVE: KOHL-FORSBERG ARCHIVES)

Three sets of large-link anchor chains sweep in smooth, flowing lines from the bow of the Emma E. Thompson *to the lake bottom.*
(PHOTO BY CRIS KOHL)

125. *GRIFFON?*

SEPTEMBER 1679   LAKE HURON

La Salle (above) *built the* Griffon (below) *in 1679, the same year it disappeared.* (BOTH: KOHL-FORSBERG ARCHIVES)

Above: *Young Richard Tappenden, Jr., gives scale to the possible* Griffon *wreckage on western Manitoulin Island in 1932.* (PHOTO BY RICHARD TAPPENDEN, SR.)
Below: *An older Richard Tappenden, Jr., shows a* Griffon *model to Joan Forsberg in 2015.* (PHOTO BY CRIS KOHL)

The greatest mystery of the Great Lakes involves the fate of a ship named the *Griffon*.

Constructed by the French explorer, Robert Cavelier, Sieur de la Salle, in 1679 at the eastern end of Lake Erie to transport an enormous quantity of prized beaver pelts for the European market and erasing his debts, the *Griffon* was the very first decked ship to sail on the upper Great Lakes ("upper" meaning upstream of Niagara Falls). It was the first ship to sail across Lake Erie, the first to sail on the Detroit and St. Clair Rivers, the first to cross Lake Huron, and the first to sail across Lake Michigan -- only to disappear with a minimal crew and a valuable cargo of furs on the return leg of its maiden voyage. La Salle and the rest of his party, stayed to explore lands beyond Lake Michigan.

The *Griffon* was never seen again by Europeans, and what happened to her has never been ascertained. Did she sink in the four-day storm that hit those parts of the lakes that the *Griffon* had to traverse? Did the *Griffon* break up on any of the thousands of uncharted rocks or reefs while seeking shelter from the storm? Did her crew, whose loyalty to La Salle was in doubt, scuttle the ship and steal the furs? Were indigenous inhabitants in northern Lake Michigan the last humans to see the *Griffon* as she sailed east into the storm? Did people at the St. Ignace mission in the Straits of Mackinac hear several blasts from a *Griffon* cannon in the middle of a stormy night? Was that a signal from a desperate crew who had lost control of their ship, perhaps due to a lost or damaged rudder, and were at the mercy of the western winds as the storm pushed them east?

Over the years, the mysterious fate of the *Griffon* has become legendary. Two dozen claims of discovery have been made regarding the *Griffon's* final resting place, nearly all of them disproven.

The western end of Manitoulin Island has a strong claim to solving the *Griffon* mystery. In the 1890s, the keeper at the Mississagi Straits Lighthouse searched the nearby forest along the shoreline for a suitable small boat mast, and came upon a cave with several skeletons in it, including one enormous skeleton (which could have been the remains of the *Griffon's* pilot, a man named Lucas, who reputedly was a very huge man.) Also in that cave, the lighthouse keeper found some brass buttons, some old French coins and tokens from the 1600s, and an ancient, silver watch case with chain. Two more skeletons were found in another cave a short distance from the first one, now totaling six -- the exact number of crew carried by the *Griffon*. These were not First Nation skeletons, as none of the tribes in the area buried their dead in caves. The lighthouse keeper also took into account the nearby, mysterious portion of a very old shipwreck that had

Three museums on Manitoulin Island, such as Meldrum Bay's Net Shed Museum, harbour pieces and artifacts that could be from the Griffon. (PHOTO BY CRIS KOHL)

been lying on the rocky shoreline about two miles north of the lighthouse since at least the late 1700s, long before the lighthouse was built. Native elders in the late 1800s could remember their grandfathers having told them about this "white man's wreck" when they were children, and that they had first seen the old wreck when they -- the grandfathers -- were children! Since at least the 1870s, local farmers had been removing the long, steel bolts from the wreck for use in plowing their fields, and local fishermen had been removing the lead caulking from the wreck for use as weights on their fish nets. However, after a severe storm in 1940, the wreckage was gone, having been washed away from the shore. The artifacts and skeletons from the two caves were all gradually lost

The oversized skull and jaw bone found in a nearby Manitoulin Island cave intrigued historians at Gore Bay in the 1930s.
(KOHL-FORSBERG ARCHIVES)

or disappeared with lighthouse keepers when those men retired. The caves themselves have collapsed due to the dynamiting at a nearby quarry since the 1920s. A jar of the cave's brass buttons was stored in a shed at the lighthouse, but the shed burned down in the 1920s, and the present shed was built in the exact same location. The caves' skulls, even the very large one, ended up on the bottom of the lake. Fortunately, three museums on Manitoulin Island share pieces of wood, iron bolts, and lead from the old wreck.

Unthinking actions (regarding artifacts that may have been used to identify the wreck as the *Griffon*) may continue to plague the western Manitoulin Island region. In the summer of 2015, the authors of this book met a scuba diver at Kagawong on Manitoulin Island who, diving earlier off the Mississagi Strait Lighthouse, raised a long, heavy timber that had a strip of lead caulking attached to one side. He used the wood to make a coffee table as a wedding gift for two friends, and he threw away the lead caulking. When we spoke with him, it was obvious that he was not familiar with the story of the *Griffon* or the old wreck that had been on the shoreline.

The route from the Mississagi Lighthouse to where the wreckage that could have been that of the Griffon *once lay is demanding.* (PHOTO BY CRIS KOHL)

One thing is certain: If the *Griffon* is found some day at a different location, then the new "greatest mystery of the Great Lakes" will be this one.

A letter "G" for "Griffon" marks the spot where the old wreck lay; it's called the "G spot." (PHOTO BY JOAN FORSBERG)

Lake Superior

Lake Superior, the largest, deepest, cleanest, and "wildest" of the five Great Lakes, contains the fewest number of shipwrecks (only about 600). The reason for this is simple: Lake Superior didn't open up to shipping traffic until 1855, relatively late in the history of the inland seas, when the Locks at Sault Ste. Marie finally were built, allowing ships to enter and exit the big lake with relative ease. And those locks were built because of the North American Industrial Revolution's enormous appetite for iron ore, which was found in the mid-1800s in vast quantities in this area.

Despite its comparatively low number of shipwrecks, Lake Superior contains wrecks to which can be attributed as many superlatives as the lake itself claims. For example, here lies the one wreck that is both the largest (729 feet, or 221 metres, long), the most recent, and the most famous shipwreck in all of the Great Lakes: the freighter, *Edmund Fitzgerald*. This disaster has been the subject of songs, books, documentaries, expeditions, theories, and myths -- in part because it is the only modern-era shipwreck that chronologically-gifted people can actually remember, recalling even where they were and what they were doing when they first heard the bad news about the "Fitz." Its loss was one of those memorably dramatic events.

Although lacking the greater variety of ship types found in the other four lakes, Superior does have an eclectic underwater fleet -- even on the less-trafficked Canadian side -- ranging from the very last shipwreck to occur in the 1800s anywhere in the Great Lakes, to cannon-mounted, steel ships of war on their way from Canada to France in 1918, to the luxury yacht that made the Jacques Cousteau expedition to the inland seas in 1980 gasp in disbelief and proclaim it to be "the most beautiful shipwreck in the world."

CANADA'S MOST FAMOUS LAKE SUPERIOR SHIPWRECKS

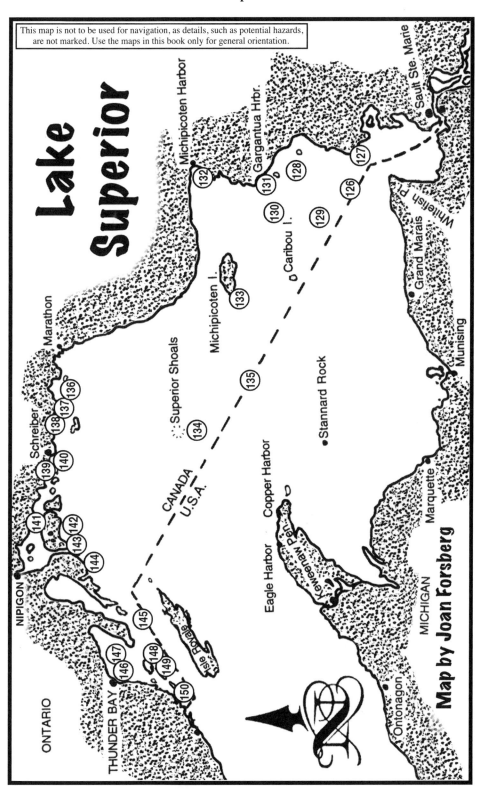

This map is not to be used for navigation, as details, such as potential hazards, are not marked. Use the maps in this book only for general orientation.

Lake Superior

Sault Ste. Marie

Whitefish Pt.

Michipicoten Harbor

Gargantua Hrbr.

127

128

126

131

132

130

129

Caribou I.

Grand Marais

Michipicoten I.

133

Marathon

Munising

Superior Shoals

Stannard Rock

135

136

137

138

Schreiber

134

140

139

CANADA
U.S.A.

Copper Harbor

Marquette

141

142

Eagle Harbor

Keweenaw Pen.

143

144

MICHIGAN

NIPIGON

145

Ontonagon

Map by Joan Forsberg

147

148

146

149

Isle Royale

150

ONTARIO

THUNDER BAY

126. *EDMUND FITZGERALD*

NOVEMBER 10, 1975   LAKE SUPERIOR

The exhilarating launch of the largest ship on the Great Lakes took place at the Detroit suburb of River Rouge on June 7, 1958. Unfortunately, a 58-year-old spectator had a heart attack and died at the scene. (KOHL-FORSBERG ARCHIVES)

The Edmund Fitzgerald *was named after the Chairman of the Board of the Northwestern Mutual Life Insurance Company of Milwaukee, a port that this ship never saw.* (KOHL-FORSBERG ARCHIVES)

The tragic, yet most famous, shipwreck in the entire Great Lakes, the enormous freighter, *Edmund Fitzgerald* (729'3" x 75' x 11'7"), which owes its fame, in large part, to a haunting, popular, 1976 ballad by Canadian songwriter, Gordon Lightfoot, lies deep in 529 feet (158.7 metres) of water.

On June 7, 1958, the hull of the steel freighter, *Edmund Fitzgerald,* was launched amidst great fanfare at the Great Lakes Engineering Works in River Rouge, near Detroit, Michigan. She was, after all, the longest and the largest ship on the Great Lakes! Her maiden voyage commenced on September 22, 1958 (after more than three months of outfitting the interior of the ship), and she sailed light to Silver Bay, Minnesota, for a cargo of iron ore pellets. She spent her entire 17-year career operating for the Columbia Transportation Division of the Oglebay Norton Company in Cleveland, Ohio. The *Edmund Fitzgerald* established cargo records when she became the first Great Lakes vessel to haul more than 26,000 gross tons in a single load.

The *Edmund Fitzgerald's* demise took

Left: *The* Edmund Fitzgerald, *the Mount Everest of Great Lakes shipwrecks, lies broken in half in deep water, the bow upright and the stern overturned.* (COURTESY OF ARTIST ROBERT MCGREEVY)
Right: *This battered and holed lifeboat, one of two found after the violent storm, both empty, is displayed at the Museum Ship* Valley Camp *in Sault Ste. Marie, Michigan.* (PHOTO BY CRIS KOHL)

place on Lake Superior in 35-foot waves that rolled and bounced out of control due to the 75-mile-an-hour winds on November 10, 1975. Heading for Detroit with 26,000 tons of iron ore (taconite) pellets from Superior, Wisconsin, the *Edmund Fitzgerald* suddenly disappeared from the radar screen of the trailing freighter, the *Arthur M. Anderson,* at 7:20 p.m., just after the *Fitzgerald's* captain, Ernest McSorley, radioed, "We are holding our own." The ship sank, apparently without warning, 17 miles from the entrance to the comparatively safe waters of Whitefish Bay, with the loss of all 29 men on board, and no bodies were ever washed ashore or found floating (the reasons being that they were trapped inside the hull, or that the water pressure at that great depth, and the water's low temperature, were too much for any decomposing gasses to lift the bodies to the surface, as they usually do).

Right: The Fitzgerald's bell is on public display in the Shipwreck Museum at Whitefish Point. (PHOTO BY CRIS KOHL)

The *Edmund Fitzgerald* plunged to the bottom of Lake Superior, apparently with engines going and propeller thrusting, when the impact of striking bottom broke her in two. A submersible expedition to the wreck site in 1994 suggested that the nose of this 729-foot-long vessel hit the bottom at 529 feet while the aft quarter was still about the water's surface. Another expedition in 1994 found a body off the bow, but its old-fashioned, cork lifejacket indicated that the body was from a much earlier shipwreck, likely from the 1920s.

Above: Detroit's Mariner's Church.
Below: Reverend Ingalls rang the church bell 29 times when he heard the news of the ship's loss, never thinking that this action would become famous.
(PHOTOS BY CRIS KOHL)

Only once, in early September 1995, have scuba divers -- specially-trained, technical divers using exotic, trimix gases -- visited the deep *Edmund Fitzgerald*. Terrence Tysall, a cave and technical dive instructor from Florida, and Mike Zee, a technical diver from Chicago, reportedly spent eight minutes on the shipwreck -- and then three hours coming back up! It was pitch black, so they could see only what fell into the range of their underwater lights, and it was bitterly cold at that depth. They have no desire to do it again.

The wreck victims' families have asked that no further visitations of any kind take place on the largest shipwreck in the Great Lakes, and the Ontario govenment has declared the wreck of the *Edmund Fitzgerald* to be off-limits to any and all activities. (Yes, the wreck does lie inside Canada by only 900 feet, or 273 metres).

Despite being off-limits to future visits, the strong, yet inexplicable mystique of the *Edmund Fitzgerald* persists.

Authors Joan Forsberg and Cris Kohl flank folksinger Gordon Lightfoot in 2005. (PHOTO SET-UP: CRIS KOHL)

Sponsored by **THE CITY OF SAULT STE. MARIE, ONTARIO**
99 Foster Drive, Sault Ste, Marie, ON P6A 5X6
Telephone: 705.759.5310   Email: csd@cityssm.on.ca   Web: www.saultstemarie.ca
Sault Ste. Marie, at the Heart of the Great Lakes, celebrates with Canada on its 150th!

127. BATCHAWANA

JUNE 26, 1907   LAKE SUPERIOR

CANADIAN BOAT BURNS

Steamer Batchawanna, Loaded With Ore, Is a Total Loss.

Crew Launched Small Boats and Easily Saved Themselves.

Sault Ste. Marie, June 27.—The Canadian steamer Batchawanna, loaded with iron ore consigned to the Algoma Steel company at Sault Ste. Marie, burned last

Left: *The 209-foot-long, wooden steamer,* Batchawana, *in an unidentified harbour.*
Right: *The ship burned to a total loss on June 26, 1907.* (BOTH: KOHL-FORSBERG ARCHIVES)

Built and launched as the ***Robert A. Parker*** in 1881 at Bay City, Michigan, for the Lehigh Valley Transportation Company in Buffalo, New York, the wooden-hulled, bulk freight steamer, ***Batchawana*** (209' x 33'8" x 16'1") ended her days 25 years later off a small island in eastern Lake Superior.

In 1902, when the vessel was already more than 20 years old, she had a close call when she partially burned off St. Martin's Island in Lake Huron on November 10th. The owner, Barry Miles of Chicago, must have viewed this as an omen, for he was never again comfortable with his ship, and he sold her to the Ganley Brothers of Sault Ste. Marie, Ontario, in 1905. They changed her name to the ***Batchawana***, after a bay and a community near the Soo, and replaced her aging boilers with those from the steamer, ***City of Collingwood,*** which had burned at Collingwood, Ontario, on June 19, 1905, with four lives lost.

Only two years later, on June 26, 1907, the ***Batchawana***, valued at $28,000 at the time, burned to a total loss just north of Coppermine Point in Lake Superior. She was loaded with iron ore consigned to the Algoma Steel Company at the Canadian Sault. Fortunately, no lives were lost, as the crew launched the small boats and landed easily on the nearby mainland. This wreck lies in a maximum of 35 feet (10.5 metres) of water to the immediate north of tiny Rousseau Island. The boiler and the engine were salvaged, but many items of interest remain: spikes, bolts, propeller and drive shaft, and large sections of wooden hull.

Left: *Bolts from the* Batchawana *lie in the shallows at Rousseau Island.*
Right: *Frank Troxell examines bolts from a missing blade on the damaged propeller.*
(BOTH PHOTOS BY CRIS KOHL)

128. ORINOCO

MAY 18, 1924   LAKE SUPERIOR

Steamer in Dry Dock,
West Bay City, Mich.

CAPTAIN AMONG 5 LOST AS LAKE SHIP SINKS IN 60-MILE GALE

16 Orinoco Survivors,
One a Woman, Battle
Way To Superior Isle

Excursion Boat
Destroyed by Fire

Vessel Founders Off Pointe Aux Mines; Tug Saves Exhausted Seamen; Missing Skipper Had Premonition of Fate; Wrote Wife He "Feared Something."

Cleveland, May 20.—Captain A. L. Lawrence, missing commander of the Orinoco, was a mate on the Chester A. Congdon, when that vessel sank in Georgian Bay in 1919, his wife declared tonight. Mrs. Lawrence said she received a letter from her husband written be-fore he sent out from Bay City

survivors, most of them still suf-fering from their 40-hour vigil as the wind-swept shores of the lake and, told grim tales of the battle against the storm, of the desperate decision to cut the barge adrift and of the fight in boats and on wreckage to reach the island, iden-tity of the Gargantua crew, com-manded by Captain D. A. Williams of the Spanish River Paper com-pany, of Sault Ste Marie, Ont., pro-vided them with clothes and food

Cleveland, May 20.—(By United Press.)—The excursion steamer State of Ohio was destroyed by fire of unknown origin at East Ninth street pier here today. John Lee, night watchman, is missing. He is believed to have lost his life in the fire.

The blaze lighted up the lake front, for miles.

The State of Ohio was built by the Cleveland and Buffalo Trans-company about 43 years ago. The ship was valued at about $100,000

Left: *The wooden giant,* **Orinoco,** *in the West Bay City, Michigan, dry dock.*
Right: *The* **Orinoco's** *loss in a 1924 storm drew many headlines.* (BOTH: KOHL-FORSBERG ARCHIVES)

In the early morning hours of Tuesday, May 20, 1924, still catching her breath from the 60-mile-an-hour gales that had swept over Lake Superior two days earlier, the rela-tively new tug, *Gargantua* (see page 146 for her story), of the Spanish River Pulp and Paper Company, suddenly steamed into a large field of floating wreckage south of Mon-tréal Island. Crewmembers could distinguish the lights of fires on the Canadian mainland at Pointe aux Mines. Cruising farther, they reached the barge, *Chieftain*, at anchor in the lee of Montréal Island, her crew safely ashore on the island. The *Gargantua* rescued them, then approached the fires on the mainland at Pointe aux Mines

Huddling in front of those fires were the survivors of the steamer, *Orinoco*, which had been towing the *Chieftain*. At the height of the storm, the tow line broke between the two ships. Fending for herself, the *Chieftain* was able to make her way behind Montréal Island for protection, where they dropped anchor and rowed to the island. But this crew was com-pletely unaware of their towing steamer's fate.

The *Orinoco* literally broke in two shortly after being torn away from the *Chieftain*. Seeing the already overburdened condition of the two lifeboats as they were being lowered over the side of his sinking vessel, Captain Anthony Lawrence of Cleveland, Ohio, refused to leave his post, and drowned when the *Orinoco* sank. Chief Engineer Joseph Wurtz of Bay City, Michigan, and Wheelsman Hugh Gordon, following the lead of their captain, knowing it was unsafe to overcrowd the undersized lifeboats, also stuck to their posts and perished. These three heroes were last seen on the deck, wearing their cork lifejackets.

The *Orinoco's* crew numbered 22 (21 men and the one woman cook). Of the 19 on the two lifeboats, two men perished from exposure before reaching shore. The remaining 17 arrived safely after many hours of freezing, terror-filled rowing. The *Gargantua* picked them up and conveyed them to the Canadian Soo (Sault Ste. Marie), where all the survivors were loud in their praise of Captain D. A. Williams and the crew of the *Gargantua*. "From the time they took us aboard, they treated us like princes," stated one survivor. "...we got a regular dinner that tasted mighty good after being without food since Sunday morning."

Numerous searches were made to try to find the bodies of the three heroes who had stayed at their posts so that others could live, and rewards were offered, but no body was found. Perhaps one of them lies off the bow of the *Edmund Fitzgerald* (see page 175).

Longtime shipbuilder, James Davidson, by bullheadedly building wooden ship after wooden ship when the new technology of steel became the obvious material of choice for vessel construction in the modern era, was the last, major holdout grasping at a dying way of life (similar to oil-industry advocates of automobile propulsion today). His yard at West Bay City, Michigan, had built the wooden giant, *Orinoco* (295' x 44' x 21'), in 1898.

129. *LAMBTON*
APRIL 19, 1922   LAKE SUPERIOR

LIGHT-TENDER
MAY HAVE SUNK

Lambton, Canadian Vessel With 17 Aboard, Thought Gale Victim on Superior.

Sault Ste. Marie, Mich., April 24. —The steamer Lambton, of the Canadian lighthouse service, carrying a crew of about 17 men, is believed to have sunk southeast of Michipicoten Island in Lake Superior during the storm last week. The Lambton, carrying light-

Left: *The government ship,* Lambton, *was built of steel in 1908 at Sorel, Québec.*
Right: *It was April 25, 1922, a week after the* Lambton *had left the Soo, that the first news accounts of the ship going missing were printed.*   (BOTH: KOHL-FORSBERG ARCHIVES)

In late April 1922, the first ships of the new season to cross Lake Superior downbound arrived at the Soo with reports that Canadian lights on the eastern side were not yet lit.

This was worrisome to Canadian authorities, since they knew that the *Lambton* (108' x 25'1" x 12'7"), the steel-hulled, government lighthouse tender that conveyed keepers to their lights at the start of the season, had left the Soo on April 18, 1922. The several lighthouse keepers on board should have arrived at their respective lighthouses by now.

By April 24, 1922, the rugged, little *Lambton*, with 19 crew and lighthouse keepers, plus their season's supplies on board, had definitely gone missing. One steamer reported spotting considerable wreckage floating approximately 25 miles southeast of Michipicoten Island. Identifiable wreckage, such as a piece of the cabin with white woodwork, was found by April 30th. It all pointed to the *Lambton* having gone down.

The freighter, *Midland Prince,* later reported actually watching the *Lambton*, battling with a sudden storm, disappear! The two vessels were travelling relatively close to each other on Wednesday, April 19, 1922, near Caribou Island, when the gale broke.

On April 26, 1922, the steel freighter, *W. C. Franz*, reported being in the ice near the location where the *Lambton* "broke her steering gear after leaving the Soo, and that the *Lambton* was forced to encounter the storm with a mended steering gear." This was given as the reason that the *Lambton* was unable to ride out the storm.

The *Franz* also reported that the light on Caribou Island was burning, indicating that someone had been put ashore there from the *Lambton* prior to the ship going missing.

The *Lambton* was not equipped with wireless, and would thus have been unable to send out a distress message when she ran into trouble. The significant lesson learned from *Titanic* exactly ten years earlier regarding the lifesaving capability of wireless radio on a ship had obviously not been learned by government vessels like the tragic *Lambton*.

130. *GOLSPIE*

DECEMBER 4, 1906   LAKE SUPERIOR

The Golspie, *formerly the* Osceola, *was equipped with a fore & aft compound steam engine, built by S. F. Hodge & Co., Detroit, while her boiler was a fire box type.*
The two Hamilton owners of the Golspie *had refused to send a tug immediately from the Sault to rescue the stranded sailors, so many of the crew arrived at a hospital eight days after frostbite had already set in. The resulting newspaper stories were so graphic and alarming that one paper was sued by the* Golspie's *owners!*
(KOHL-FORSBERG ARCHIVES)

Built as the 980-gross-ton, wooden vessel, *Osceola* (183'6" x 34' x 22'), at West Bay City, Michigan, and launched on June 15, 1882, this ship, after numerous mishaps over a 20-plus-year career, including being wrecked and abandoned in late 1887 off Michigan's "thumb" in Lake Huron, but being recovered and repaired the following spring, was sold to two Canadians from Hamilton, Ontario, in July 1905. They changed her name to *Golspie*, after a maritime community in northern Scotland, revealing the new owners' heritage.

On December 4, 1906, on the proverbial "last trip of the season," the *Golspie* was stranded and wrecked in Brulé Bay (today's Old Woman Bay), south of Michipicoten Harbour, Ontario. She was loaded with oats and a general cargo at Fort William, Ontario, bound for Owen Sound, when she ran off course. Weather conditions were severely adverse, with freezing temperatures and thick, mad-swirling snow. The ship, broadside on the gravel beach, took quite a pounding. Fourteen of the 20 crew took to the lifeboat to obtain assistance in Michipicoten, but a few became badly frozen from the severe cold. Meanwhile, a tug rescued the men from the stranded vessel, and, after three days, the *Golspie* broke up.

There are varying accounts of the hardships experienced by the *Golspie's* crew in reaching civilization and safety. The entire crew initially survived, but many of them paid a heavy price, as reported by the *Sault Star* on Thursday, December 20, 1906:

> The five sailors of the wrecked steamer *Golspie*...reached the Soo on the tug *Andrew J. Smith* last Friday morning, and being all found suffering from frost bite, were sent at once to the General Hospital.
>
> It was found there that several amputations would be necessary, but Soo people had no idea at the time that the men were so badly frost bitten as to necessitate twelve operations.
>
> All day Friday, two of the hospital medical staff were busy on these five sailors. Every one of the frozen men lost both feet, and one lost both his hands [this Scotsman reportedly later succumbed to shock and died]....
>
> It is reported that the five men, fresh from the old country [England, Scotland, Ireland], were not aware of the severe weather that is experienced on Lake Superior, and that after the vessel stranded, they neglected to take blankets and warm clothing with them, when getting to shore, although orders had been given them to do so.

The *Golspie's* boiler is the one lying in about 10 feet (3 metres) of water at the mouth of Old Woman River (still visible, according to reports made in 1937 and 1991). The propeller is alleged to be buried in the sand between the mouth of Old Woman River and the cliffs. There is wreckage of a wooden ship found sparingly in the shallows. One scuba diver told one of the authors of this book that the main wreckage lies in about 100 feet (30 metres) of water in Old Woman Bay, close to shore, but this has not been verified.

131. *COLUMBUS*

SEPTEMBER 10, 1909   LAKE SUPERIOR

The Columbus *burned to a total loss at remote Gargantua Harbour.* (INSTITUTE FOR GREAT LAKES RESEARCH, BOWLING GREEN STATE UNIVERSITY, OHIO)

A nine-mile (15-km.), 1 hour, rough road ride will get one close to the wreck. (PHOTO BY CRIS KOHL)

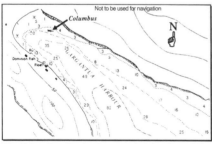

The Columbus *lies in the once-thriving bay of Gargantua Harbour.*   (KOHL-FORSBERG ARCHIVES)

A two-mile (3-km.) trek is necessary from the end of automobile access to the wreck of the Columbus.
(PHOTO BY CRIS KOHL)

"If you make it in there, you'll join the ranks of a handful of divers who have explored the wreck of the *Columbus*," we were informed back in the 1980s by our Lake Superior friend, Ryan LeBlanc, who was sharing one of the North's best-kept secrets with us.

Remote Gargantua Harbour is a wilderness gem, well worth the hour it takes to drive the nine miles from the paved Trans-Canada Highway west along a winding, pot-holed, dirt road interrupted periodically by rickety Bailey bridges spanning fast-moving streams. The once-flourishing fishing community is a ghost town today, but its history remains evident on land -- and especially below the bay's waters.

That rough road ends at a rough, waterfront parking lot -- with Gargantua Harbour still about two miles (three kms.) away, accessible only by trail or by inflatable boat carried across the rock-strewn beach and launched there.

Gargantua Harbour must be one of the prettiest natural bays ever created, with its long, curving swath of sandy beach at the end of the rounded harbour, and the very gradual deepening of its crystalline waters to the sudden drop-off point. An azure sky of deepest summer often crowns this beautiful setting. But this quiet, relaxing serenity belies the bustling activites of its past.

At the turn of the 20th century, commercial fishing created the community of Gargantua Harbour. Catches of herring and lake trout were busily packed on ice there and shipped to larger markets. But by the 1950s, the invasive sea lamprey had devastated commercial fishing, and the town fell into ruin. A couple of abandoned buildings and the foundations of several others are all that can be seen on land.

But the main, historic attraction at this backwoods harbour site is the wreck of the large, wooden tugboat, the **Columbus**. The top of the steam engine protrudes above the water, making this shipwreck easy to find. Gazing at the steam engine's exposed metalwork, one becomes aware of the fact that something big happened here a long time ago.

Launched as the *John Owen* (136'2" x

Left: *Although in a remote area, the wreck of the* Columbus *is easy to locate from the surface.*
Right: *The* Columbus' *steam engine leans in Gargantua Harbour.* (BOTH PHOTOS BY CRIS KOHL)

25'2" x 11'8") on March 7, 1874, by the Detroit Dry Dock Company, she was the largest of the early Detroit River tugs. According to the Inland Lloyds insurance ratings, the *John Owen* was valued at $36,000 in 1875, when the ship was nearly new, but by 1906, the value of this 32-year-old vessel was only $15,000.

The *John Owen* worked as a wrecking (which meant "salvaging") tug in the 1890s, helping recover vessels that became stranded on various shorelines, but for most of the *Owen's* career, she towed enormous log rafts from Lake Superior, through the Soo Locks, and down to harbours in the southern Great Lakes. This was dangerous work, akin to a bull being loose in a china shop. Once, while downbound, emerging from the Detroit River with just such a huge log raft, the logs snagged a tugboat which was at anchor and carried it, with the logs, into Lake Erie, where it sank. Fortunately, no one was injured.

Sold in 1907 to a Canadian named Joseph Ganley of Sault Ste. Marie, Ontario, who changed her name to the *Columbus*, the vessel spent three seasons transporting supplies to Canadian backports on Lake Superior until, on September 10, 1909, she caught fire while docked at Gargantua Harbour and was cut loose to save the dock. No lives were lost.

The hull and machinery offer visitors (boaters, kayakers, swimmers, snorkelers, scuba divers) ample opportunities for either casual explorations or detailed examinations. The *Columbus,* which rests on her port side, offers, as attractions, the steam engine, the boiler, the four-bladed propeller, a capstan, and much of the wooden hull. Fishing community cast-offs, such as a tea kettle, are found near the former docks, and a sunken barge lies nearby opposite the *Columbus*. This remote area is part of Lake Superior Provincial Park, so it becomes doubly important not to take any souvenirs from the ghost town or its waters.

Left to right: *Joyce Hayward takes a close look at the* Columbus' *rudder. Gary Gentile approaches a propeller blade. Joan Forsberg glides over the massive boiler.* (PHOTOS BY CRIS KOHL)

132. *ACADIA*

NOVEMBER 5, 1896   LAKE SUPERIOR

The Acadia *was a very early "composite ship," having been built of both iron and wood. But that sturdier construction could not protect it from the hard rocks and boulders along Lake Superior's shoreline, nor the inhospitable weather conditions found in the month of November.*

(ONTARIO ARCHIVES)

Launched at Hamilton, Canada West (renamed Ontario 60 days later), on May 1, 1867, exactly two months before Canada became a country, the graceful, white, 806-gross-ton steamer, *Acadia* (176'6" x 25'6" x 10'4", final measurements after an 1882 rebuild), is a likely candidate for being the first ship built in the Great Lakes of composite hull construction, that is, the combination of an iron frame planked with wood (like the *Clarion* shipwreck off Lake Erie's Point Pelee; see pages 92-93).

The *Acadia's* Captain Chamberlain gave this account of his ship's loss:

"We left Fort William at 11 a.m. [on Wednesday, Nov. 4, 1896],... and had a good run down Lake Superior until in the vicinity of Michipicoten Island. There, on account of heavy weather, I determined to seek shelter in the bay at Michipicoten river. A heavy snow storm was on, and we went aground on a rock bottom at 10 o'clock Thursday night, staving a hole in the bottom. The wind shifted and the steamer commenced pounding and driving farther up the rocks. At 2 o'clock the next morning, the pumps were stopped and the vessel allowed to settle.

"The crew of seventeen took a supply of bedding and provisions ashore and constructed a rude shelter. We remained there two days waiting for the weather to moderate, and leaving two of the crew on the shore to watch the steamer, started in the two yawl boats. We rowed fifteen miles to Gargantua [Harbour], arriving there Saturday night. Sunday morning I, with four of the crew, borrowed the lighthouse tender and leaving the remainder of the crew, started for the Soo. Near Mamainse we were detained for four days and nights by rough weather. The provisions ran out and we were compelled to carry flour from a settlement some distance inland on our backs and live on cakes made of that.

"The weather moderated sufficiently this morning to enable us to reach the Soo. All the way down we encountered scarcely any persons except at Gargantua and at the settlement. The shore was rocky and bold, and exceedingly inhospitable. There was no food of any kind to be obtained in the woods, and we suffered extremely from the cold."

The steamer had completely disappeared by the time the captain returned on a tug.

The *Acadia*, surprisingly, lies broken and scattered over a wide area in shallow water along the shoreline west of Michipicoten River, Ontario. In between boulders on this rocky bottom are various broken hull pieces, steam fittings, and tools in a maximum of 30 feet (9 metres) of water. In 1991, the generic ship's bell from the *Acadia* was found and displayed in a museum in the Canadian Sault. Deeper explorations have yielded nothing further.

133. *CHICAGO*

OCTOBER 23, 1929   LAKE SUPERIOR

Left: *The propeller,* Chicago, *departing Buffalo, New York.*   (KOHL-FORSBERG ARCHIVES)
Right: *Salvage efforts to save the 28-year-old* Chicago *failed.*   (GREAT LAKES HISTORICAL SOCIETY)

At one of the most remote locations in all of the Great Lakes, the wreck of a large, steel freighter, the *Chicago* (324'2" x 44' x 14'), lies in 10 to 70 feet (3 to 21 metres) of water. That location is Shafer Bay, at the extreme western end of Michipicoten Island. This massive land entity, third in size after Isle Royale and St. Ignace Island among all of the Lake Superior islands, sits about 35 miles (56.7 kms.) from the nearest mainland marina at Michipicoten Harbour, Ontario. On Michipicoten Island, a handful of commercial fishermen make Québec Harbour their temporary summer season residence. There are no stores, no accommodations, no restaurants, no marinas, and no airfill stations for scuba divers anywhere on this wilderness island.

The 3,195-ton *Chicago*, built at Buffalo, New York, and launched on September 28, 1901, succumbed to the rocky reefs at the western end of Michipicoten Island on October 23, 1929, during a blinding snowstorm. The crew's travails began many miles away, when their captain decided that the weather was too severe to enter their ship into the Portage Lake Ship Canal on the Keweenaw Peninsula, so they steamed north to round the peninsula's tip. Blinding snow, enormous waves, and 50 mile-an-hour winds gripped the vessel tightly, pushing the ship, its compass now gone awry, eastward across Lake Superior out of control. When they finally hit the rocks, the confused captain thought they had stranded on Parisienne Island, far to the south! No lives were lost from the 31 people on board at the time. They camped on the island after removing provisions from their damaged, stranded ship. Days later, Coast Guard Cutter No. *119* and the tug, *Seminole,* launched their lifeboats to remove the crew, with the *Seminole* taking them to Sault Ste. Marie.

During salvage operations on December 19, 1929, the ship, valued at $167.500, slid off the rocks down a submerged slope, making the *Chicago* a permanent island feature.

This shipwreck lies on her port side on that slope and the site offers good visiblity, with views of a capstan on the stern deck, the cargo of zinc ingots (each one stamped with "Anaconda Brass Special," most of which have been recovered by salvagers and visitors over the years), two chains running down a stern hawsepipe, a chain locker, a propeller and its hub, the large boiler, and a stream anchor. The bow, in the shallows, is badly broken up, but it still exhibits a windlass and a popped-out hawsepipe with chain still running through the opening.

Any visitor who makes it this far to this site will definitely take a very good look!

134. *Bannockburn*

November 22, 1902   Lake Superior

Above: *The* Bannockburn *was named after the June 23-24, 1314, "Battle of Bannockburn" that resulted in Scotland's independence from Britain.* Right: *The Montréal Transportation Company, which owned the* Bannockburn, *soon gave her up as lost.*   (Both: Kohl-Forsberg Archives)

ALL HOPE ABANDONED.

BANNOCKBURN GIVEN UP FOR LOST AT KINGSTON.

Buffalo Schooner Celtic Foundered in Lake Huron—Crew of the Steamer Hebard Saved.

(Special Dispatch to The Globe.)

Kingston, Dec. 2.—All hope of the missing steamer Bannockburn has been given up by the M. T. Company's officials and friends of those aboard the boat. Of a crew of 21 Kingston claimed eleven—George Booth, chief engineer; Charles Selby, second en-

Built in Middlesborough, England, in 1893, the 1,620-gross-ton, steel freighter, **Bannockburn** (245' x 40'1" x 18'4"), survived crossing the Atlantic Ocean, but succumbed to Lake Superior, the greatest of the Great Lakes.

The **Bannockburn** worked on the Great Lakes hauling bulk cargoes, mostly grain, between the Lakehead ports at western Lake Superior clear across to Montréal, frequently towing the huge schooner-turned-barge named the **Minnedosa** carrying the same cargo.

But the **Bannockburn** was traveling solo, without any tow, due to the risk of bad weather that late in the season when she made her final trip. Downbound with a cargo of grain from Port Arthur (Thunder Bay), Ontario, on November 21, 1902, the **Bannockburn** passed the passenger steamer, **Hamonic**, that night, which noticed nothing amiss or out of the ordinary with the freighter. This was, however, the last time that anyone ever saw the **Bannockburn** or her 22 crew. Somewhere along the stormy wind's trail that pushed the ship southeast, the **Bannockburn** disappeared. The strong "ghost ship" aura that surrounds her arose because hardly a trace of remnants or bodies was found from her, other than a lifebelt located more than a year later, and, several years after that, an oar with the ship's named barely visible on it.

The **Bannockburn** had sailed into infinity. Over the next few years, several alleged sightings of the **Bannockburn**, sailing at night or in the hazy distance, earned her the nickname, "The Flying Dutchman of the Great Lakes."

Since the **Bannockburn** was last seen in the middle of Lake Superior, she could lie in either U.S. or Canadian waters. The weather might have pushed her onto Superior Shoal, which would not be located by hydrographers for nearly another 40 years, identified as a dangerous series of pinnacles rising from hundreds of feet in the bottom of Lake Superior to within about 22-to-28 feet below the surface. Several shipwrecks probably lie there.

One year, soon, a submersible exploring the depths of Lake Superior will send photos and video of a shipwreck with a smokestack that displays the letters, "MTCo," for the Montréal Transportation Company, which owned the **Bannockburn** at the time of loss.

Much of the mystery, and that "Flying Dutchman" aura, will then disappear.

135. *CERISOLES* AND *INKERMAN*

NOVEMBER 24, 1918   LAKE SUPERIOR

Left: *The* **Navarin** *was one of the lookalike sister ships to the* **Cerisoles** *and* **Inkerman.**
Right: *Newspapers followed the search for the missing minesweepers on a daily basis.*
(BOTH: KOHL-FORSBERG ARCHIVES)

We're going to view two similar shipwrecks as a single entity in this case.

Twelve French ships of war were under construction in 1918 by the Canadian Car and Foundry Company of Fort William, Ontario, in efforts to speed up World War One's end. Three of these trawler-minesweepers, the *Cerisoles*, the *Inkerman*, and the *Sebastopol* (each measured 135′6″ x 26′2″ x 12′7″), left Fort William on November 23, 1918, headed for Europe by way of the Sault, the St. Lawrence River, and Boston. Each was truly a ship of war, armed with a 100mm cannon on the forward deck and another at the stern.

But the gales of November blew devastatingly hard on Lake Superior that year, and ocean-going sailors have long decried the stormy terrors of the Great Lakes as being worse than those which any ocean could hurtle their way. These three ships became separated off the Keweenaw Peninsula, with only the *Sebastopol* reaching the Sault on November 26, 1918. The *Cerisoles* and the *Inkerman,* with their French crews totaling 76 men, along with two Canadian pilots, were never heard from again. Ironically, World War I had ended 12 days earlier.

The *Cerisoles* had been launched on September 25, 1918, and the *Inkerman*, on October 10, 1918; both were completed and ready to leave the yard by late November.

Wreckage likely from the two minesweepers came ashore near Grand Marais, Michigan: an unpainted lifeboat and some broken lumber painted lead-gray, the traditional war colour of ships. In July 1919, the bodies of two men, believed to have been from the missing minesweepers, were found on the north shore of Lake Superior.

The remaining ten warships made it safely to Boston where the vessels were disarmed due to suspicions of their heavy cannons causing stability problems. Many experienced Great Lakes sailors believed that the missing ships probably had their bottoms torn out when they scraped over shoals (either at the Keweenaw or on the as-yet-undiscovered Superior Shoals) during the storm. Either or both of these two vessels could be in Canadian or U.S. waters of Lake Superior. The day that a submersible exploring the bottom of Lake Superior first spies a World War I cannon mounted on a pocket battleship will be the day that the mystery of the *Cerisoles* and the *Inkerman* will be solved.

Sponsored by the **Thunder Bay Museum**
425 Donald Street East, Thunder Bay, ON P7E 5V1   Tel.: 807-623-0801
Go to www.thunderbaymuseum.com or view us on Facebook, Twitter, Flickr & Pinterest
A year-round museum, historical society, and archives for Thunder Bay and N.W. Ontario

136. WHALEBACK BARGE *115*

DECEMBER 18, 1899   LAKE SUPERIOR

Barge 115 *was launched on August 15, 1891, at Superior, Wisconsin.*   (KOHL-FORSBERG ARCHIVES)

Whaleback barge *115* (256' x 36'1" x 18'9"), the last Great Lakes shipwreck of the 1800s, disappeared somewhere in northern Lake Superior when people on land were busily preparing for Christmas. Regular folks went Christmas shopping, while eight sailors fought for their lives in mid-December in the harshest of the Great Lakes.

At Two Rivers, Minnesota, the 1,169-gross-ton barge *115* was loaded with 3,000 tons of iron ore, attached to the whaleback steamer, *Colgate Hoyt,* and the two vessels headed for the Soo on December 10, 1899, on their final run of the season. They sailed right into one of the worst storms of the year. Three days later, the ships were somewhere off northern Lake Superior when the tow line parted due to the storm strain. The towing *Hoyt* lost its helpless barge *115,* along with the eight crewmembers who were on board.

The frantic *Hoyt* zigzagged back and forth searching for its lost partner, but barge *115* was gone. There was nothing to do but to steam to Sault Ste. Marie and find tugs to help scour the lake. This was done, but also to no avail. Lake men feared that barge *115* had gone down and its crew had drowned. The searches were called off.

But on board barge *115*, Captain Arthur A. Boyce and his seven men were only lost, not dead, but they did drift helplessly in the blizzard for five terrifying days before *115* stranded off some wilderness shore. A small life raft took the entire crew, in shifts, safely to land (their main lifeboat had washed away). The next day, the men began walking along the shoreline, wading through thick snow past precipitous cliffs. Before long, they became aware that they were on an island. However, they could see the mainland in the distance.

In an abandoned log cabin, they found spikes, nails, and enough wood to fashion a large raft (since they had left their small life raft on the other side of the island) which, by some miracle with all eight men often standing in freezing water up to their knees, conveyed them to the mainland, eagerly propelled by their makeshift paddles.

PIG BARGE

IS ADRIFT

The Whaleback No. 115 May Have Gone Down.

HAD CREW OF EIGHT MEN

LOST ON SUPERIOR IN TERRIFIC STORM LAST MONDAY NIGHT.

Early Report Was of Very Sensational Nature to the Effect That the Hoyt and No. 115 Had Probably Gone Down With Crews, Including Extras Numbering Nearly Fifty Men—Only One is Missing.

MARQUETTE, Mich., Dec. 15.—A special to the Mining Journal from Houghton tonight contains a statement

Left: *Early newspaper accounts presumed that* 115 *was permanently lost.*
Below: *The wreck site on Pic Island.*
     (BOTH: KOHL-FORSBERG ARCHIVES)
Right: *Wreckage from Barge* 115 *can be found 50 feet (15 metres) up the cliff on Pic Island.*   (PHOTO BY CRIS KOHL)

NOT TO BE USED FOR NAVIGATION

Once across, they struggled to find any humans who could help them. They stumbled upon the Canadian Pacific Railroad track and reached the nearest town, more dead than alive. But all of them were, indeed, alive. The first search for missing whaleback barge *115* was over.

The First Mate of barge *115* personally recounted details of the crew's experiences:

...Some of the men took extra clothes with them and in the party we had two loaves of bread and a ham, besides our pockets full of candles....We landed in a small cove and began to climb up the steep bluff....The snow was about three feet deep....The first night we camped in the woods and the next day we started along the shore line. It was then that we found that we were on an island. As we followed the shore we came across a log cabin.... It was without a roof and had a part of an old sheet iron stove. We had taken ashore from the barge an axe and some matches and we all began to cut boughs and make a roof for the shanty and to make a fire in the stove.... [The next] morning we could see the mainland, about three miles away. We ripped the old shanty down and made a raft... and sank knee deep in the water when we all boarded her...but we started out. ...we landed....after struggling four days in search of human beings, we struck the tracks of the Canadian Pacific road. ...At last we met two section hands, who told us that the nearest town was Middleton, a mile and a half away....The Canadian Pacific people took good care of us....

The wild, rough, rocky shoreline of Pic Island is as inhospitable today as it was in 1899. Joan Forsberg stares from an inflatable boat, amazed by this wilderness setting. (PHOTO BY CRIS KOHL)

The single fairlead on 115's *bow, mounted on a blunt nose, identifies this wreck as a whaleback.* (PHOTO BY JOE LARK)

A diver approaches the most intact part of the 115's *wreckage, the bow.* (PHOTO BY JOE LARK)

You will need a boat to take you out to Pic Island, a few miles off Neys Provincial Park on the Canadian mainland. The broken, steel wreck of this whaleback, located by Ryan LeBlanc in 1980, ending the second major search for barge *115*, lies on a rock bottom 40 to 80 feet (12 to 24 metres) deep. Only the bow, with its deck house, is intact, with braided steel wire wrapped around a large windlass. Immense twisted steel sheets, all that remain of the hull, lie scattered nearby.

The crew of the whaleback barge *115* lost their ship and cargo, but their lives were saved. All of them made it home just in time to be with their overjoyed families for Christmas 1899, the last holiday of the nineteenth century, and for New Year's Day 1900, the first day, the dawn, of a new century and a new era.

A large deck winch on the 115 *sits in place near the superstructure.* (PHOTO BY JERRY ELIASON)

137. *JUDGE HART*

NOVEMBER 27, 1942   LAKE SUPERIOR

On Wreck in Blizzard 36 Hours, Crew Rescued

Men of Grain Carrier Judge Hart Reach Toronto After Terrible Ordeal in Lake Superior

Twenty survivors — the entire crew—of the ill-fated grain carrier, Judge Hart, which now lies 276 feet below the ice-encrusted surface of Lake Superior, are in Toronto to-day, little the worse for wear after thirty-six harrowing hours of a blizzard that rocked them under the impetus of a fifty-three-mile-an- frozen solidly, could not be closed. Later, when a wheelsman came on duty, the door froze behind him and could not be closed.

The John Ericsson, in attempting to get near the sinking Judge Hart, dragged her anchor for two hours, before getting it down in forty-six fathoms—about 276 feet—of water.

It was learned that insurance on

Left: *The freighter,* **Judge Hart,** *was built in England to fit perfectly in the Welland Canal locks.*
Right: *Despite wartime conditions, the loss was publicized.* (BOTH: KOHL-FORSBERG ARCHIVES)

The steel propeller, ***Judge Hart*** (252'2" x 43'2" x 24'), struck Simon's Reef in Ashburton Bay, northern Lake Superior, on November 28, 1942, while cruising downbound from Fort William, Ontario, to Toronto with 101,500 bushels of wheat. Help was nearby in the form of the steamers ***John Ericsson*** and ***James B. Eads***, which, with their combined horsepowers, pulled the ***Judge Hart*** free from her rocky perch. Unfortunately, the hole in her hull was too huge for the pumps to control the rushing waters; the 21 crewmembers on board were rescued by the steamers, and their ship drifted and sank in deep water.

The 1,729-gross-ton ***Judge Hart*** had been built at Cowes, England, in 1923. Owned by Eastern Steamships Ltd. of Port Colborne, Ontario, from 1923 until 1937, she ended her career belonging to the Upper Lakes & St. Lawrence Transportation Company Ltd. of Toronto for the last five years of her active life. The ship carried twin scotch boilers, and her triple expansion engine could produce 900 horsepower.

Discovered by well-known Lake Superior shipwreck hunters/scuba divers Jerry Eliason from Minnesota and Kraig Smith from Wisconsin in mid-June 1990, the ***Judge Hart*** sits upright in about 180 feet (54 metres) of water in near-perfect condition. The underwater images presented by James Marshall of this shipwreck that co-author Cris Kohl first viewed in Sault Ste. Marie, Ontario, in November 1990, were absolutely incredible, revealing jaw-dropping sights such as the pilothouse, with the radio headphones still sitting on the counter, the wooden ship's wheel solidly in place next to an upright telegraph, or chadburn, and the binnacle, with the compass inside its housing, perfectly intact.

The magnificently intact nature of the **Judge Hart** *can be seen from the condition of the ship's binnacle and railings* (left) *and the pilothouse interior* (right). (BOTH PHOTOS ARE BY DARRYL ERTEL)

138. *RAPPAHANNOCK*

JULY 25, 1911   LAKE SUPERIOR

Above: *The* Rappahannock *was named after a river in Virginia, the site of a major US Civil War battle.*
Right: *The huge, wooden steamer,* Rappahannock, *docked at Fort William, Ontario.*
(BOTH: KOHL-FORSBERG ARCHIVES)

A mid-summer storm in 1911 pounded the *Rappahannock* (308'1" x 42'5" x 21'2") with 70-mile-an-hour winds on the open waters of northern Lake Superior. The steamer and her tow, the 360-foot-long barge, *Montezuma*, were both loaded with coal from Ashtabula, Ohio, heading towards Duluth, but at 5:30 that morning, the towline broke and the ships were separated (the tow was later picked up by another steamer). His ship already leaking badly, with his crew sweating from hours of nonstop pumping to keep the vessel afloat, Captain W. Z. Ratley knew that it was time to retreat. The only safe retreat was Jackfish Bay, which they managed to reach that night at 10:30, right when their steering gave way. The crew ran their ship aground at 11 p.m. However, instead of being able to stay put on the stranded ship and relax, the tired crew soon realized that the ship's stern, hanging over deep water, was sinking. They abandoned ship in lifeboats at 12:40 a.m., and the ship sank half an hour later in water 35 to 85 feet deep. The crew camped on the shore that warm night.

The *Rappahannock,* built at West Bay City, Michigan, and launched on June 6, 1895, was found by Ryan LeBlanc in 1979, its hull, decks, and housings, including a walkway with carved, wooden supports in excellent shape.

Left: *Joe Lark approaches an open doorway on the lower deck of the* Rappahannock; *considerable white paint remains on the walls and posts in this walkway.*   (PHOTO BY JOYCE HAYWARD)
Right: *Ryan LeBlanc, who found the* Rappahannock *in 1979, poses with the huge ship's wheel, which he was instrumental in getting returned to the wreck.*   (PHOTO BY CRIS KOHL)

139. GUNILDA

AUGUST 11, 1911   LAKE SUPERIOR

The fabulous, luxury yacht, Gunilda, *underway at full speed.* (KOHL-FORSBERG ARCHIVES)

The fabulous, luxury yacht, Gunilda, *dead stopped on rocks.* (KOHL-FORSBERG ARCHIVES)

Shipwreck hunter Ryan LeBlanc examines the Gunilda's *mast in front of the Rossport Inn, where the yacht's people stayed after their ship sank.* (PHOTO BY CRIS KOHL)

Proclaimed to be "the most beautiful shipwreck in the world" by leading authority Jacques Cousteau in 1980, the *Gunilda* lies in deep water off Rossport, Ontario.

The 385-gross-ton, palatial, steel steam yacht, *Gunilda* (195' with her bowsprit -- x 24'7" x 14'2"), built at Leith, Scotland, in 1897, was powered by a triple expansion engine, capable of producing 109 horsepower, and her two scotch boilers, all built by the same firm that constructed the hull.

The *Gunilda* was a beautiful yacht used for entertainment and travel by William Harkness, a wealthy capitalist (or "robber baron," which was the expression in popular use by some people at the turn of the twentieth century.) Harkness, living in Cleveland, Ohio, was one of the original investors with John D. Rockefeller in the Standard Oil Company.

On August 29, 1911, the *Gunilda* cruised past wilderness islands along the nothern shore of Lake Superior. On board were Mr. Harkness, his family, a number of friends, and his crew. Harkness had not hired a local pilot because he considered the $15 fee for his services to be a waste of money. Suddenly, tragedy struck when the *Gunilda* grounded solidly on McGarvey's Shoal on the northeast side of Copper Island near Rossport, Ontario. No one was injured, but the front third of the vessel was high and dry.

Mr. Harkness was nonplussed. He calmly arranged for the tug, *James Whalen,* and the barge, *Empire*, to release his yacht so he could be on his way; this was, after all, only a minor inconvenience. Fortunately, the passengers and crew were removed to the Rossport Inn before the salvage commenced. When Harkness was told that a second tug would be required to keep the *Gunilda* upright as it was being towed off the rock, Harkness balked, refusing to hire another boat. So, on August 11, 1911, the *Whalen* pulled, the *Gunilda* moved, and, once off the rock, she listed to starboard and sank, stern first,

Sponsored by **DISCOVERY CHARTERS AND TOURS**
224 Church Street, Box 99, Rossport, ON P0T 2R0
Tel.: (807) 824-3323 Email: discoverypb@yahoo.ca www.discoverycharters.ca
Tour Lake Superior's North Shore and Dive the Wrecks of the *Gunilda* and *Judge Hart*!

in 257 feet (78 metres) of water next to the shoal. Now there was absolutely no hope of salvage.

The ship was valued at over $100,000. William Harkness paid off his crew, and his party simply returned home by means of the Northern Navigation steamship, *Huronic*, and land travel. He bought himself another boat to replace the one which he had just lost.

Eight years later, the *Gunilda* was mentioned as a highlight in Mr. Harkness' obituary in the *New York Times* of May 11, 1919:

> **William L. Harkness, capitalist and yachtsman, died of heart disease at his home, 12 East Fifty-third Street....**
>
> **He was the owner of the *Gunilda*, a $100,000 yacht which was stranded eight years ago on the north shore of Lake Superior. His family and a party of guests from the city were aboard, but no one was injured. Mr. Harkness was a member of the New York Yacht Club and the Corinthian Club.**

Rumours that this wealthy yacht carried jewels in a safe, fine china, precious silverware, and rare vintage wines soon circulated. Several attempts over the years have been made at salvage of this incredible vessel, but all failed due to the immense depth of water. One Thunder Bay, Ontario, diver named Charles King Hague died on August 8, 1970, while exploring the wreck; another diver died under rather mysterious sircumstances in 1989. This deep site is unforgiving of any errors.

In the early 1980s, diver Ryan LeBlanc of nearby Schreiber, Ontario, was part of a team that experimented with mixed gas, and he made 16 dives to the *Gunilda* to film her, but called it quits when the risk factors became too great.

A mast from the *Gunilda*, recovered years ago by means of a grappling hook, has been beautifully restored as a flagpole in front of the Rossport Inn, which itself contains an interesting *Gunilda* display.

This shipwreck was legally purchased from the insurance company by diver Fred Broennle, who succeeded in recovering a number of artifacts, but when he passed away in April 2013, he had succeeded mainly in raising the public's awareness of this part of Great Lakes History.

The *Gunilda* proudly sits upright and intact, and is carefully watched by the local residents because it is their small town's personal treasure.

The ship's wheel remains one of the most impressive sights on the Gunilda.
(PHOTO: DAN LINDSAY, SEA-VIEWDIVING.COM)

Ahead of the ship's wheel is the binnacle, which houses the Gunilda's *main compass.*
(PHOTO: DAN LINDSAY, SEA-VIEWDIVING.COM)

A deck-mounted searchlight on the Gunilda *has stayed dark for more than a century.*
(PHOTO: DAN LINDSAY, SEA-VIEWDIVING.COM)

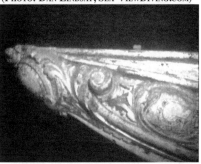

The gold foil covering the ornate wooden bow scrollwork still glitters and shines.
(PHOTO: DAN LINDSAY, SEA-VIEWDIVING.COM)

140. *ONTARIO*

AUGUST 10, 1899   LAKE SUPERIOR

A TOTAL LOSS.

ONTARIO RAN ASHORE IN A DENSE FOG YESTERDAY MORNING.

Jackfish, August 10.—The Canadian steamer Ontario, bound for Nipigon with a cargo of coal, went ashore this morning near Rossport and is a total loss. The steamer went on the beach in a dense fog about 3 o'clock. Her crew were rescued and her consorts escaped to the beach. The Ontario was formerly a passenger steamer, and is owned by Capt. John Cornwell and others, of Sombra, Ont.
The steamer had in tow the schooners

Left: *The steamer,* Ontario, *built in 1874, sank in a storm during the summer of 1899.*
Right: *Since no lives were lost, many witnesses could tell reporters their story of the* **Ontario's**
loss.   (BOTH ITEMS: KOHL-FORSBERG ARCHIVES)

The wooden, passenger/freight steamer, *Ontario* (181' x 35' x 12'2"), rebuilt as a 723-gross-ton bulk carrier in the year before her career ended, smashed onto the rocks in the shallows just off the eastern end of Battle Island in northern Lake Superior about seven miles (11 kms.) from Rossport, Ontario, on August 10, 1899, during an unusual summer snowstorm. The ship was bound for Nipigon, Ontario, with a cargo of coal at the time of loss. No lives were lost.

This shipwreck was located on October 23, 1977, by Ryan LeBlanc, at that time living in Schreiber, Ontario, and his team. They found a clue on shore -- one of the *Ontario's* huge boilers -- despite the fact that this boiler was totally covered in logs, tree branches, and other debris! The *Ontario's* other boiler lies just off this shore in about ten feet (three metres) of water. The wreck, broken up and scattered, rests on a rock and sand bottom, with timbers and other wreckage extending around the point to the north of the land boiler. By August, visibility can be low due to algae blooms forming in the warmed-up water.

In 1882, the *Ontario* carried a regiment of Northwest Mounted Police from Sarnia to Duluth, from whence they continued to the Canadian West just before the transcontinental railroad (the Canadian Pacific Railway) was finished. The *Ontario* also hauled food supplies, such as beef cattle for fresh meat, to the construction teams of the C.P.R.

Left: *Joyce Hayward and Ryan LeBlanc explore the huge* **Ontario** *boiler that nature beached on the rocky shore adjacent to the wreck site. Ryan's team found this wreck in 1977.*
Right: *Ryan LeBlanc explores some of the* **Ontario's** *wreckage.*   (BOTH PHOTOS ARE BY CRIS KOHL)

141. *MARY E. MCLACHLAN*

NOVEMBER 7, 1921   LAKE SUPERIOR

The **Mary E. McLachlan,** *an enormous, four-masted (later reduced to two as a barge) schooner, experienced a tragic launch in 1893 at West Bay City, Michigan.*   (KOHL-FORSBERG ARCHIVES)

The huge, four-masted schooner, *Mary E. McLachlan* (251′ x 41′ x 16′2″), built as hull number 96 by Frank Wheeler & Company at West Bay City, Michigan, was launched on March 2, 1893, an event that killed several people when 30 spectators on board a nearby ship were knocked into the water, despite having been warned to move. This was not a good beginning for the *McLachlan*. Named after the owner's mother (who died in 1899 at the age of 81 without ever having seen her namesake), the *Mary E. MacLachlan* provided an unusual rescue in October 1913. When the steamer, *Lackawanna*, lost her rudder gear, the engineless *Mary E. McLachlan* was lashed to the bigger boat and steered for both of them while the steam from the *Lackawanna's* engines furnished the motive power.

The *Mary E. McLachlan* was sold to Canadian interests in 1916. She foundered in a storm in shallow water with no lives lost on November 7, 1921.

Located by Ryan LeBlanc on May 16, 1981, the wreck of the *Mary E. McLachlan* lies in 15 to 35 feet (4.5 to 10.5 metres) of water east of the town of Nipigon, Ontario, one mile off the mainland in Mountain Bay, halfway between Rossport, Ontario, and Vert Island to the west. Water visibility is often poor here because two rivers flow into the wreck.

Left: *The* McLachlan's *bell was raised years ago and donated to a local historical society.*
(PHOTO BY CRIS KOHL)

Right: *Co-author Cris Kohl and early Lake Superior shipwreck hunter, Ryan LeBlanc, at the latter's home in 1995.*
(PHOTO SET-UP BY CRIS KOHL)

Sponsored by **The Township of Nipigon,**
52 Front St., PO Box 160, Nipigon, ON P0T 2J0
Contact: Suzanne Kukko (807) 887-3135 ext 26   edo@nipigon.net   www.nipigon.net
Nipigon is a unique community one hour east of Thunder Bay, Ontario

142. *MARY ANN HULBERT*

DECEMBER 13, 1883   LAKE SUPERIOR

Left: *The 67-foot-long* **Mary Ann Hulbert** *resembled this vessel, the 65-foot-long* **Experiment,** *which was wrecked in 1902 on Lake Michigan with several lives lost.*

Right: *The steamer,* **Kincardine,** *was towing the* **Hulbert** *when the latter sank with all hands. Nine years later, the* **Kincardine** *was wrecked on Lake Huron.* (BOTH: KOHL-FORSBERG ARCHIVES)

One of the smallest sailboats ever to sail on Lake Superior holds the tragic record for the most lives lost in any sailing vessel shipwreck on that lake.

The two-masted, 62-ton schooner, *Mary Ann Hulbert* (67'1" x 20'2" x 7'1"), built in 1856 at Sandusky, Ohio, was used by the U. S. government in 1862 as a supply vessel serving indigenous people in the Lake Superior region.

The *Mary Ann Hulbert*, by this time owned in Ontonagon, Michigan, left Port Arthur, Ontario, on December 13, 1883, very late in the shipping season, under tow of the steam barge, *Kincardine,* both vessels loaded with construction materials for the Canadian Pacific Railroad at Michipicoten Harbour, near Wawa, Ontario. Besides her five crew members, the *Hulbert* carried 15 railroad construction workers. By 10 p.m., when both ships were off St. Ignace Island, a violent storm arose. The seams on the *Hulbert* opened and the ship began to sink. Although those on board the *Kincardine* could hear the cries for help coming from the *Hulbert,* they were powerless to assist in these mountainous waves. When the *Hulbert* was clearly on the verge of sinking, the *Kincardine* cut the towline so their vessel would not be dragged to the bottom with her.

All 20 people crammed on board the small schooner, *Mary Ann Hulbert,* perished in this sinking. The press condemned this tragic loss, clearly stating that such an old vessel should never have been on Lake Superior waters in December. The *Hulbert* was worth only about $2,000 at the time of loss, but no price could be put on the 20 lives lost.

The Port Huron newspaper reported, on December 18, 1883, that

> The schr. *Mary Ann Hulbert* went down during the severe gale last Wednesday on the north shore of Lake Superior near Duluth with 20 men on board.

and six days later, the same paper reported on the misfortunes of the towing steamer:

> The Canadian steamer *Kincardine* in trying to force her way through the ice at Jackfish Bay, Lake Superior had a hole stove in her bow, filled rapidly and sunk. Her stern lies in 20' of water at the entrance of Jackfish Bay and cannot be raised this winter....

Clearly, December was not a time to be on Lake Superior. The *Kincardine*, recovered in the spring of 1884, was permanently wrecked on a rocky shoreline near the tip of the Lake Huron's Bruce Peninsula in 1892. The *Mary Ann Hulbert* wreck awaits discovery.

143. *Neebing*

September 24, 1937   Lake Superior

Left: *The* **John B. Ketcham II**, *seen in this picture taken by famous photographer Louis Pesha, was renamed* **Coalhurst** *in early 1927 and, in 1928,* Neebing.
Right: *The loss of lives in 1937 prompted big headlines.*   (Both Items: Kohl-Forsberg Archives)

Six lives were lost when the gravel carrier, *Neebing* (193' x 40'5" x 12'3"), keeled over and foundered in a severe southeast gale on September 24, 1937, one quarter of a mile off the north tip of Moss Island in the Nipigon Straits, and only one-third of a mile off the mainland. The *Neebing's* captain, the chief engineer, a fireman, the male cook, and his wife, the assistant cook, were the five immediate victims. A small rowboat was launched by the three men on board the *Coteau*, eventually picking up ten men, including two who had swum to Moss Island. A sixth life was lost when one of the picked-up crewmen, temporarily knocked uncouscious when a hatch cover struck him as the *Neebing* sank, died in hospital from injuries (a fractured skull) received in the disaster. The *Neebing*, with the barge, *Coteau*, in tow, was hauling a load of gravel from Paradise Island bound for Red Rock, Ontario, for its owner, the Sin-Mac Lines Company of Montréal.

Another Sin-Mac Lines boat, the 81-foot-long tug, *Strathmore* (launched as the *D.S. Pratt* at Midland, Ontario, in 1911), steaming out of Red Rock, Ontario, passed through shipwreck debris, including a *Neebing* nameboard. Seeing the *Coteau* anchored in the distance, the *Strathmore* changed course and headed towards the barge, later removing the *Neebing's* survivors and taking them to Red Rock. A reported explosion on board the *Neebing* was only the lake water as it hit the boiler and "forced smoke out of the funnel more than 50 feet high with a loud puff," according to the *Coteau's* captain.

Three days after the sinking, the wreck was found by the *Strathmore* using sounding and dragging operations carried out under the supervision of the Sin-Mac Lines. A hardhat diver, who was sent down after a ship's anchor pulled up a section of the *Neebing's* forward cabin, reported absolutely no visibility and was thus unable to search for bodies. Six days after the sinking, one of the five missing bodies was recovered. In mid-November 1937, the 365-foot-long salvage ship, *Maplecourt* (formerly the *North West* -- see page 43), owned by Port Arthur's United Towing & Salvage Company which may have purchased the wreck for possible recovery, put a hardhat diver on the *Neebing*, but he could not locate the remaining four bodies.

This wreck, lying in approximately 60 to 108 feet (18 to 32 metres) of water, is intact, with even the huge crane that was sitting on its deck; unfortunately, the remains of drowned crewmembers have reportedly been seen by scuba divers recently on this shipwreck.

The *Neebing* was the second steel-hulled lumber carrier on the lakes when she was built as the *John B. Ketcham II* at Toledo, Ohio, and launched on May 21, 1892. Valued at $75,000 in 1892, age, and inactivity for most of the 1930s, rusted much of her steel hull.

144. *St. Andrew*

September 20, 1900   Lake Superior

The Canadian, wooden propeller, St. Andrew, *was wrecked in 1900.*   (Kohl-Forsberg Archives)

Launched originally as the 157-foot-long *W. B. Hall* at the Louis Shickluna Shipyard at St. Catharines, Ontario, in 1885, the *St. Andrew* received her name change, as well as 35 feet (10.5 metres) of length, in 1897, the year she was sold by Toronto's William B. Hall to James Playfair & Company of Midland, Ontario. Her engine came from the tug, *W. T. Robb*, which had been built at Stromness near Port Maitland, Ontario, in 1864, and which was dismantled in Toronto in 1883, with the *Robb's* hull later being turned into a pier at Toronto's Victoria Park. The *St. Andrew's* final dimensions were 192'6" x 27'9" x 12'4".

The *St. Andrew* ran hard onto the rocks off the southern edge of Blanchard Island (itself only about half a mile long, running north and south, and one-quarter of a mile wide) on Thursday, September 20, 1900, while enroute during a storm from Jackfish Bay to Port Arthur, Ontario, to pick up a cargo of wheat for delivery to Kingston. Three of the 16-person crew jumped safely to the island before large waves carried the ship 100 feet (30 metres) farther off shore, and only a strong, young fellow swimming with a line from the ship to the three men already on the island allowed the entire crew to reach land unharmed. Soon the vessel slid off the rocky ledge into 60 feet (18 metres) of water. The tug, *Georgina,* rescued the marooned crew the next day and took them to Port Arthur.

The *St. Andrew's* machinery was salvaged, and she lies broken with numerous artifacts, such as blocks and carts, scattered about. There is metal strapping around part of the wooden hull. In 1975, the first divers to explore the site picked up, among other items, the ship's bell (it's gone now). A small island, about six miles (10 kms.) southwest of the wreck, was named St. Andrew Island in commemoration of this ship.

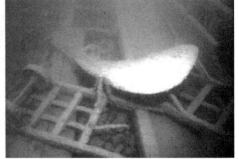

Left: *Broken timbers from the* St. Andrew *lie on the lake bottom.* **Right:** *Hand carts and a spare propeller blade remain interesting items on this shipwreck.*   (Both Photos: Joyce Hayward)

145. *SCOTIADOC*

JUNE 20, 1953   LAKE SUPERIOR

Lake Freighters Ram One In Crew Drowns

Left: *The wheat-laden* Scotiadoc *sank within 30 minutes after colliding with the freighter,* Burlington.
Right: *The* Scotiadoc *loss was reported in the* Toronto Evening Telegram *on June 22, 1953.*
(BOTH: KOHL-FORSBERG ARCHIVES)

In dense Lake Superior fog at 6:40 p.m. on June 20, 1953, the upbound, 443-foot-long, 4,568-gross-ton steamer, *Burlington*, which carried no cargo, collided with the downbound, 4,432-gross-ton steamer, *Scotiadoc* (424′ x 48′1″ x 23′9″), loaded with 234,000 bushels of wheat bound for Prescott, Ontario. The *Scotiadoc*, rammed just aft of midship, sank in deep water about six miles (ten kms.) east of Thunder Cape off Trowbridge Island.

The only fatality was Wallace McDermid of Sault Ste. Marie, Ontario, the night cook on the *Scotiadoc*. As the lifeboat with him and four others in it was being lowered, it upset, spilling everyone into the lake. All except McDermid, who, being a polio victim, wore a heavy, steel leg brace, were able to grab onto lines hanging from the ship. No one saw him again after he fell into the water. The remaining 29 crew were rescued by the *Burlington*. Chief Engineer Albert Chalmers of Collingwood survived his third shipwreck; the first was the *Agawa* when it stranded on Manitoulin Island on December 7, 1927, and the second, the *Prindoc,* which sank in a collision off Isle Royale on June 1, 1943.

The *Scotiadoc* was launched as the *Martin Mullen* on May 14, 1904, at Cleveland, Ohio. Her triple expansion engine and twin scotch boilers produced 1,460 horsepower. Renamed *Scotiadoc* in 1947, this ship was owned by the Paterson Steamship Lines, while the *Burlington*, launched in 1899 as the *Henry W. Oliver* at Lorain, Ohio, and owned by the Canada Steamship Lines, was scrapped at Hamilton, Ontario, in 1967.

The wreck of the *Scotiadoc*, located in 2013 by Jerry Eliason and his team in 870 feet (263.6 metres) of water, is the deepest shipwreck found in the Great Lakes to date.

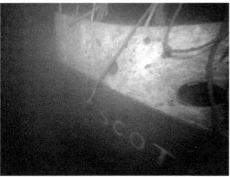

Scotiadoc *machinery and the ship's name on the hull.*
(ROV IMAGES COURTESY OF JERRY ELIASON)

146. *MARY ANN*

1933   LAKE SUPERIOR

The **Mary Ann,** *a tug built in 1867, has a unique claim to fame.* (BOTH: KOHL-FORSBERG ARCHIVES)

A wooden tug named the **Mary Ann** (78' x 15' x 8'), built by George Hardison at Stromness, Ontario (close to Port Maitland on eastern Lake Erie), holds a unique place in Canadian history -- she was the very first vessel registered in the new Dominion of Canada on July 1, 1867, the day Canada became a country.

This little boat picked up the crew of the steamer, *A. Neff,* when it was wrecked in October 1886, at northern Lake Superior's Edwards Island.

But by 1901, the 34-year-old **Mary Ann** was condemned and abandoned and, much later, in 1933, was scuttled off the Welcome Islands near Fort William/Port Arthur, Ontario.The 1920s and 1930s saw major clean-ups all around the Great Lakes, as old, wooden ships, which had been abandoned and allowed to sink along the shorelines of rivers, bays, and harbours, and had become serious eyesores due to their large numbers sticking out of the shallow waters where they rested, were raised, temporarily patched, towed out into deeper water, and scuttled. In those environmentally worry-free days, "out of sight" meant "out of mind." These ships, sunk so silently, were quickly forgotten.

Then, in the post-World-War-Two era, scuba divers came along, and they have been finding, whether by accident or by design, these scuttled wrecks ever since.

The **Mary Ann** was initially reported to have been one of the scuttled wrecks found in 2001 off Thunder Bay, Ontario, lying in 200+ feet of water. However, in 2013, two scuba divers taking their boat towards another wreck, found what was believed to be the **Mary Ann** sitting in 70 feet (21 metres) of water. Closer examination since then indicates that this ship might not be the **Mary Ann**. Stay tuned for further developments in the continuing story of what became of Canada's first, registered vessel!

147. GREEN RIVER

NOVEMBER 5, 1932   LAKE SUPERIOR

The **Green River,** *formerly the* **Gogebic,** *received her last name in 1921 when the ship was re-duced to a barge.*   (KOHL-FORSBERG ARCHIVES)

This huge, wooden ship, lying in 50 to 80 feet (15 to 24 metres) of water in the Welcome Islands just off shore from Thunder Bay, Ontario, is one of the more popular dive sites in the region due to the intact nature of its large hull and its comfortable depth.

The *Green River* (final dimensions: 275' x 40' x 22') was towed out and purposely sunk in one of Thunder Bay's "ships' graveyard" areas on November 5, 1932, simply to get rid of a leaky, old vessel that was too old to work and no longer worthwhile to repair.

Launched on October 1, 1887, as the 227-foot-long *Gogebic* at West Bay City, Michigan, by F. W. Wheeler & Company, mainly for the coal and ore trade (hauling coal from Lake Erie to Lake Superior, and returning to Lake Erie with iron ore), the ship cost $125,000 to build, an enormous sum in1887. For 33 years, the propeller was owned in a variety of locations, including Chicago, Detroit, Alpena, Erie, and Duluth, and in 1897 was lengthened by 50 feet (15 metres). The ship, however, stranded on June 13, 1919, with heavy damage, on Deadman's Island just east of Flatland Island, six miles (10 kms.) south of present day Thunder Bay, Ontario. The *Gogebic* was claimed for the salvage bill when Mr. James Whalen's Canadian Towing & Wrecking Company of Fort William recovered the vessel, reportedly at the high cost of $25,000. Reduced to a barge and renamed the *Green River* in 1921, the ship saw very little activity before it was stripped and scuttled in 1932. Sport divers accidentally found the wreck in late 1979 while heading to a different one.

148. *MONKSHAVEN*

NOVEMBER 28, 1905   LAKE SUPERIOR

Left: *The* Monkshaven *docked at the Canadian Soo.* Right: *The* Monkshaven *in October 1906, ashore again after a failed salvage attempt.*   (BOTH: KOHL-FORSBERG ARCHIVES)

The steel propeller, *Monkshaven* (249' x 36'1" x 17'5"), was a canaller-type freighter built at South Shields, Great Britain, by J. Readhead & Company in 1882. The vessel was purchased in 1900 by the Algoma Central Steamship Company of Sault Ste. Marie, Ontario.

The *Monkshaven* has the distinction of being the first victim of the Great Storm of 1905 -- which was actually the third severe, ship-sinking storm of that bad year on Lake Superior. Some of the other, well-known, Lake Superior victims of this November 28-30, 1905, storm (also called "The *Mataafa* Storm") are the *Mataafa*, the *LaFayette*, and the *Madeira*. The *Monkshaven* stranded on one of the tiny islets in a strip of several, rocky, treeless outcroppings called the Angus Islands, just one mile to the southeast of the much larger Pie Island near present-day Thunder Bay, Ontario. The 21 crewmembers, fearing that their ship would break up or be pushed into deep water and sink, jumped onto the barren islet. There they suffered from hunger and freezing exposure to the strong winds for three days on these inhospitable rocks. Only when the winds subsided did they dare return to the above-water bow section of their battered ship, where they found some clothing and food. Thirteen of the crew decided to row one of the yawlboats to the Lakehead for help, and, a few hours later, once they were in the main shipping lane, the freighter, *Sylvania*, picked them up and convyed them quickly to Fort William, from which point a tug was sent to the Angus Islands to save the remaining eight members of the crew.

Famed wrecking master, James Reid, was able to refloat the *Monkshaven* by August 10, 1906, and the ship remained secured to Angus Island while Reid was away working on another salvage job. During a storm on October 10, 1906, the *Monkshaven* ended up on the rocks again after having torn loose from her moorings. More autumn storms soon broke up the vessel, which was valued at $70,000.

The wreck of the *Monkshaven* was found in modern times by scuba divers Ken Engelbrecht, Randy Saulter, and Ken Merryman in 1978.

Although the *Monkshaven* was dynamited as part of the scrap metal salvage efforts during World War II, portholes and other items of interest remain at this site. Personal effects of crew members, such as razors, can still be seen in different pockets of sand.

The pieces of the *Monkshaven* can be seen beginning in knee-deep water, and extending to a depth of 70 feet (21 metres). The wreck is scattered and very broken up, and the propeller has no blades left.

149. *LEAFIELD*

NOVEMBER 9, 1913   LAKE SUPERIOR

The Leafield, *built in England following their tradition of the pilothouse in mid-ship, disappeared with all hands near Thunder Bay, Ontario, on November 9, 1913.*   (KOHL-FORSBERG ARCHIVES)

Towering waves lashed by hurricane-force winds are credited with destroying the steel propeller, *Leafield* (249' x 35'2" x 16'6"), during the notorious Great Storm of November 1913, but this loss was not in Lake Huron, where most of the storm's destruction was focused. Lake Superior experienced such a tempest that two freighters on that lake were victims of the gales of November: the *Leafield* off Canada's Lakehead, and the 525-foot-long *Henry B. Smith*, also lost with all hands, north of Marquette, Michigan.

The *Leafield* almost made it to safe harbour on November 9, 1913. She was only 14 miles (21 kms.) away from the twin cities of Port Arthur and Fort William (amalgamated and renamed Thunder Bay in 1969), carrying a cargo of steel rails and railroad track fastenings for the Canadian Pacific Railroad. The last people to see the *Leafield* (reportedly hard aground on Angus Island) were those on board the passenger steamer, *Hamonic*, which, after this incident, developed a morbid reputation for final sightings; see the story of the *Bannockburn* on page 184.

The *Leafield* disappeared after either diving into a huge wave trough offshore, or striking the rocks at Angus Island before sliding into deep water, accompanied by all 15 to 18 (depending upon one's sources of information) of her crew. It is rumoured that she lies at this latter location at a depth of 440 feet (133.3 metres).

The 1,454-gross-ton, steel-hulled *Leafield* was built in 1892 at Sunderland, England, and carried a triple expansion engine with one scotch boiler. The ship, valued at $100,000, was insured for $74,100; the cargo was insured for $70,000.

150. *HOWARD*

JUNE 13, 1921   LAKE SUPERIOR

The tug, Howard, was 57 years old when she stranded in fog, caught on fire, and burned to a complete loss off Victoria Island on Lake Superior in the spring of 1921.

(REV. PETER VAN DER LINDEN COLLECTION)

For a wooden ship built during the U.S. Civil War to stay active into the 1920s is nothing short of amazing. This vessel outlived most of the people who were born in 1864!

Built at Wilmington, Delaware, in 1864 as a Union gunboat during the tail end of the U.S. Civil War, and launched as the *Admiral D. D. Porter,* this ship was renamed *Howard* after a new owner, Henry Howard of Port Huron, Michigan, had her rebuilt there in 1889.

The large tug, *Howard* (114'5" x 22'2" x 10'), with a crew of 14 on board, met her end when she stranded in fog on June 13, 1921, at Victoria Island, south of Thunder Bay, Ontario, while on her way to pick up a barge loaded with pulpwood for delivery to Erie, Pennsylvania, on Lake Erie. The tug's mate took the lifeboat, and, solo, rowed west to Cloud Bay, struggled through the forest and underbrush to Scott Highway (today's Hwy. 61), hitched a ride into town, and arranged for the tug, *Strathbogie,* to aid the *Howard.* But by then, the *Howard* had caught on fire and sunk, with no lives lost.

In 1961, an early diver to this wreck site removed the *Howard's* brass whistle and donated it to the museum in Thunder Bay, Ontario. A barge reportedly lies underneath the wreck of the *Howard*; one source says this barge is what remains of the 160-foot-long *James P. Donaldson*, but the *Donaldson*, after burning at her dock, was stripped and scuttled on May 6, 1923, so it could not possibly be resting underneath the *Howard*, which sank two years earlier. Reports also give the location of the *Donaldson's* scuttling as being off the Welcome Islands, a fair distance away from Victoria Island.

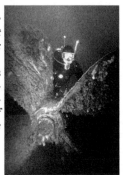

Left: *Don Edwards takes a close look at the* Howard's *firebox door.*
Right: *The* Howard's *four-bladed propeller catches Don's attention in 50 feet of water; the wreck lies in 45 to 120 feet.*
(BOTH PHOTOS: JOE LARK)

Canadian Ships Lost in U.S. Waters of the Great Lakes

As a counterbalance to the many U.S. vessels lying in Canadian waters are many Canadian ships that were wrecked in U.S. waters, and thus they are now the property of the state upon whose bottomlands they repose. Some of the more famous ones are:

Roy A. Jodrey
November 21, 1974   St. Lawrence River

The Algoma Central Railway motor vessel, *Roy A. Jodrey*, (640′6″ x 72′ x 40′), hauling 20,000 tons of iron ore pellets towards Detroit, struck a shoal near Wellesley Island at 3 a.m. and sank in very deep (250 feet; 75 metres) water. No lives were lost. The depth and the fast current make this a challenging site for technical divers.

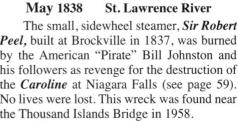

(KOHL-FORSBERG ARCHIVES)

Sir Robert Peel
May 1838   St. Lawrence River

The small, sidewheel steamer, *Sir Robert Peel,* built at Brockville in 1837, was burned by the American "Pirate" Bill Johnston and his followers as revenge for the destruction of the *Caroline* at Niagara Falls (see page 59). No lives were lost. This wreck was found near the Thousand Islands Bridge in 1958.

(KOHL-FORSBERG ARCHIVES)

H.M.S. *Ontario*
October 31, 1780   Lake Ontario

This 77-foot-long, British sailing ship sank in a violent storm during the Revolutionary War with about 130 people, including soldiers, women, children, and possibly 30 U.S. prisoners of war, perishing. This wreck, found by Jim Kennard, Dan Scoville, and Chip Stevens on May 31, 2008, rests in about 400 feet (120 metres) of water, masts up and cannons on deck!

The H.M.S. Ontario. (COURTESY OF THE ARTIST, PETER RINDLISBACHER)

The Frontenac. (ART BY C.H.J. SNIDER, COURTESY OF THE TORONTO REFERENCE LIBRARY)

Frontenac (steamer)
September 1827   Lake Ontario

The first steamship on the Great Lakes, the *Frontenac* (170' x 32' x 11'), built at Ernestown, Upper Canada (later Ontario), by several Kingston merchants, was powered by a British-built, Boulton-Watt, 50-horsepower steam engine. Although launched on September 7, 1816, her maiden voyage, from Kingston to York (Toronto), did not commence until June 17, 1817. This historic ship was destroyed near the mouth of the Niagara River by an arsonist's fire; her recovered engine was put into another ship.

Sand Merchant
October 17, 1936   Lake Erie

A steel sandsucker built at Collingwood, Ontario, in 1927, the *Sand Merchant* (252' x 43'6" x 17'5"), foundered in strong winds on October 17, 1936, with the loss of 19 lives, in Lake Erie, four miles northeast of Avon Point, Ohio. The ship was loaded with sand from the Point Pelee area bound for Cleveland. The wreck lies upside-down in 65 feet (19.5 metres) of water.

The sandsucker, Sand Merchant.

Regina
November 9, 1913   Lake Huron

A victim of the Great Storm of 1913, the worst storm in recorded Great Lakes history, the *Regina* (249'7" x 42'6" x 20'5"), built in Dumbarton, Scotland, in 1907 and owned by the Canadian Interlake Line, sank with the loss of all 15 hands in Lake Huron 6.5 miles (10 kms.) northeast of Lexington, Michigan. The wreck, upside-down in 83 feet of water, was found on July 1, 1986.

The steel freighter, Regina.

Minnedosa
October 20, 1905   Lake Huron

The largest sailing ship ever built on the Canadian side of the Great Lakes, the four-masted *Minnedosa* (243' x 35'6" x 16'9") was launched on April 26, 1890, at Kingston, Ontario. She sank in Lake Huron while under tow in a severe storm on October 20, 1905, with the loss of all hands. This wreck was located in 1991 after a long search by Dave Trotter and his team. The *Minnedosa* sits upright in 210 feet (63.6 metres) of water.

The mighty Minnedosa (THE ABOVE THREE IMAGES ARE FROM THE KOHL-FORSBERG ARCHIVES)

Magellan
November 9, 1877   Lake Michigan

The 330-gross-ton, three-masted schooner named the *Magellan* (137' x 23' x 11'8") was built by renowned shipbuilder, Louis Shickluna, at St. Catharines, Ontario, in 1873. This ship, a full-sized canal schooner, while bound from Chicago to Toronto with a cargo of 20,000 bushels of corn, encountered strong head winds off Two Rivers, Wisconsin, and dropped her anchor to wait for calmer weather. There is strong evidence that a steamer collided with the stationary *Magellan* that night. All eight men (seven were Canadians and one was reportedly from Clayton, New York) on board the *Magellan* were killed and, while a few bodies were found, only bits and pieces (hands, arms, legs) of the others were located, indicating severe, physical trauma that could have been delivered only by the propeller of a steamer. In the end, the strongest evidence pointed to the steamer, *Joseph L. Hurd*, as having collided with the *Magellan*. The *Hurd*, built in Detroit in 1869, had a long, accident-filled career, including several collisions, before finally being abandoned at Sturgeon Bay, Wisconsin, in 1913. The wreck of the *Magellan* has not yet been located.

The Armistice Day Storm
November 11, 1940   Lake Michigan

A disastrous day in Lake Michigan's maritime history saw three, steel freighters destroyed, two of them lost with all hands. Only one of the three was a U.S. ship, the 420-foot-long *William B. Davock,* which went down in deep water (240 feet, or 72.7 metres) with all hands.

The stories of the other two ships, both Canadian vessels, are told below.

This historic marker commemorating the "Veteran's Day Storm" of 1940 stands in Pentwater, Michigan. (PHOTO BY CRIS KOHL)

Anna C. Minch
November 11, 1940   Lake Michigan

Although built at Cleveland in 1903, the 4,139-gross-ton, steel freighter, *Anna C. Minch* (387' x 50'2" x 23'9"), went into Canadian ownership, specifically by the Western Navigation Company out of Fort William, Ontario, in 1928. This ship sank in 45 feet (13.6 metres) of water off Pentwater, Michigan, with the loss of all 24 lives on board.

The Canadian freighter, **Anna C. Minch.** (KOHL-FORSBERG ARCHIVES)

Novadoc
November 11, 1940   Lake Michigan

The steel freighter, *Novadoc* (420' x 52' x 23'), built in England in 1928, was stranded and broken in two by the storm in 15 feet (4.5 metres) of water off Pentwater, Michigan. Two lives were lost before a small tug with three commercial fishermen on it daringly ventured to the wreck and rescued the remaining 17 crewmembers, an act of courage that was recognized and commended by the Canadian government.

The wrecked **Novadoc.** (KOHL-FORSBERG ARCHIVES)

Algoma   November 7, 1885   Lake Superior

The wrecked stern of the **Algoma** *at Isle Royale, Lake Superior.*

In the worst maritime accident at Isle Royale, the steel, passenger steamer, *Algoma* (262'8" x 38'2" x 23'3"), built at Glasgow, Scotland in 1883, stranded on Mott Island, southwest of Rock Harbor, with the loss of 45 of the 59 people on board. Those lost were on the bow when the ship broke in half. The bow remains missing, swept into deep water, while the stern half lies broken and scattered in three gullies. Most of the mechanical parts were salvaged in 1886.

Monarch   December 6, 1906   Lake Superior

The wooden passenger and freight steamer, *Monarch* (240' x 35' x 14'8"), launched at Sarnia, Ontario, in 1890, grounded hard onto the inhospitable and uninhabited shoreline called the Palisades at the eastern end of Isle Royale, Lake Superior's largest island, during a blinding snowstorm. One man reached shore with a rope, which he tied to a tree so that the other 60 people on board could escape the sinking ship hand over hand along that line. One life was lost when a young crewman slipped from the rope.

Massive pieces of hull and decking, as well as some scattered machinery (the steam engine and the boiler were salvaged) comprise this site, which is extensive in shallow water (between 10 and 70 feet, or 3 to 21 metres), but less so in deeper water (from 70 to 150 feet, or 21 to 45 metres).

Left: *The regal* **Monarch** *proudly underway, with officers and passengers on the pilot house.*

Right: *The* **Monarch** *dethroned at Isle Royale's Palisades.*

Glenlyon   November 1, 1924   Lake Superior

The **Glenlyon** *steaming through the Soo Locks.*

Another one of the several Canadian ships that failed to get past the obstacle named Isle Royale while bound from the Soo to the Lakehead was the steel freighter, *Glenlyon* (328' x 42'5" x 20'5"). Launched as the *William H. Gratwick* at West Bay City, Michigan, in 1893, new Canadian owners changed her name to *Glenlyon* in 1914. Stranded on a reef on the island's south side while seeking storm shelter, the ship and its wheat cargo (but fortunately no lives) were lost. Wreckage is scattered in 10 to 100 feet.

(ALL IMAGES ON THIS PAGE ARE FROM THE KOHL-FORSBERG ARCHIVES)

Kamloops   December 6, 1927   Lake Superior

The *Kamloops* story is one of the more tragic Isle Royale shipwreck tales. Built in England in 1924, this steel freighter (250' x 42'9" x 24'3") foundered in a severe, early winter storm alongside rocky Isle Royale. Not all of the crew of 20 men and two women perished immediately; some reached the island by lifeboat and froze or starved to death slowly. One of the women left a heart-wrenching note in a bottle to her parents. The bodies were found the following spring.

The *Kamloops,* lying about 300 feet (90 metres) off Twelve O'Clock Point on the north shore of Isle Royale, was located in 1977, with divers Ken Merryman, Randy Saulter, and Ken Engelbrecht being the first to explore and identify her. This intact wreck lies on her starboard side in about 270 feet (82 metres) of water, with the bow deeper than the stern. The perfectly preserved ship's wheel is chained in place to avoid loss.

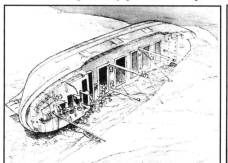 

Left: *The wreck of the Canadian freighter,* **Kamloops**.   (COURTESY OF THE ARTIST, ROBERT MCGREEVY)
Right: *The Fort William newspaper headlined the search on Dec. 12, 1927.*   (KOHL-FORSBERG ARCHIVES)

Emperor   June 4, 1947   Lake Superior

At the time of her launching at Collingwood, Ontario, on December 17, 1910, the 7,031-gross-ton, steel, bulk freight steamer, *Emperor* (525' x 56'1" x 27'), was the largest ship ever built in Canada. (Compare this with the *James Carruthers* on page 132). Hauling a heavy, iron ore cargo downbound in fog from Port Arthur to Ashtabula, the ship struck Canoe Rocks off eastern Isle Royale and sank with the loss of 12 of the 33 lives on board.

The hull, although split, forms a long line of massive, cracked steel running down a rocky slope in depths from 25 to 175 feet (7.5 to 53 metres), with the ship's propeller and rudder sitting at the deep end. This shipwreck is so enormous that scuba divers cannot see the entire thing in one dive (or even a few!) The shallow bow and the deep stern are buoyed by the National Parks personnel separately. At the bow, the large anchor and open holds are impressive, while the stern offers the ship's galley, crew's quarters with bunkbeds in them, skylights, and large dorades, or air vents.

Left: *The* **Emperor** *served her second owner, Canada Steamship Lines, well for 34 years.* (KOHL-FORSBERG ARCHIVES). Right: *The well-stocked galley stove in the* **Emperor's** *deep stern.* (PHOTO BY JOYCE HAYWARD)

Canadian Ships Lost near the Waters of the Great Lakes

There are several famous/infamous shipwrecks that repose in waters that do not flow into the Great Lakes system and, finally, there is also one extremely significant and tragic wreck lying in a briny current in an area that naturally mixes the fresh waters of the Great Lakes with the salt waters of the Atlantic Ocean.

The Lake Simcoe steamer, **J. C. Morrison.**
(Toronto Reference Library)

The Muskoka propeller, **Waome**
(Kohl-Forsberg Archives)

The **Mayflower** *sank in Lake Kamaniskeg.*
(Library and Archives Canada)

J. C. Morrison
August 4, 1857   Lake Simcoe

The sidewheel steamer, *J. C. Morrison,* built in 1854, burned to a total loss at Barrie, Canada West (later Ontario), on August 4, 1857. Cut loose to save the dock, the flaming ship drifted across Kempenfelt Bay and sank. The wreck, in a maximum of 40 feet (12 metres) of water, was located by Barrie diver Ron Marshall in 1975.

Waome
October 6, 1934   Lake Muskoka

Launched in 1912 as the propeller, *Mink,* at Gravenhurst, ON, this ship was renamed the *Waome* (78' x 14') in 1929. A sudden, powerful gust of wind knocked the ship onto her port side, filling her with water, and she sank in 74 feet (22.4 metres). The captain, the passenger (a minister), and one sailor drowned, with the other four crew surviving. The *Waome* ("water lily" in Ojibwa) is a popular scuba dive site.

Mayflower
November 12, 1912   Lake Kamaniskeg

The 59-ton sternwheeler, *Mayflower* (77' x 18' x 4'), sank in a storm near Barry's Bay, Ontario, while underway with 12 people and a corpse in a coffin. The floating coffin saved three people, but the other nine drowned. The wreck lies in 20 feet (6 metres) of water, about 500 feet (150 metres) off the eastern shore of the lake.

The worst maritime disaster in all of Canada was the sinking of the passenger liner, **Empress of Ireland,** *after colliding with another ship; 1,012 people perished.* (KOHL-FORSBERG ARCHIVES)

R.M.S. *Empress of Ireland*
May 29, 1914   St. Lawrence River

The sinking of the R.M.S. (Royal Mail Ship) *Empress of Ireland* (570' x 65'7" x 40') in 130 feet (39.4 metres) of briny water in the lower St. Lawrence River near Rimouski, Québec, after an early morning collision with the Norwegian collier, *Storstad* (439'6" length), became Canada's worst maritime disaster in peacetime.

Launched in Scotland on January 27, 1906, the 14,191-gross-ton *Empress of Ireland* was commissioned by the Canadian Pacific Railroad. Captain Henry Kendall was on his first voyage down the St. Lawrence River on his new command as master of the *Empress*, which was commencing her 96th voyage across the Atlantic, on May 29, 1914.

Fog set in, and the approaching *Storstad's* bow sliced into the *Empress of Ireland's* starboard side; while the *Storstad* remained afloat, the *Empress* quickly listed to starboard, sinking within 14 minutes of impact. There was too little time to close the ship's watertight doors, and the vessel's fast list allowed only five lifeboats to be launched on one side. Of the 420 crew, 172 died; from the 1,057 passengers, 840 perished (51 of the 87 1st Class passengers died; 205 of the 253 2nd Class; and 584 of the 717 3rd Class). Truly tragic was the fact that only one boy and three girls from the 138 children on board survived. From 1,477 people on the *Empress*, only 465 survived (248 crew and 217 passengers).

In 1999, the Canadian government placed the *Empress of Ireland* on the register of Historic Sites of Canada, thus providing the wreck with protection.

Many divers in the 1960s and 1970s removed items from the Empress of Ireland, *with little thought to the ship's significance in Canadian history and to its archaeological value. One diver amassed an entire dining room of* Empress *china and galley items -- which today, fortunately, repose in a museum in Ottawa.*

(COURTESY OF PHILLIPE BEAUDRY)

AFTERWORD

From the 1985 book, *Dive Southwestern Ontario!*, the first flicker of the flame smoldered into the fire seen in the 1990 book, *Dive Ontario, The Guide to Shipwrecks and Scuba Diving*, and was vigorously fanned by the celebration of Canada 150 into the blazing inferno of passion for Canadian Great Lakes Maritime History shining in this book, *Canada's 150 Most Famous Great Lakes Shipwrecks*. There have been about 20,000 different commercial vessels that have sailed on the Great Lakes over the last 300 years, and about 2,000 of them discovered their final resting place at the bottom of the waters of the Canadian freshwater seas – Canada's icewater museums.

Why would anyone care so much about the past as reflected in the historical treasures found in the inland seas that Canadians call their own? These amazing submerged cultural rarities are pieces of a puzzle that, when added to the rest of Canadian land-based history much more easily witnessed, enable us to complete the picture of where we are now and, most importantly, why.

Canadian Great Lakes maritime history – so often overlooked and under-rated – yet it's essential to the story of Canada's entire history. It would not be the country it is today without the Great Lakes. The lakes were the highways of yesteryear, moving people and goods and the stuff of industry to propel the nation forward. The steamers, schooners, paddlewheelers, huge steel freighters, small wooden package haulers, tugs, and humble barges were the cars, trucks, trains, and planes that we depend on today for transportation. There was a time when all we had for travel was ship, horse, or foot! The technology to improve transportation by ship developed because of commercial requirements, for example, the building of enormous freighters able to more efficiently carry larger and larger loads, and also, sadly, as a response to tragic happenings, for example, the use of steel vessels rather than too-easily-burned wooden boats.

Canada has a rich, colorful maritime history, which only in recent years has begun to be appreciated for its true value and connection to the overall history of Canada, North America, and to the rest of the world. The uniqueness and nonrenewability of Canada's submerged cultural resources elevate them to a lofty position in comparison to those in other locales.

We have the best preserved shipwrecks in the world lying in the cold, fresh waters of the Great Lakes! The maritime legacy of the inland seas, which includes those many significant ships which facilitated westward expansion and the economic development of Canada, plus the many workhorses: the schooners, the steamers, the ships which built Canada, must be neither ignored, nor pillaged, nor forgotten.

Bibliography

A. Books

A Centennial Tribute to the Great Lakes Storm: 1913. Goderich, ON: Great Lakes Storm of 1913 Remembrance Committee, 2013.

Amos, Art, and Patrick Folkes. *A Diver's Guide to Georgian Bay*. Toronto, ON: Ontario Underwater Council, 1979; reprinted in 1986.

Barrett, Harry B. *Lore & Legends of Long Point*. Don Mills, ON: Burns & MacEachern, 1977.

Barry, James. *Georgian Bay, The Sixth Great Lake*. Toronto, ON: Clarke, Irwin & Company Ltd., 1968.

Cain, Emily. *Ghost Ships, Hamilton and Scourge: Historical Treasures from the War of 1812*. Toronto: Musson, 1983.

Cameron, Scott L. *The Frances Smith, Palace Steamer of the Upper Great Lakes, 1867-1896*. Toronto, ON: Natural Heritage Books, 2005.

Carroll, Paul. *The Wexford: Elusive Shipwreck of the Great Storm, 1913*. Toronto, ON: Natural Heritage Books, 2010.

Crisman, Kevin J., ed. *Coffins of the Brave, Lake Shipwrecks of the War of 1812*. College Station, TX: Texas A&M University Press, 2014.

Curtis, Andrew. *Into The Blue, Family Secrets and the Search for a Great Lakes Shipwreck*. Toronto, ON: Random House Canada, 2003.

Cuthbertson, George. *Freshwater, A History and Narrative of the Great Lakes*. New York, NY: The MacMillan Company, 1931.

Dear Ella,...I hope this is not like this in the fall, June 1913. A Tribute to Lost Mariners & Ships in the Great Lakes Storm of 1913 as Told by Their Descendants. Goderich, ON: Great Lakes Storm of 1913 Remembrance Committee, 2013.

DesRochers, Claude. *Wawinet, September 21st, 1942*. Penetanguishene, ON. Published by the author, 2015.

Echo Soundings, Marine News from the Amherstburg Echo, a series of volumes for the years 1874-1914, and 1936 -1937, Amherstburg, ON: Marsh Historical Collection, 1998-2016.

Filey, Mike. *I Remember Sunnyside, The Rise & Fall of a Magical Era*. Toronto, ON: The Dundurn Group, 1996.

Floren, Russell, with Andrea Gutsche and Barbara Chisholm. *Alone in the Night, Lighthouses of Georgian Bay, Manitoulin Island, and the North Channel*. Toronto, ON: Lynx Images, 1996.
...............*Ghosts of the Bay, A Guide to the History of Georgian Bay*. Toronto, ON: Lynx Images, 1994
...............*The North Channel and St. Mary's River*.Toronto, ON: Lynx Images, 1997.
...............*Superior, Under the Shadow of the Gods*. Toronto, ON: Lynx Images, 1998.

Folkes, Patrick. *Shipwrecks of the Saugeen, 1828-1938*. Published in 1970; 85 numbered pages, plus several unnumbered pages of maps and photographs.
...............*Shipwrecks of Tobermory, 1828-1935*. Published in 1969; 38 numbered pages, plus several unnumbered pages of maps and photographs.

Gillham, Skip. *The Ships of Collingwood, Over One Hundred Years of Shipbuilding Excellence*. St. Catharines, ON: Riverbank Traders, 1992.

Gillians, Dave. *For the Love of Bayfield*. Bayfield, ON: Bayfield Historical Society, 2012.

Harrah, Backward and Forward. Harrah, OK: Harrah Historical Society, 1999.

Heyl, Eric. *Early American Steamers, Volumes I-VI.* Buffalo, NY. Published by the author, 1961-1969.

Higgins, Robert. *The Wreck of the Asia, Ships, Shoals, Storms and a Great Lakes Survey.* Waterloo, ON: Escart Press, 1995.

Humphries, William. *Great Fury.* London, ON:Concept Printing. Published by the author, 1975.

Investigating...Canada's Deep South. A 1980 reprint of an informal Parks Canada publication entitled *Insite and Information, Point Pelee National Park*, originally produced in 1975.

Kohl, Cris. *The 100 Best Great Lakes Shipwrecks, Volumes I and II.* West Chicago, IL: Seawolf Communications, Inc., 1998; revised editions, 2005.
...............*Dive Ontario, The Guide to Shipwrecks and Scuba.* Chatham, ON. Published by the author, 1990; revised, enlarged edition, 1995.
...............*Dive Ontario Two! More Ontario Shipwreck Stories.* Chatham, ON. Published by the author, 1994.
...............*Dive Southwestern Ontario!* Chatham, ON. Published by the author, 1985; rev. ed., 1988.
...............*The Great Lakes Diving Guide,* 2nd edition. West Chicago, IL: Seawolf Communications, Inc., 2008.
...............*Shipwreck Tales: The St. Clair River (to 1900).* Chatham. Published by the author, 1987.
...............*Shipwreck Tales of the Great Lakes.* West Chicago: Seawolf Communications, Inc., 2004.
...............*Treacherous Waters: Kingston's Shipwrecks.* Chatham, ON. Published by the author, 1997

Kohl, Cris, and Joan Forsberg. *Great Lakes Shipwrecks, Recent Discoveries and Updates.* West Chicago, IL: Seawolf Communications, Inc., 2016.
...............*The Wreck of the GRIFFON, The Greatest Mystery of the Great Lakes.* West Chicago, Illinois: Seawolf Communications, Inc., 2014.

Leaves from the War Log of the Nancy, Eighteen Hundred and Thirteen. Huronia Historical Development Council and Ontario Department of Tourism and Information. n.d.

Lewis, Walter, and Rick Neilson. *The River Palace* (the *Cornwall*). Toronto: Dundurn Press, 2008.

Long, Megan. *Ghosts of the Great Lakes.* Toronto, ON: Lynx Images, 2003.

Longhurst, G. I. "Buck." *Steamers of the Turkey Trail.* Gore Bay, ON: Gore Bay & Western Manitoulin Museum, 2011.

Mansfield, J. B., ed. *History of the Great Lakes, Volumes I and II.* Chicago: J.H. Beers & Co., 1899.

Marcolin, Lorenzo. *A Great Lakes Treasury of Old Postcards, Canadian Harbour Scenes 1894-1960.* Midland, ON: Huronia Museum, 2007.

McGoogan, Ken. *Fatal Passage, The Untold Story of John Rae, the Arctic Adventurer Who Discovered the Fate of Franklin.* Toronto, ON: HarperCollins Publishers, 2001.

McGreevy, Robert. *Lost Legends of the Lakes, An Illustrated History.* Harbor Beach, MI: Robert McGreevy, 2011.

Metcalfe, Willis. *Marine Memories.* Picton, ON: The Picton Gazette, 1975.
...............*Canvas & Steam on QuinteWaters.* South Bay, ON: The South Marysburgh Marine Society, 1979.

Mills, John M. *Canadian Coastal and Inland Steam Vessels, 1809-1930.* Providence, RI: The Steamship Historical Society of America, Inc., 1979, plus various supplements.

O'Brien, Brendan. *Speedy Justice, The Tragic Last Voyage of His Majesty's Vessel Speedy.* Toronto, ON: The Osgoode Society, 1992.

Ouderkirk, Capt. Gerry. *Shipwrecked on the Bruce Coast.* Published ca. 1995; 31 numbered pages; no other publishing information given.

Powers, Tom. *In the Grip of the Whirlwind, The Armistice Day Storm of 1940.* Holt, MI: Thunder Bay Press, 2009.

Prothero, Frank & Nancy. *Tales of the North Shore*. Port Stanley, ON: Nan-Sea Publications, 1987.

Salen, Rick and Jack. *The Tobermory Shipwrecks*. Tobermory, ON: The Mariner Chart Shop; numerous editions between 1974 and 2012.

Smith, Arthur Britton. *Legend of the Lake, The 22-Gun Brig-Sloop Ontario, 1780, New Discovery Edition*. Kingston, ON: Quarry Heritage Books, 2009.

Stanton, Samuel Ward. *American Steam Vessels*. New York: Smith & Stanton, 1895.

Stein, C. E. *The Wreck of the Erie Belle*. Wheatley, ON: Ship 'N Shore Publishing Company, 1970.

Stone, Dave. *Long Point, Last Port of Call*. Erin, ON: The Boston Mills Press, 1988.

Stonehouse, Frederick. *The Wreck of the Edmund Fitzgerald*. Au Train, MI: Avery Color Studios, 1977.

Van der Linden, Rev. Peter J., ed. *Great Lakes Ships We Remember*. Cleveland, OH: Freshwater Press, 1979; revised 1984.
...............*Great Lakes Ships We Remember II*. Cleveland, OH: Freshwater Press, 1984.
...............*Great Lakes Ships We Remember III*. Cleveland, OH: Freshwater Press, 1994.

Wachter, Mike and Georgann. *Erie Wrecks & Lights*. Avon Lake, OH: CorporateImpact, 2007.
...............*Erie Wrecks East, A Guide to Shipwrecks of Eastern Lake Erie*. Avon Lake, OH: CorporateImpact, 2000.
...............*Erie Wrecks West*. Avon Lake, OH: CorporateImpact, 2001.

Weir. Stephen. *Sinking of the Mayflower, lost November 12, 1912*. Burnstown, ON: General Store Publishing House, Inc., 1990.

Wolff, Julius F., Jr. *Lake Superior Shipwrecks*. Duluth, MN: Lake Superior Port Cities, Inc. 1990.

Wrigley, Ronald. *Shipwrecked, Vessels Meet Doom on the North Shore* (of Lake Superior). Thunder Bay, ON: RW Publishing, 2013.

B. Periodical Literature

Alford, Terry. "Kingston's Newest Wreck Dive (the *Wolfe Islander II*)." *Diver Magazine*. Vol. 12, No. 1, (March, 1986) 18-21.
..............."Time Capsule in Kingston, Queen of Kingston's Wrecks (the *Wolfe Islander II*)." *Diver Magazine,* Vol. 14, No. 1 (March, 1988), 19-20.

Barker, Gerry. "The Loss of the Steamer *Atlantic*." *Inland Seas*, Vol. 20, No. 3 (Fall, 1964), 211-214.

Bellefeuille, Monique J. "Wreck Facts: The St. Lawrence River's *Conestoga*." *Skin Diver* Magazine. Vol. 39, No. 8 (August, 1990), 18, 48, 57.

Bellefeuille, Monique and Mike. "*Lillie Parsons*." *Diver Magazine*. Vol. 16, No.7 (Nov., 1990), 18-19.

Birke, Scott. "Under The Bay." Interview with Cris Kohl and others. *On The Bay Magazine* (Georgian Bay). Vol. 8, No. 3 (Summer, 2011), 62-69.

Dekina, Vlada. "The Two Lives of *Northwind* [sic]" *Wreck Diving Magazine*. Issue 5 (2005), 67-73.

Folkes, Patrick. "The Schooner *Sweepstakes,* A Mystery Solved." *Save Ontario Shipwrecks Newsletter*. (Spring-Summer, 1984), 12-13.

Gilchrist, David. "Diving Weekend at Port Colborne (Wreck of the Steamer, *Raleigh*)." *Diver Magazine*. Vol. 20, No. 5 (August, 1994), 14-15.

Golding, Peter. "Inner Space Adventure, *Comet* in Lake Ontario." *Diver Magazine*, Vol. 5, No. 4 (June, 1979), 21-24.

..............."Lady of Muskoka, The *Waome*." *Diver Magazine*. Vol. 6, No. 4 (June, 1980), 20-21.
..............."*Maple Dawn* [sic]." *Diver Magazine*. Vol. 6, No. 4 (April-May, 1980), 36-37.

................"Tale of Two Wrecks, *Sweepstakes -- City of Grand Rapids*." *Diver Magazine*. Vol. 6, No. 1 (January-February, 1980), 24-25.

................"The Wreck of the *George A. Marsh*." *Diver Magazine*, Vol. 5, No. 8 (November-December, 1979), 38-40.

Hall, Judy. "Save the *Sweepstakes*, Completion of Phase I." *The Canadian Diving News* (January, 1972), 9-11.

Harvey, Robert. "Survey Report -- S.O.S. Quinte, *Annie Falconer*." *Save Ontario Shipwrecks Newsletter* (Spring/Summer, 1985), 11-14.

Hoover, Pierce. Underwater photos by Cris Kohl."Shipwreck City" (Kingston, Ontario). *Sport Diver Magazine*. Vol. 9, No. 3 (April, 2001), 56-61.

Kohl, Cris. "The 12-Fathom Lady of Lake Erie (the *Willis)*." *Wreck Diving Magazine*. Issue 26 (2012), 56-61.

................Backwoods Secret (the *Columbus*)." *Diver Magazine*. Vol.17, No. 5 (Aug., 1991), 33-35.

................"Battle for the *Atlantic*" *Diver Magazine*. Vol. 19, No. 3 (May, 1993), 36-37.

................"The Dead Captain's Secrets (the *George A. Marsh*)." *Wreck Diving Magazine*, Premier Issue, 2004, 40-47.

................"The Dredge, *Munson*." *Diver Magazine*. Vol. 23, No.6 (Sept., 1997), 26-27.

................"Ghost Fleet of the St. Clair River." *Wreck Diving Magazine*. Issue 37 (2015), 48-55.

................"The *George A. Marsh* Mystery." *Diver Magazine*. Vol. 24, No. 5 (July-August, 1998).

................"Great Lakes, Great Wrecks." *Skin Diver* Magazine. Vol. 51, No. 6 (June, 2002), 52-55.

................"Great Lakes Shipwrecks." *Sport Diver* Magazine. Vol. 12, No. 6 (July, 2004), 63, 94-96.

................"A Great Lakes Queen Turned Widow Maker (the *Merida*)." *Wreck Diving Magazine*, Issue 6 (2005), 32-38

................"Great Lakes Treasure: Paddlewheeler *Comet*." *Wreck Diving*. Issue 18 (2009), 36-41.

................"The Great Storm of 1913." *Wreck Diving Magazine*. Issue 31 (2013), 28-35.

................"Honeymoon Wreck: Lake Huron's *Joyland*." *Diver Magazine*. Vol. 22, No. 2 (April, 1996), 30-31.

................"Lake Erie's Lost Steamer, *Colonial*." *Diver Mag*. Vol. 20, No. 4 (June, 1994), 22-23.

................"A Lake Huron Gem: The *Emma E. Thompson*." *Diver Magazine*, Vol. 23, No. 4 (June, 1997), 18-19.

................"The Once-Mighty *Metamora*." *Diver Magazine*. Vol. 23, No. 5 (July-Aug., 1997), 18-19.

................"Lake Ontario's Lost Team: *Condor* and *Atlasco*." *Diver Magazine*. Vol. 22, No. 7 (November, 1996), 24-25.

................"*Manola* -- Half a Shipwreck." *Diver Magazine*. Vol. 21, No. 9 (February, 1996), 28.

................"The Mystery of the Shipwrecked Barges (*Atlasco* and *Condor*)." *Wreck Diving Magazine*. Issue 25 (2011), 32-39.

................"An Oddly Named Shipwreck, The *Joyland*." *Wreck Diving Mag*. Issue 15 (2008), 12-21.

................"The Power of a Simple Schooner (the *Annie Falconer*)." *Wreck Diving Magazine*. Issue 13 (2007), 64-73.

................"The Shipwreck Which Lies in Two Lakes (*Manola* and *Mapledawn*). *Wreck Diving Magazine*. Issue 9 (2006), 52-57.

................"Freshwater Barnacles Threaten Shipwrecks."*Diving Times*. Vol. 12, No.2. Summer, 1989

................"The Short, Unhappy Life of Duane Precious (the tug, *Monarch*)." *Wreck Diving Magazine*. Issue 20 (2010), 28-37.

................"A Small Workhorse Among Giants (the *Munson*)." *Wreck Diving Magazine*. Issue 32 (2014), 60-65.

................Steamer *Northern Indiana*, Lake Erie Tragedy." *Diver Magazine*. Vol. 22, No. 9 (February, 1997), 20-22.

................"Ten Great Wrecks of the Great Lakes." *Rodale's Scuba Diving Magazine*. Vol. 13, No. 3, Issue 115 (April, 2004), 43-50, 105.

................"Terror on the *Clarion!*" *Wreck Diving Magazine*. Issue 35 (2015), 36-45.

................"The Tragic Wreck of the *Olive Branch*." *Wreck Diving Magazine*. Issue 39 (2016),72-79.

................"Tragic Wreck on Lake Erie (*Merida*)." *Diver Mag*. Vol. 22, No. 4 (June, 1996), 24-26.

................"Triumphs and Tragedies of the *Arabia*, Part 1 and Part 2." *Wreck Diving Magazine*. Issue 27 (2012), 42-49, and Issue 28 (2012), 54-61.

................"Workhorse in the Wilderness" (the tug, *Columbus*.) *Wreck Diving Magazine*. Issue 38 (2016), 36-45.

................"The Wreck of the *William H. Wolf*." *Ontario Diver's Digest*. August, 1990.

Kuss, Dan. "Wreck of the *Rappahannock*." *Diver Magazine*. Vol. 16, No. 8 (Dec., 1990), 19-21.

Lenko, Borys. "*J. C. Morrison* Found." *Dive Canada*. November-December, 1976, 7.

Lewis, Steve. "Discovery of Lake Huron's Elusive *Wexford*." *Advanced Diver Magazine*. Issue 7 (Fall, 2000), 30-31.

McDaniel, Neil. "Fathom Five's Deep Treasure, the Barque *Arabia*." *Diver Magazine*. Vol. 13, No. 3 (May, 1987), 22-23.

Miller, Al. "The Search for *Barge 115*." *The Nor'Easter*. Vol. 19, No. 1 (Jan.-Feb., 1994), 1-5.
................"The 'Lucky' Boat (*City of Cleveland*)." *Nor'Easter*. Vol. 18, No. 6 (Sept. 1992), 18-19.

Mullings, Ken. "The Fate of the *Falconer*." *Diver Magazine*. Vol. 18, No. 6 (Sept., 1992), 18-19.

Neilson, Rick. "The Sidewheeler, *Cornwall*." *Diver Magazine*. Vol. 17, No. 4 (June, 1991), 32-33.

Orr, Dan. "The Barque, *Arabia*: 1853-1884." *Diver Magazine*. Vol. 11, No. 6 (Sept., 1985), 30-32.

Robnik, Diane. "New Light on 1918 Minesweeper Mystery (the *Cerisoles* and *Inkerman*)." Thunder Bay Historical Museum Society, *Papers and Records,* Vol. XLII (2014), 3-14.

Soegtrop, Michael. "*Mapledawn*, Wreck in Southern Georgian Bay." *Diver Magazine*. Vol. 18, No. 4 (June, 1992), 20-21.
................"The *Mayflower*." Vol. 17, No. 3 (May, 1991), 36-37.
................"Tobermory's Classic Shipwreck, *City of Cleveland*." *Diver Magazine,* Vol. 13, No. 1 (March, 1987), 24-29.
................"Twice Lost by Fire (the *Atlantic* in Lake Huron)." *Diver Magazine*. Vol. 7, No.3 (April-May, 1981), 27-29.

Van Heest, Valerie. Underwater video "captures" by Dan Scoville and Jim Kennard, "Seek and Ye Shall Find, 228-year-old British warship found intact in Lake Ontario (the *Ontario*)." *Wreck Diving Magazine*. Issue 16 (2008), 68-73.

Wachter, Mike and Georgann. "Lake Erie's Schooner, *C. B. Benson*." *Advanced Diver Magazine*. Issue 8 (Winter, 2000), 16-17, 48.

Weir, Stephen. "The *City of Sheboygan*." *Diver Magazine*. Vol. 26, No. 2 (April, 2000), 18-19.
................"Double Dip Kingston's *Marsh* and *Comet*." *Diver Magazine*. Vol. 26, No. 7 (October-November, 2000), 8-9.

C. Newspapers

Various issues of the following newspapers were utilized:

Amherstburg (Ontario) *Echo*
Belleville (Ontario) *Daily Intelligencer*
Blenheim (Ontario) *News Tribune*
Buffalo (New York) *Evening News*
Chatham (Ontario) *Daily Planet*
Chicago (Illinois) *Daily Tribune*
Chicago (Illinois) *Inter Ocean*
Cleveland (Ohio) *Herald*
Cleveland (Ohio) *Plain Dealer*
Cleveland (Ohio) *Press*
Detroit (Michigan) *Free Press*
Detroit (Michigan) *Times*
Duluth (Minnesota) *Evening Herald*
Fort William (Ontario) *Daily Times-Journal*
Goderich (Ontario) *Signal Star*
Kingston (Ontario) *Whig*
London (Ontario) *Free Press*
Manitoulin (Ontario) *Expositor*
Manitoulin (Ontario) *Recorder*

Midland (Ontario) *Free Press Herald*
Milwaukee (Wisconsin) *Sentinel*
Owen Sound (Ontario) *Daily Sun*
Picton (Ontario) *Gazette*
Port Huron (Michigan) *Daily Times*
Port Huron (Michigan) *Times Herald*
Sandusky (Ohio) *Register-Star-News*
Sarnia (Ontario) *Daily Observer*
Sault Ste. Marie (Michigan) *Evening News*
Sault (Ste. Marie, Ontario) *Daily Star*
Toledo (Ohio) *Blade*
Toronto (Ontario) *Globe*
Toronto (Ontario) *Globe & Mail*
Toronto (Ontario) *Daily Star*
Toronto (Ontario) *Evening Telegram*
Wiarton (Ontario) *Echo*
Windsor (Ontario) *Border Cities Star*
Windsor (Ontario) *Evening Record*
Windsor (Ontario) *Star*

Index

Words in *italics* denote a publication or a ship's name.
A number in **bold** denotes a photograph or a drawing on that page.

Sponsor Index

About the Kohl-Forsberg Archives

It started as a hobby in the 1970s: collecting items about Great Lakes maritime history. After Cris Kohl's first book about Great Lakes shipwrecks was published in 1985, the collecting became serious. Several decades and many dollars later, the accumulation of maritime ephemera has grown so much that it exceeds any designation as a "collection" and has become "archives" -- 3,300+ books, 6,800+ archival photos of ships, 6,300+ archival maritime postcards, 6,400+ individual file folders (each one containing information about one Great Lakes shipwreck) in 22 filing cabinet drawers, 140 3-inch binders of photocopied newspaper articles (61,000+ pages), many maritime brochures, many hours of audiotaped interviews, plus 21,000+ underwater shipwreck photos/slides taken by Cris Kohl, and many hours of underwater video shot by both Cris Kohl and Joan Forsberg. The archives also include all of the late Joyce Hayward's Great Lakes images. We are currently searching for a responsible, accessible, permanent repository for the Kohl-Forsberg Archives.

About the Authors

Cris Kohl and Joan Forsberg, well-known maritime historians, divers, photographers, videographers, authors, and speakers, are a husband-and-wife team who love to explore shipwrecks, particularly those in the Great Lakes. Starting with a double major in French and Russian for a diplomatic career, Joan switched to completing a degree in History. Cris has degrees in English and Education, and a Master of Arts degree in History. Both have underwater archaeology certifications from Great Britain's Nautical Archaeology Society (NAS). Their maritime history archives are one of the largest privately-held collections in the Great Lakes.

Joan, from Chicago, has been the Chairman of the Shipwrecks and Underwater Archaeology Room at Chicago's annual "Our World -- Underwater" Show since 1996. She is the author of the scuba celebrity cook-and-tell book, *Diver's Guide to the Kitchen*, and articles in magazines such as *Immersed, Great Lakes Boating*, and *Wreck Diving Magazine,* for which she became the Copy Editor in 2006. Joan appears behind the camera shooting underwater video, and in front of the camera as Cris' underwater model. In her three terms as President of the Underwater Archaeological Society of Chicago (2008, 2009, 2010), she spearheaded several significant maritime history projects and was the recipient of the 2011 UASC Award "for many years of leadership and dedication." Joan is a member of the international Women Divers Hall of Fame, has served as a Trustee of WDHOF for several years, and is currently in her third term as WDHOF's Chairman of the Board.

Cris, described in 2002 by California's *Skin Diver Magazine* as being "widely recognized as the world's preeminent Great Lakes wreck guru," is a prize-winning underwater photographer from Windsor, Ontario. He started writing about Great Lakes shipwrecks in 1982, with sixteen books and 300+ magazine and newsletter articles published since then. Several dozen of his articles have been published in Canada's *DIVER Magazine*, and his work has appeared in every issue of the international *Wreck Diving Magazine* since it began operations in 2003. He has helped locate and identify several Great Lakes shipwrecks. He served on the Executive Board of the Ontario Underwater Council (1988 to 1997), is a Past President of the Underwater Archaeological Society of Chicago (2004), is the 2008 recipient of the annual "Our World -- Underwater" Outstanding Achievement Award, and in 2013, he received the Save Ontario Shipwrecks Marine Heritage Award "for his extensive body of work contributing to widespread appreciation of Ontario's maritime heritage." His expanded edition of *The Great Lakes Diving Guide* is the most comprehensive book ever published about Great Lakes shipwrecks.

Both Cris and Joan have appeared on numerous television programs, including on the History Channel, Discovery Channel, CBS, and Chicago's WTTW, and their underwater video has been broadcast on PBS and Canada's CTV network. They wrote the book detailing the first 40 years of Chicago's annual "Our World -- Underwater" Scuba Show. Co-authors of the recent books, *The Wreck of the GRIFFON, The Greatest Mystery of the Great Lakes* and *Great Lakes Shipwrecks, Recent Discoveries and Updates,* and producers of many Great Lakes shipwreck maps, shipwreck postcards, and maritime history documentaries, Cris and Joan look forward to their next big adventure.

The following articles provide more information about Cris Kohl and Joan Forsberg:

Hildebrand, Dick. "Shipwrecks of the Great Lakes, A World Class Dive Destination." (Biographical information about Cris Kohl and Joan Forsberg in this entry, as well as the next). *Windsor Life Magazine*. Vol. 22, Issue 5 (Summer, 2015), 20-24.

.............."Great Lakes Shipwrecks." *Windsor Life Magazine,*. Vol.23, Issue 6 (Sept., 2016), 23-24.

Steinburger, Heather. "Dynamic Duo." *Lakeland Boating*. Vol. LXIV, No. 8 (September, 2010), 30-33.

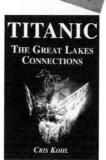